Making the
Technical
Sale

D0956609

Rick Greenwald
and
James Milbery

Real-World Training for
The Successful Sales Consultant

Making the Technical Sale

Copyright ©2001 Muska & Lipman Publishing

All rights reserved. No part of this book may be reproduced by any means without written permission from the publisher, except for brief passages for review purposes. Address all permission requests to the publisher.

All copyrights and trademarks used as examples or references in this book are retained by their individual owners.

Technology and the Internet are constantly changing, and by necessity of the lapse of time between the writing and distribution of this book, some aspects may be out of date. Accordingly, the author and publisher assume no responsibility for actions taken by readers based upon the contents of this book.

Library of Congress Catalog Number 00-100911

ISBN: 0-9662889-9-8

5 4 3 2 1

Educational facilities, companies, and organizations interested in multiple copies or licensing of this book should contact the publisher for quantity discount information. Training manuals, CD-ROMs, and portions of this book are also available individually or can be tailored for specific needs.

MUSKA&LIPMAN

Muska & Lipman Publishing
2645 Erie Avenue, Suite 41
Cincinnati, Ohio 45208
www.muskalipman.com
publisher@muskalipman.com

This book is composed in Officina Sans, Officina Serif, and Eurostyle typefaces using QuarkXpress 4.1.1, Adobe PhotoShop 5.0.2, and Adobe Illustrator 8.0.

Credits

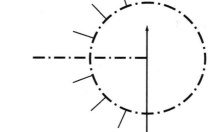

Publisher
Andy Shafran

Managing Editor
Hope Stephan

Development Editor
Joyce Rappaport

Copy Editor
Martin Sterpka

Proofreader
Molly Flynn

Cover Designers
Michael Williams
John Windhorst

Production Manager
Cathie Tibbetts

Production Team
DOV Graphics
    Michelle Frey
    Stephanie Japs

Indexer
Kevin Broccoli

Printer
R.R. Donnelley and Sons

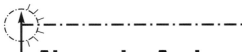

About the Authors

James F. Milbery, of Easton, Pennsylvania, is principal of Kuromaku Partners LLC—working with a diverse group of clients such as Oracle Corporation and William Blair Capital Partners. Before founding his own business, he spent many years as a technical sales force manager, most recently with software providers Revere Inc, Uniface, Ingres Corp. and Compaq (Digital Equipment).

Richard E. Greenwald, of Evanston, Illinois, is a competitive analyst with Oracle Corporation and principal of Strategic Computing Services. He has been a senior technical sales professional with management and training responsibilities as well as territory development over the course of his 16+ years in the industry. He has been published in numerous professional journals, and has written *Oracle Power Objects Developers, Mastering Oracle Power Objects, Special Edition: Using Oracle Web Server, The Oracle WebDB Bible, Oracle Essentials*, and more.

Dedication

From Jim Milbery—To my lovely wife, Renate—without her love and support, none of this would be possible.

From Rick Greenwald—For my family—LuAnn, Elinor, and Josephine Greenwald, who have sold me on the meaning of happiness.

Acknowledgments

In the process of writing this book, we both inevitably spent a lot of time thinking back to the individuals with whom we have worked over the past two decades. Most, if not all, of the lessons we have learned in our careers and tried to pass on through this book came with the assistance and analysis of our professional colleagues. To quote David Rudder, "to mention any one would perhaps make the others feel small, but several people stand out in sharp relief."

Jim Milbery: I believe it would be impossible for me to thank all of the people that have made this book possible, since so many of you have shaped my experiences in working with a sales team. There are two people that bear special mention due to the profound and positive way in which they have influenced my career in technical selling. John Calandrello is one of my oldest and closest friends and he is also the first salesperson whom I worked with as a technical sales consultant. John is an extremely talented sales representative and businessman, and I have to give him complete credit for getting me started down the right path as a technical rep. Without his help, guidance and continuing friendship, I would never have been able to create this book. For those of you in the software business, the name Michael J. Wilson should be familiar to you. Michael has championed the cause of software as a vice president of sales, president and CEO for a number of highly successful companies. I have had the great pleasure of serving under Michael in a variety of technical capacities for many, many years. I would challenge you to find any leader with more spirit, enthusiasm and overall business acumen than Michael. He has helped to shape my career in too many ways to count. In addition, Bob Howatt is one in a million and a great sales rep to boot (war eagle back atchya, coach!). I have had the honor and privilege of working with some of the best technical sales consultants and sales representatives in the business. It is my hope that I have been able to capture some of their collective insight and experiences in the creation of this book.

Rick Greenwald: I would like to specifically mention a select few—Chuck Quakenbush and Vince Finley, the first two truly great outstanding reps with whom I worked; Ray Schwartz, my first manager, who set me on the right path and imbued me with an excitement and professionalism that still remains; Paul Rasmussen, a true friend; Richard Heaps, who proved to me that it was possible to be great at my job and also be a great human being; and Tony Espinosa, who taught this old dog a few new tricks.

We would like to thank the gang at Muska & Lipman—Elizabeth Agnostinelli, Hope Stephan, and Andy Shafran, for believing in this project and helping us shape it into the book in your hands.

And last, but certainly not least, we both would like to make special mention of Paul Senatori, the boss who brought us together and encouraged us on this work.

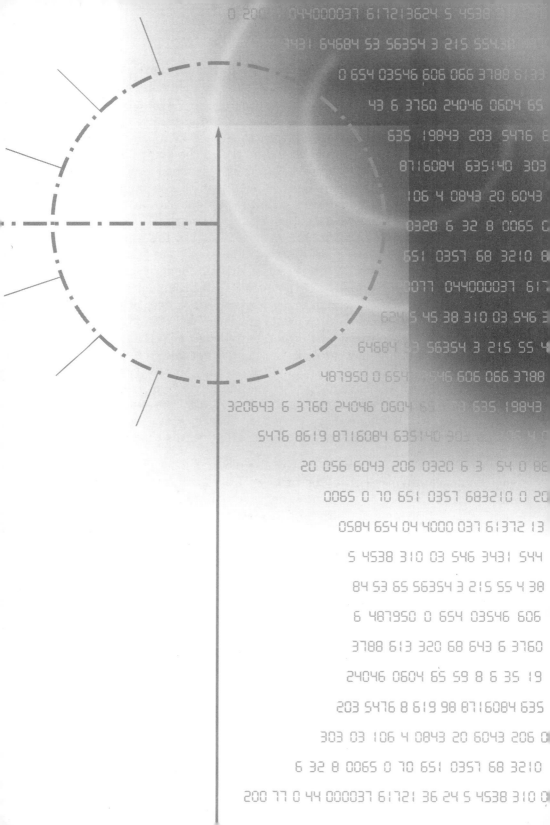

Contents

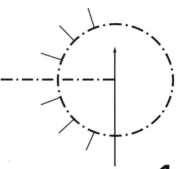

4—Understanding the Buyer 51

5—Working with People 69

15—Working the Competition 295

16—Eight Challenging Prospects 315

17—The Seven Deadly Sins
of Sales Consultants 335

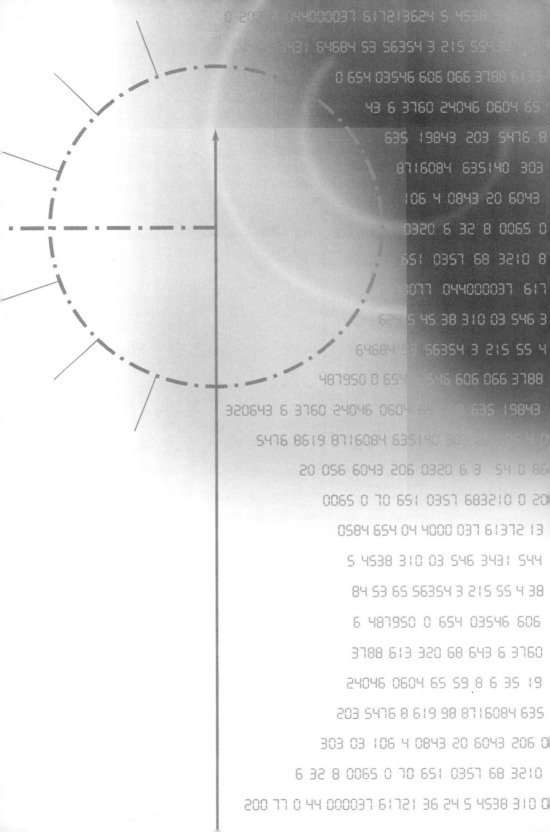

Introduction

The book you are holding in your hands is both a labor of love and a product of necessity. Its co-authors both have been in the IT industry for more than 16 years, and both spent a great deal of their time in the industry as either sales consultants or in positions that worked to support sales consultants.

When we met in 1996, Jim mentioned his long-standing idea that the world really needed a comprehensive training manual for sales consultants. Rick immediately agreed with him. The job of a sales consultant is unique—part sales person, part technical guru, and part professional problem solver. There were a wide variety of titles that touched on some aspects of this job, but none that really focused on the complete scope of activities that make up the daily life of a sales consultant.

We also agreed that there are common denominators for all sales consultants. With our three decades of experience, we felt that we had a firm grasp on the essential nature of the position—mainly because we had learned from the many mistakes we had made personally and had seen in others.

A mere five years later, this book was completed. We believe that it has fulfilled its original goal by giving readers a thorough understanding of the skills needed to be a successful sales consultant. We have also included many real-world experiences and examples which illustrate the facets of the sales consulting life.

What This Book Contains

This book aims to be the basic training manual for sales consultants. It delivers information about three of the most important disciplines that contribute to the position of sales consultant:

- **The world of technology**—All technical products and services have some characteristics in common. The Technology Life Cycle, as described by Geoffrey Moore and others, describes how products are brought to market and accepted by the user community. This Life Cycle has a direct bearing on how you will present your products and how they will be seen by your potential audience of prospects.

- **The world of sales**—Although sales consultants do not sell products or services directly, they are a part of a vendor organization and a sales team whose ultimate responsibility is to sell. If you ignore the essentials of sales, you will not be able to be a successful sales consultant.

- **The world of people**—A sales consultant is always a member of a team. By understanding how to best interact with the different members of that team, you can maximize your effectiveness and your job satisfaction.

The job of the sales consultant resides at the intersection of these three main areas. We have tried to not only provide a basic understanding of these areas in themselves but to also show how they relate to a sales consultant's every-day activities and to each other. In this way, we feel that the book has fulfilled its early goal. With this single volume, you will be able get an essential grasp on the full breadth of this fascinating job. And, we hope, the wisdom presented on these topics will give this book the ability to guide you through your entire career in the technology industry.

Who Should Read This Book

The primary audience for this book is, of course, sales consultants. Although we describe the particulars of this job more fully in Chapter 1, a sales consultant is essentially someone who provides technical support for the sales of technology-based products. These products are primarily computer hardware and software products. The technical support provided for the sales of these products involves working with customers to understand the features and benefits of those products. As a sales consultant, you will perform demonstrations, create customized solutions for sales prospects, and respond to requests for information. Your job will usually also extend to working with larger groups of customers at trade shows and user groups.

We believe that this book is an ideal training companion for all types of sales consultants—those who sell hardware, those who sell software, those who sell services, those who are new to the role, and those who have been sales consultants for many years.

We also think that this book will provide great value for anyone who consistently works with sales consultants, such as sales representatives and management. We have frequently seen situations where even the companies that employ sales consultants seem to have a less-than-complete understanding of the job and the people who fill it. By providing a more explicit understanding of sales consulting, this book will help all of those who are peripherally involved with sales consultants to work with them more effectively and to appreciate their unique strengths and weaknesses more fully.

The birth of the Internet has caused a virtual explosion in the need for trained sales consultants. Software and technology are no longer a luxury for most businesses; these are absolute necessities in order for them to remain competitive. More technology and more customers translate into an ever-increasing need for specialists who can translate the arcane language of technology into brick-and-mortar business benefits. And these are the exact skills that are at the core of the sales consultant's role in the selling process.

Cardinal Rules, Maxims, and Red Flags

Throughout this book, you will occasionally see short pieces of text highlighted on a page. The information is emphasized because it conveys one of the essential points of this book. We mean to both drive home the importance of the information and make it easy for you to review these points by rapidly skimming through the text. These pieces of text fall into three categories: cardinal rules, maxims, and red flags.

A Cardinal Rule is a talisman for your actions.

Cardinal rules are guidelines for your actions and conduct in your job. You can think of cardinal rules as a talisman that will guide your actions in your job. You should keep the cardinal rules in the back of your mind and try to never take an action that will counteract a cardinal rule.

Because cardinal rules are such strict guides for behavior, they are the least common types of special information in this book.

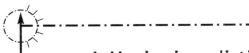

A Maxim is a distilled piece of wisdom, culled from experience.

Maxims are different from cardinal rules in that they do not provide direct guidelines for your actions. A maxim is a piece of wisdom that you can use to understand the different situations that you will face in your job. As with cardinal rules, we have derived maxims from our long experience as sales consultants and working with sales consultants. We use maxims to help you to understand the situations you will find yourself in, without having to go through the long process of trial and error.

**A Red Flag is a warning
that something is amiss.**

A red flag, as the name implies, is a sign of danger. When your encounter a red flag in your job, it is a signal that there is a problem ahead. Typically, a red flag is a seemingly innocent event that indicates an underlying problem that you should deal with. Red flags can alert you to a problem and help you deal with it before it jeopardizes your interaction with your customers and prospects.

We don't intend for the cardinal rules, maxims, and red flags to replace a careful reading of the text. The text surrounding these points provides valuable explanations and illustrations of the points. These points will act more as an internal outline, which both summarizes the essence of the surrounding text as well as acts as a bookmark for the explanations in the chapter.

In addition to these eye-catching formats, we have used two other special formatting conventions throughout the book.

> Whenever you see text set off in this manner, you will be reading a story or explanation that is based on a direct personal experience of one of the authors. We have chosen to use the first person singular pronoun in these experiences, so you will read about what "I" have done, rather than what "we" have done.

In all cases, the names of the companies and individuals have been obscured—not to protect the innocent, but to hopefully expand the range of the lessons learned from the experience.

We have also used running examples to help to illustrate some of the points we are discussing in the book. These examples are indented and set in italic type, as in the following:

> *The primary example we use in the book is the fictitious SuperServer, which is an application server software product. It doesn't really matter if the products and services that you will be involved with have anything to do with this type of product. We have chosen this imaginary product because it has many of the generic features of a broad spectrum of products. In fact, neither of the co-authors have ever worked explicitly as a sales consultant with an application server product. However, you will be able to apply the SuperServer example case directly to the current market place.*

We hope that you get as much out of this book as we have tried to put into it. Please feel free to pass on any suggestions on ways that you think the book can be improved through our publisher's Web site:

http://www.muskalipman.com/techsale/

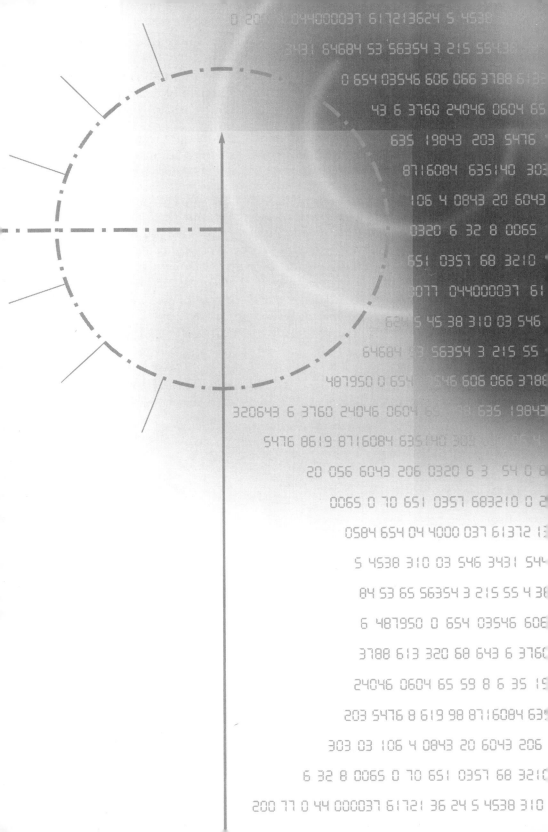

Your World

Welcome to *Making the Technical Sale!* Congratulations on selecting this book that will help you maximize the success and enjoyment of being a sales consultant. We have packed this text with techniques and tips that will help you succeed in the world of technology.

You are about to start on an exciting journey. Sales consulting is an extremely exciting and rewarding career. You will find your days filled with cool technology and interesting challenges—and this book will act as a comprehensive training manual for you, the sales consultant. But before we can jump right into the tips and techniques we have gathered over three decades, we will have to define the world that you work in.

What Is a Sales Consultant?

In some ways, the job description of a sales consultant is difficult to describe. Your day-to-day work will bridge a wide variety of tasks, from spokesman to programmer. In fact, although this position is common to virtually every type of company that sells technology, there are even many different names for it. Your own company may refer to you as a sales consultant, a systems engineer, a sales engineer, a technical sales person, technical evangelist, or simply describe you by reputation, such as a product master or guru. In this book, we will use the term "sales consultant" to describe a position where your primary focus is to provide the technical expertise needed to make sales.

The term "sales consultant" is probably the most common name for the job, because it illustrates one of the great realities of your position:

"Sales" comes before "consultant."

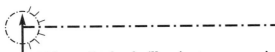

This cardinal rule illuminates your primary value to your organization—you contribute to the sales effort. You should always keep this rule uppermost in your mind. You may find yourself naturally tending towards the "consultant" part of your job title—the part where you can continually establish your technical prowess with customers. But the money for your salary comes from the revenue gathered from making sales.

What Is Your Primary Responsibility?

Your primary job is to help your sales team to acquire and retain customers—also known as "closing deals." In the process of landing customers, you are helping to make the world a better place by leveraging the power of technology for the greater good. This may sound a bit far-fetched, but it is remarkably close to the truth.

Whom Do You Work With?

Nearly as important as what you do is the context in which you do it. The defining elements of this context are the people you interact with as part of your job.

Prospects and Customers

Your job revolves around the production of revenue, so naturally, the most important people in your world are those individuals who can be the source of that revenue. In sales terms, you could be dealing with *prospects*, those who do not yet have a relationship with your company, or *customers*, those who already own one or more of your company's products or use your company's services.

Although many companies differentiate between these two types of sales opportunities, we will use the two terms interchangeably throughout this book. Since someone who owns your products might also purchase more of your products, many of your existing customers will also be prospects for future sales. In fact, studies have shown that it is much easier to make a follow on sale to an existing customer than it is to create a new customer from a fresh prospect—no matter how willing the prospect. For this simple reason, you should always treat your customers with the same consideration that you would show towards a new prospect.

The other important fact to remember is the uniqueness of every customer situation.

Every sales opportunity is different.

In my first year as a sales consultant, I was talking with a prospect who began his conversation with the phrase, "You've probably never seen another company like ours." Sure I have, I thought in the confidence of my own mind— you guys are all alike.

But, in fact, he was right. And in all the time since, I have yet to find a single sales situation that is exactly like any other.

And even if one opportunity is very much like another, each individual is different. By treating each opportunity as a unique experience, you are also treating each person at your prospect account as a unique individual—a show of respect that is usually rewarded with a better working relationship.

A Team

Your focus as a sales consultant is to generate sales revenue. This is also the focus of your company. You are an important part of a larger team, all united with this common goal. You will be able to contribute the most to your team effort by understanding a little more about the responsibilities of others on your team.

Sales Representatives

The most important member of your immediate team is your sales representative. He or she is responsible for guiding the sales effort from start to finish. The sales rep will find your sales opportunities, prioritize them, and handle all the financial details of the deal.

In many areas, though, your tasks overlap those of the sales rep. You are both working towards a common goal—closing the deal. However, there are two areas where virtually all teams of sales reps and sales consultants differ.

You are responsible for handling the technical details of your products and services, and with a high level of accuracy. When it gets down to the nitty-gritty of how to use your product, you are the one stepping to the forefront.

This simple differentiation does not mean that your representative does not fully understand the technology. He surely does. But the prospect will look to you for explanations of the details, while the sales representative typically presents the big picture.

All other aspects of the deal are handled by the sales rep. The sales rep is in charge and holds the ultimate responsibility for closing deals—the rep always handles the money.

These simple facts lead to your first maxim:

Never talk about money with your customers.

If your customer brings up the topic, gently defer to your sales representative. The sales rep is the person who is ultimately responsible for the revenue you generate. The sales rep's compensation, and even his or her continued employment, is directly related to the sales he or she produces. Because of this, your sales rep is solely responsible for managing the sales effort.

The sales representative is the captain of the team.

This cardinal rule does not mean that you cannot contribute your own ideas about the direction of a sales cycle. A good sales representative will take advantage of the insights and information that may be apparent only to the sales consultant and treat you as a partner. But the sales rep will always have the last word on decisions about any particular opportunity or account.

Your Colleagues

If you work for a medium-sized to large company, you will probably be one of a group of sales consultants. Although no sales situation is like any other, one of the best ways to learn is from the mistakes and successes of others.

Your colleagues can provide valuable insights into your products and the way to handle sales opportunities, as well as acting as a source of specific technical wisdom. Not only can your colleagues help you in your job, but having a mutually sharing relationship with your colleagues can make your working life much more enjoyable.

Perhaps, in the old days, you would see your equals as your competitors for some of the benefits of your job, but in the wildly expanding world of technology, there is plenty to go around. Interaction with your colleagues will help all of you succeed.

Your Corporate Support Team

Although your sales team is on the front lines, trying to increase business, your organization will usually include two types of support teams—corporate resources and administrative resources.

Most companies have headquarters marketing and management staffs, whose job is to create materials to help you in your selling efforts. These materials tend to be broadly focused—remember, since no two sales situations are alike, a general piece of collateral (sales material) must be broad.

Corporate Marketing

Although you may be tempted to create all of your own presentation materials from scratch, it is good practice to try to use the corporate materials as your starting point, for two reasons:

1. **Corporate marketing has better resources to put together attractive materials:** Although you, as a technical person, may think that an attractive look and feel is not that important, most prospects are more open to a better looking presentation.

2. **Corporate marketing will, in most cases, be champions of the official company line, which the combined resources of your organization will be pushing:** This line is the same tack being taken in many other marketing materials, which your prospect has seen, so using the corporate materials as your basis will leverage this existing mindshare.

Technical Support Team

Another corporate resource, which is often overlooked, is the technical support team. The technical support department is the only other section in a company that has direct contact with customers. When your customers have problems, be they trivial or dire, they will contact tech support. If you can, you should try to establish contact with the people in your tech support organization who handle calls from your significant customers. Therefore, when you are aware of problems your customers are having, you can help improve your relationships with them by taking a

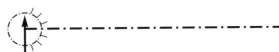

proactive approach. You can also sometimes help the technical support staff by giving them background information about the account. By understanding the situation and personality of the people at the customer site, you may be able to guide tech support to the most effective solution to the problem.

If your work situation allows prospects to call for technical support, it is imperative that you establish this contact, since such a call can signal the first warning of a potential land mine that could destroy your sales effort.

You can understand what a difficult job technical support is. All day long, these people answer phones, and the customers on the other end of the phone are calling only because they have a problem. We have found that technical support people really respond well to positive interaction with sales consultants, since taking a call from a sales consultant is inevitably a pleasant change for them. This makes it pretty easy to include technical support workers as members of your team, letting you reap the benefits of a good relationship with them.

Your Administrative Support Team

Your administrative support team is made up of those people who help to keep your organization running—from your local IT staff to the administrative people in your office and elsewhere.

Since the focal point of your company is to make sales, and since you are part of the sales team, you may develop the attitude that your administrative team should simply offer you unqualified support without expecting anything in return. While, at a high level, this may be an accurate statement, everyone works better as part of a team. And your administrative staff plays a crucial role in keeping your organization functioning.

The support staff is the lifeblood of your office.

If you take the time and effort to make your administrative staff feel like part of the team, you will reap the rewards in improved support.

How You Do Your Job

I hate having others telling me how to do my job. One of the joys of being a sales consultant is being able to manage your own set of tasks. But there are some standards of behavior that apply to your job as well as to any other professional position.

Professional Conduct

The role of a sales consultant has traditionally carried with it a reputation for eccentricity. The expertise of a sales consultant is highly valued, so some deviation from the norms of professional behavior are frequently tolerated.

You may very well be allowed to come into the office dressed more casually than your counterparts in sales, and your general attitudes about the world may also be different than your sales representatives.

Your character falls somewhere between the professional demeanor of sales and the anything-goes attitude of development.

However, don't let the leeway you have within your organization be reflected in your interaction with your customers and prospects. You should always conduct yourself in a professional manner with people outside your company. You should dress well, take care of your personal grooming, and not use inappropriate language in front of customers.

The key word in the last paragraph is *inappropriate*. Every situation has its own context, and you do want to fit in. If you are going on a sales call on a Friday, you should find out from your prospect in advance if the company recognizes "casual Friday" dress codes.

Although you may occasionally feel out of place coming to a meeting in a suit and tie when others appear in jeans and casual shirts, the discomfort of this mismatch is far less than if the situation were reversed. Appearing in casual clothes when your prospect is in business attire could ruin your credibility for good.

We do not believe that jeans and a T-shirt are appropriate for any customer interactions, at least within working hours.

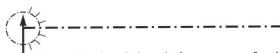

A good rule of thumb for your professional conduct is what I call the "Customer + 1":

Customer + 1 is a safe formula for judging the level of professional conduct.

This rule states that you can be *almost* as informal as your customer. If your customer appears wearing jeans and an Aloha shirt, you can wear khakis or slacks and a golf shirt. If your customer wears slacks and a polo shirt, you can appear in a sports coat.

If your customer uses the word "damn" in your conversation, you can feel free to use "dang," and so forth.

Of course, there is always an upper limit on these rules. If your customer shows up in a business suit, this doesn't mean you have to appear in formal wear!

By using the Customer + 1 rule, you can always err on the side of caution, which will denote your respect for the customer without causing too glaring a contrast.

Lateness

Being prompt is more than just being polite. It is the basic foundation of a professional relationship.

There is no excuse for lateness.

You should never be late for any appointment, internal or external, because your attitude sets a tone for the meeting and silently speaks volumes about your respect for the other party who was kept waiting.

Your quest for promptness does not mean you will always be successful in arriving on time to an appointment. There are always unforeseen events that can delay your schedule, from heavy traffic to a flight being canceled to a late start from home because you have a sick child. But in any and all of these cases, you should make every effort to contact your prospect as soon as you see a delay looming. Inform him or her of the possibility that you may be late. Even if you can only leave a voice mail, the prospect will at least understand that you did your best to meet at the appropriate time.

Learning How to Listen

I'm sure you've all heard this simple maxim before:

> ## You have two ears and one mouth, so you should listen more than you speak.

As trite as it may sound, this statement is especially relevant to the job of a sales consultant. You will be dominating the conversations in many parts of your interactions, especially with your prospects. When you do a product demonstration or a chalk talk, you will, in essence, be lecturing to your somewhat attentive audience.

But you must never forget to pay attention to the reactions of your audience. In virtually every part of the sales process, your primary goal is to *get* information from your prospect, not to give information to them. You can get information only by listening to the responses to what you and the other members of your sales team are saying.

In fact, some of your most valuable listening comes when your sales rep, or some other member of your sales team, speaks.

> ## In most sales situations, the sales team has four ears and one mouth.

Both you and your sales representative can listen to your prospect, while only one of you can talk at a time.

Don't take the attitude that you can sit back and relax when your sales rep is speaking, even if you have heard the pitch dozens of times before. You can contribute more to the success of your sales effort by carefully listening to the reactions of the prospect. It is easier for the person who has not been speaking to judge the reactions of an audience, since the silent member can focus all of his or her attention on the audience.

Keep notes on the listeners' reactions to share with the sales rep later, so both of you can adjust your future efforts to address any areas that might seem problematic.

Of course, the word *listen* should be taken in its broadest sense. You listen with more than your ears, since your counterparts communicate with more than their mouths. Their body language can tell you a world about their attitude, so you should also concentrate on listening with your eyes throughout the sales process.

First Principles

Before we get into the rest of this book, we must discuss two concepts that are so important that we refer to them as "first principles"—and you should consider these two principles at every level of your work as a sales consultant.

Maintaining Control

Uncertainty is a part of our lives, especially our lives as sales consultants. A wide variety of potential actions can make our decisions much more difficult—mainly because people are involved. A person's reactions are not always predictable, unlike those of a computer, which will always make the same decision in the exact same circumstance. No, people are affected by such an incredibly high number of variables that it seems virtually impossible to control the actions of even a single person, let alone the group of people that is involved with most prospect teams.

On top of this, each individual and group is different, so applying general rules about control in a job when you encounter many different people in the course of each working day may seem like an impossible task.

Added to this difficulty is the simple fact that most people don't like being controlled—especially by a sales team. Despite this, the first golden rule is all about control:

Maintain control of the sales process, to as great a degree as possible.

Notice the wording of this cardinal rule. Though you won't be able to control the *actions* of your prospects and customers, you can, to some extent, control the *process*. Your prospects and customers will always be in control of the final outcome of the process—that's why they call it selling, rather than buying—but you can still guide the course of the process.

Controlling the process means that you are the one who sets the course for the sales cycle. In an ideal situation, you can reach agreement with your prospect on the steps of a sales cycle in your initial meetings. You can set up a timetable that will include each step in the cycle and the action that will follow from that step.

As you move into each step, you will work at creating an even finer degree of control. For instance, you might start by establishing that an evaluation will center around a particular set of criteria. Your next step in establishing control of the process is to create a list, in cooperation with your prospect, as to what those criteria are. Another step in increasing your control over the sales process is to determine how each of the criteria will be weighted in making the final purchase decision.

Remember that your prospect may be leery of readily giving up too much control early on in the process. Keep your eyes open for opportunities to establish even more control over the cycle. The more control you have over the sales process, the greater your ability to influence its outcome.

If you can gain control over the substance of one or more steps in this process, you will be in an extremely favorable position. For instance, if you were to gain control of the actual creation of the criteria, you would be able to set the ground rules for the sales engagement.

Be careful, though, because an overaggressive attitude can lose you some easily spooked customers. If you seem to be trying to dominate the sales process, some prospects may back away. Even worse, they may simply turn off the flow of information.

A good sales team is never surprised by the outcome of a sales cycle.

As you work through the sales cycle and achieve a greater level of control, you should also come to a greater understanding of how your product or service matches up with the needs of the prospect.

If you suddenly find yourself surprised by a twist or turn in the sales cycle, it should be a sign to you that you have lost control of the process. And as you move deeper and deeper into the sales cycle, you should find your scope of control gradually increasing.

**If you find your scope of control
decreasing at any point in a sales cycle,
take it as a danger sign.**

There are two basic reasons why you might find your scope of control decreasing as you reach the later stages of the sales cycle:

1. **You made a miscalculation at some point earlier in the sales cycle**—Perhaps you made an incorrect assumption about your prospect. This might show up only later in the sales cycle as a reduction in control. For instance, you may have assumed that your chief contact on the prospect team was totally in charge of the evaluation process. All of a sudden, it turns out that the evaluation has to go through another group of people.

2. **Your prospect has begun to withdraw**—Someone, somehow, drove the nice and orderly progress of your sales cycle off the rails. The reason could be extremely indirect, such as a report in The Wall Street Journal that your company is on the verge of bankruptcy. The reason could be extremely direct, such as the fact that your sales rep made an inappropriate comment to a member of the prospect team.

In the end, it doesn't matter *why* your control of the sales process has decreased: It just matters that it has. If you find yourself in this position, you should beat an orderly retreat until you and your sales team can figure out how to re-establish yourselves in the account.

The Finite Resources of the Sales Cycle

Your time and resources are limited, as are the time and resources of your prospect. Because of this simple fact, you should always be aware that no sales cycle is infinite. This restriction is the basis for the second golden rule.

> *There are always limitations on resources in the sales cycle.*

This is a somewhat self-evident cardinal rule, but it should shape virtually all of your actions while you work with an account. Each of the resources in a sales cycle—your time, your prospect's time, your prospect's budget, your ability to satisfy all of your prospect's wishes—has some type of limit. Don't ever make the mistake of believing otherwise.

Once you have been in the sales business for a long time, you will have heard a prospect tell you things that contradict this basic rule. Nonetheless, beware of what appears to be the "boundless" prospect.

If a prospect says to you, "We don't have a time limit for the evaluation process," the sales cycle is in trouble. If the prospect doesn't have to buy a product at any fixed point in time, they obviously have no immediate plans for using the fruit of the purchase, which, of course, means that the purchase is not really required.

This situation does not necessarily mean that you and your sales team get up and walk away from the prospect. Instead, you should factor this lack of an immediate need into your calculations on how to deal with the prospect.

Of all the resource limitations in a sales cycle, the most stringent limitation is time. As you already know, you will be trying to balance the demands of many different sales opportunities. However, the limitation on *your* time is not the most crucial time limit in the sales process. Instead, the following is true:

The most limiting restraint on a sales cycle is face-to-face time with the prospect.

Every real sales cycle is made up of only a limited amount of time for you to spend with the prospect. The amount may vary from account to account and may very well be stretched over an extended period, but you have to continually be aware that the amount of time you have for direct contact with your prospect is finite.

To be successful in your overall efforts, you will have to learn how to use your limited time in the most efficient manner. In Chapter 18, we discuss how to manage your overall time, but you should always keep in mind that this limited resource affects every step in the sales cycle. The entire process of qualification, which is discussed in detail in Chapter 8, is basically a precursor to deciding how much time to spend with any particular account. You should plan your demos, as will be discussed in Chapter 10, to make efficient use of time in presenting the strong points of your product.

Even dealing with the competition, which is discussed in Chapter 15, comes down to a matter of time management. You don't want to spend too much of your valuable face-to-face time with your prospect discussing the competition, since this time will be subtracted from the time you

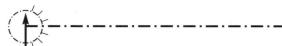

have to present the advantages of your own products. Similarly, if you can set up an objection that forces your competition to spend an inordinate amount of their time dealing with your team, you will have gained an advantage in the sales cycle by taking away from their selling time.

In the world of online sales, the face-to-face aspect of the sales cycle can virtually disappear. However, the pressure of limited contact is even greater, since a typical prospect may only spend a few minutes visiting your site.

Why This Book?

If you've gotten this far, we hope you have begun to see the value of this book. But what, exactly, is the purpose of the book?

We bill this volume as "a comprehensive training manual." It will focus on helping you to improve on the two essential qualities that make up a successful sales consultant.

- Technical skills
- People skills

These two qualities are present in wildly varying degrees in different individuals. In fact, technical ability and interpersonal skills are frequently seen as antithetical to each other, as depicted in the classic image of the anti-social technician. The combination of skills makes your job quite unique and challenging.

These two qualities have another similarity. You can never attain true mastery of either of these qualities. (It's a Zen thing!) As you work with your particular products and solutions, you will gain a greater familiarity with them, but you will continually be faced with new sets of problems from your prospects and customers that will require you to continually find new ways to apply your knowledge. Of course, in the fast-changing world of technology, your products will also continue to evolve.

Your people skills can also be continually improved. Just as you will continually face new technical challenges, each sales situation you enter will be slightly different. Even if the technical nature of a particular sales cycle is exactly the same as another, each opportunity will have a different cast of characters, with their own interpersonal dynamics that you will have to adjust to. There is an infinitely wide variation in people and their attitudes, so you will continually be challenged to find new and better ways to interact with your customers and prospects.

If there is such a wide range of technical and people skills needed, how can this book help you? While it may be difficult to master technical skills and people skills, there is a process you can follow to be successful. We have walked this road before, so we can offer you two types of help:

- **Experience**—This stems from our thirty years in the business, both as sales consultants and working with sales consultants.

- **A framework to understand your primary tasks**—Although we cannot train you on the specifics of your products and environment, we can give you a context that will help you to understand the wide variety of tasks in your working life.

This book can help you examine and re-examine your job and yourself. It is always difficult to realize the need for this type of re-examination. If you have been a sales consultant for very long, you no doubt already feel that you know a great deal about how to do your job—and you do. But you can always gain from further contemplation on the tasks that make up your professional life.

A good sales consultant can always find ways to improve. And a truly great sales consultant will be able to use experience as a way to hone his or her skills. This book is meant to help you polish your own natural abilities.

We firmly believe that there is no "best" prescription for a generic solution to the problems you will face in your job. But we are confident that this book will help you to gain a deeper understanding of the essential tasks that make up your job and allow you to use your own strengths most effectively.

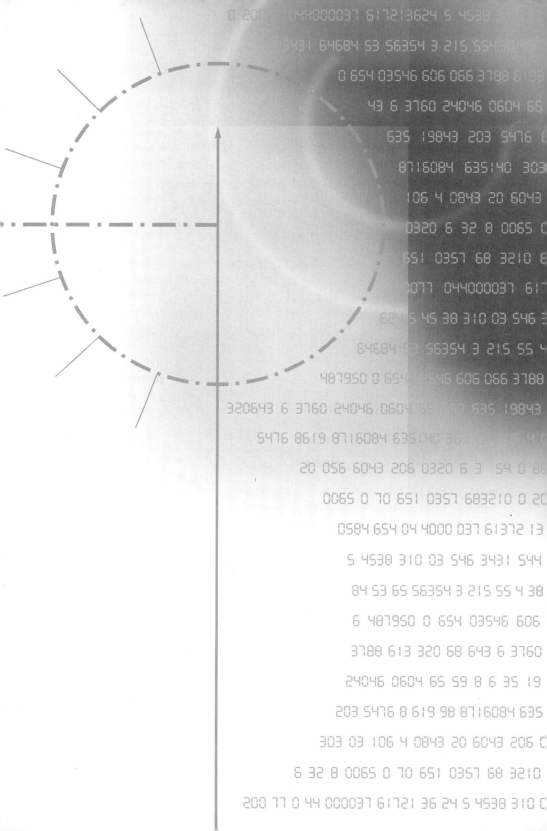

CHAPTER 2

The Sales Process

The goal of any sales team is to close deals and acquire customers. The steps that you follow to attain these goals make up what is called the sales process. Most technical sales follow a similar pattern from lead acquisition to closure, but some variations are found along the way.

Because you are a sales consultant, your presence is critical to the sales process, even though you are not necessarily in command of the overall process. In this chapter, we are going to look at the overall sales process so that we can show you the "big picture." Some elements will not affect you directly, but you will find it helpful to understand how the overall process works. This way, you will better appreciate your place in the grand scheme.

As with the introduction to basic sales terminology in Chapter 1, this chapter is not intended to be a replacement for any of the fine books and methodologies surrounding the sales process. Instead, it will lay the groundwork for further discussion of your primary goal—closing technical sales.

Sales Funnel

One of the most crucial activities your sales team will engage in is determining which sales opportunities you will focus on. In order to help to categorize your opportunities, we use the *sales funnel,* as shown in Figure 2.1.

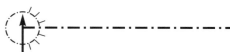

Figure 2.1
Sales Funnel.

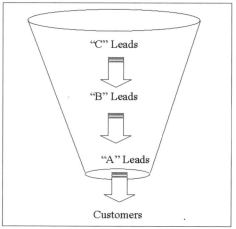

"C" Leads

"B" Leads

"A" Leads

Customers

The visual image of the funnel is appropriate—a greater number of prospects are at the top than at the bottom. After all, many are called on, but few are closed.

Sales teams use different terminology to refer to the prospects located at the various phases of the funnel. We have chosen a basic terminology for our funnel, calling the different prospects "A," "B," and "C." The higher the letter grade, the closer a prospect is to making a purchase.

Prospects labeled "C" leads are generally in the preliminary phase of their evaluations. They are surveying the marketplace but may not yet have a specific timetable or criteria upon which to make a decision. They are in the funnel because they have reached the "lead generation" phase of the sales cycle, and perhaps have attended a seminar or sent in a "bingo card" from a trade magazine, which is used to request information from an advertiser. Thus, they are on the sales radar screen, but because you serve as a sales consultant, you are less likely to find them on *your* radar screen. Over a period of time, some of these prospects will become "B" leads.

While there are many "C" leads, there are always comparatively fewer "B" leads. Your sales rep partner will generally have had several telephone conversations and maybe even some face-to-face meetings with prospects at the "B" level of the funnel. You may even be asked to accompany the sales rep to these meetings to help qualify these prospects. We'll talk more about this process in Chapter 8.

It is possible that as a sales consultant you will have some interaction with "B" prospects. Your activities may include qualification meetings, conference calls, and short demonstrations. However, it is unlikely that you will be conducting detailed product evaluations with "B" prospects. Sales consultants are a precious resource, so most sales reps will not expect you to devote your time and energy working "B" leads. This is especially true when you are in a territory that has an active and full sales funnel. You will normally only be deployed on the "A" leads, while the sales rep will work the other accounts without your involvement. Prospects in the "B" category are not necessarily bad prospects; they just have not come far enough along in the sales cycle to warrant a concerted effort to close them.

> As a sales consultant for a relational database vendor, I came across many accounts controlled by people who were planning to buy an application off the shelf and then choose a database engine on which to run the application. It did not make much sense to work these accounts heavily until they had decided upon the application software. My sales partner would keep an eye on the account and leave it as a "B" lead, since it was clear that the prospect was going to buy a database at some point, and that we were in the running. Once the "B" account had made the application decision and made the transition to the "A" list, I would typically get involved with beginning the detailed demonstration and evaluation phases of the sales process.

As prospective clients make their way down the funnel, the number of accounts gets smaller and smaller, in keeping with the "many are called on, few are closed" concept. The smallest, but most important, category is composed of the "A" leads, since these are the accounts that are the most likely to make a buy decision within the expected time frame. From a sales perspective, time frames are almost always calculated on a quarterly basis.

"A" leads are accounts that exhibit the following characteristics:

- They have the budget (money to spend)
- They are in the market for a product in your product category
- They have established criteria and are actively looking for a solution
- Your product's capabilities roughly match the prospect's technical requirements

The first point on our lists concerns money. Your sales rep will always immediately try to qualify the account for budget. If there is no money, there will not be a sales cycle. The sole exception to this rule involves accounts that are pursuing corporate site licenses. Sometimes, large companies will evaluate the leading products within a product segment and then select a particular product as the "standard" for all of their subdivisions. In such cases, the budget requirement may be waived with the understanding that the selected vendor will have the exclusive ability to sell to all of the divisions.

The second major criteria demands making sure that the customer is in the market for a product that fits your description. This is just like the *Sesame Street* jingle, "One of these things is not like the others." If the prospect is looking at three sports cars and a bulldozer, and you are the bulldozer, it is probably time to reclassify the prospect out of the sales cycle. The third point on the list involves checking to see if the customer has established an evaluation process. Has he or she put together a criteria document? Has he set a deadline? Does he or she have a business need that dictates finding a solution?

The final point involves checking to see if the potential client's technical requirements match your product's capabilities. Even products in the same basic category have different capabilities, so part of the ticket to the "A-List" category calls for roughly matching their requirements to your features. This point is the one where you will be expected to give the most input. Since you are the technical expert on your team, your sales representative may ask your help in ranking "A" level prospects on this criteria.

The lower down the sales funnel you go, the further along in the sales process you are—and the faster the cycle may progress. At the "A" point, the process is likely to proceed much faster. A single prospect might linger around as a "B" lead for months, but then make the transition to the "A-List" with closure in a matter of weeks or even days.

Prospect Status

Sales leads that pass the basic qualifications process are granted status as prospects. They typically enter the funnel. In most cases, prospects will be classified as "C" leads, but this is not always the case. Sometimes, a new prospect will jump right into the "A-List" from the start, but this is a rarity.

Up to this point, the corporate marketing department might have taken the active role in "managing" the account by inviting the prospect to seminars or just keeping them on the mailing list. But once a lead is officially recognized as a prospect, the sales team will take responsibility for the account.

Once a sales lead becomes a prospect, it usually also becomes part of a sales forecast. As the name implies, the sales forecast is designed to predict the timing and amount of future sales. Forecasts include a list of all accounts in the funnel, although some "C" level prospects may not be included if the sales rep does not have enough information on them. The sales rep provides details about the prospect's status, next steps, an estimate of the dollar value of the deal, and the expected closing date. Once the prospect has been placed on the forecast list, the sales team becomes responsible for the maintenance of the account. Although you will not necessarily be responsible for each account in the forecast, you should always have a copy of the current forecast.

The sales forecast is just as important to you as it is to the sales rep.

The forecast represents the game plan for your team in the current quarter. Although you might not be responsible for accounts in the "C" and "B" categories, it is important for you to keep an eye on these accounts. As the sales process with these prospects proceeds, you will undoubtedly be involved in the qualification, demonstration, and evaluation stages. The forecast gives you a road map to the workload that you can expect over the current quarter. It also gives you some direction about where you should be spending your time. If you find yourself spending hours on the phone answering questions from a "C" prospect, something is wrong. It's time to get the sales rep involved either to move the account up in the funnel, or to find a way to reduce the effort you are spending on this distant potential sale.

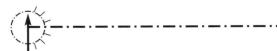

How will you know which accounts are important if you don't have a copy of the forecast? Some sales reps will be reluctant to share the details of their forecast with you. You may need to point out that there are advantages for both of you if you have access to the forecast. Your time and abilities are a valuable resource in the sales cycle, and they can be most effectively applied where they will do the most good. In addition, you may be able to contribute information to the sales rep that will help make his or her forecast more accurate.

Stages in the Sales Cycle

There are several broad stages that most sales cycles pass through. These cycles are

- Qualification
- Presentation and demonstration
- Product evaluation
- Selection and negotiation
- Closure

Not all sales cycles go through all of these stages, and not all of these stages are equal in time or importance. For instance, some sales opportunities may involve extensive product evaluation periods, while others may not require any. However, these stages are always presented in this order, and you will usually engage in most of them in a sales cycle.

Qualification

In qualifying a prospect, you match the needs of the prospect with the capabilities of your product and solution. If you are selling bulldozers and the prospect is looking for sports cars, then the account isn't qualified.

Both your sales rep and you will engage in some form of qualification. The sales rep will qualify the account as to the budget, the purchasing process, and contractual issues. As a sales consultant, your role will be to determine the technical fit between the prospect's needs and your product's capabilities.

Qualifying is an ongoing process rather than a single event, but the sales process still includes a specific qualifying stage between the identification of the prospect and the demonstration/evaluation phases. Demonstrations and evaluations require a significant investment of time and energy, so it is important to make sure that the prospect's technical requirements are a good fit before you invest additional resources in the account.

In Chapter 8, we will be more specific about the details of managing the qualifying process. At this point, you only need to keep in mind that the qualification phase will be the first stage that involves a significant amount of your time. Spending this time up front will ensure that the team doesn't waste time working accounts that are unlikely to result in sales.

Properly qualified accounts are ready for more aggressive action on the part of the sales team. Typically, you will be needed in qualified accounts to at least perform a product demonstration. Your sales rep will steer the less-well-qualified prospects to seminars or trade shows in hopes of later leading them deeper into the sales funnel.

Presentation and Demonstration

Once an account transitions into the "A" category, it is time to schedule a presentation and demonstration. (Some "B" category prospects will fall into this category as well.)

Presentations and demonstrations are the heart and soul of the technical selling process. At this point in the sales cycle, the prospect has responded to an advertising and marketing campaign, has been introduced to the sales team, and has been qualified as a basic technical fit for your product or service. Now, the prospect wants to be sold on a solution. The presentation and demonstration give you the chance to starting selling with a vengeance. Chapter 9, "Making Effective Technical Sales Presentations," will introduce you to the presentation process in detail, and Chapter 10, "Delivering Effective Product Demonstrations," will walk you through the product demonstration event. This phase of the sales cycle signals the start of your heavy involvement in the account.

Your job during this phase of the sales cycle is to position your product as the key solution for the prospect. To do so, you will leverage your thorough understanding of your product's capabilities and you must understand your prospect's technical needs in detail.

Inadequate and ineffective presentations and demonstrations mean that the prospect likely will drop out of the sales process. A prospect might still buy a product, but it will probably not be *your* product. Conversely, if you score well in this point in the sales cycle, you will be well positioned to win the evaluation phase of the sales process.

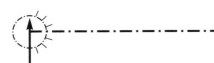

I have worked with products that do not require a demonstration, such as utility programs and certain compilers. If your buyer is the technical decision maker, and your product is more of a commodity technical product, you may sometimes skip the demo and give the prospect a trial copy of the software. You can then move right to the evaluation phase. Skipping the demonstration stage can shorten the sales cycle, but it puts incredible pressure on you as a sales consultant to manage the qualification and evaluation phases.

Giving a prospect a copy of the software may replace the need for a demo, but it does not replace the information-gathering aspect of the demo.

Never simply drop off a trial of the software without follow-up, and consider it part of the sales cycle.

If you want to close a deal, you will have to do more than simply wait for a prospect to evaluate the software without your assistance.

Product Evaluation

For complex and expensive software, prospects rarely decide to purchase a product after seeing just a presentation and demonstration. In most cases, the prospect will move into the evaluation phase, a phase that can take several forms. Prospects verify the features and benefits of your solution through product evaluation.

Sometimes, the evaluation process is as simple as checking customer telephone references or visiting a site where your product is used. Often, the customer will want to work with your product directly by attending customer training sessions or conducting a trial of your product or service at their location. We will take a detailed look at managing evaluations in Chapter 11, but it is important even now for you to understand the value of this stage in the overall sales process.

Most prospects won't go to the evaluation phase with all competing products. Instead, they will typically identify a front-runner (either formally or informally) and then move to the product evaluation stage with this product and one or two secondary competitors.

> ## The sales rep decides whether or not to proceed with any evaluation, but the sales consultant manages the evaluation on a daily basis.

As a sales consultant, you will be more involved with the *daily* workings of the evaluation process than with any other phase of the sales process. Most issues that come up during an evaluation are technical, so it falls to you to handle these issues as they arise. Evaluations can be incredibly time-consuming, but winning the evaluation is usually the ticket to closing the deal.

Selection and Negotiation

If you win in the technical decision phase, the next stage in the process is negotiation. As a sales consultant, you will not be heavily involved in this part of the sales process, but you still must be diligent. Your prospect will likely start negotiating heavily with the selected vendor, but the second-place vendor may still have a chance at winning the deal if the prospect cannot come to terms with the primary vendor. Many times, the negotiations will proceed while the product evaluation phase winds down, especially if the prospect has been building or implementing a prototype with your product. Even after the prospect has selected your product on its technical merits, he or she might want to show the prototype to other members of the organization in order to capture the organization's enthusiasm.

> ## The negotiation phase is a time of peril for sales consultants.

There are two kinds of peril to be wary of at this point. If yours is the selected product, you have to keep up your enthusiasm and technical oversight while negotiations proceed. After all, the last thing you want to have happen is for a showstopper to crop up and interrupt the negotiations. On the other hand, if yours is not the selected product, you must work with your sales rep to shut down the evaluation phase and walk away from this last opportunity.

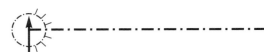

For a sales consultant, being in second place like this is one of the worst possible situations. You've essentially lost the deal but still have to waste large blocks of time finishing up with what is probably a lost cause. This is a good time to work with your sales rep to close down the evaluation prematurely. If the leading product fails to close the account during negotiations, you can always return to the evaluation. The final decision is up to the sales rep, and there will be cases where he will decide to "hang in there," especially if the competitor's position is weak from a negotiation perspective.

A good sales rep will usually gain some agreement about pricing and making the deal with the prospect before the evaluation phase begins. Reps want to make sure that the prospect has a basic idea of how much the product will cost, so they start preliminary negotiations early on. The "best and final offer" or BAFO negotiation comes at the end of the evaluation period. After all, your sales rep will be negotiating from a much stronger position if your product has won the technical evaluation. The hardest negotiating still takes place at the end of the sales cycle.

Large, complex application products such as enterprise resource planning (ERP) and customer relationship management (CRM) tend to be expensive solutions, as they include extensive service costs. Most companies quote list prices for the software until they reach the end of the sales cycle. Prospects will typically negotiate with several selected vendors to get the best price. In such cases, a deep discount can overcome an inferior technical solution. (Sometimes a "good enough" product is really good enough for a particular customer.)

Closure

You can choose your cliché here—"It's not over 'til the fat lady sings" or Yogi Berra's "It ain't over 'til it's over." You win the business only when the customer signs the contract and provides your company with a purchase order. Period. Although you will not be involved in the actual closing process, you should remember to take the time to enjoy the win.

Most sales departments have a routine to signify the closing of a deal. The "ringing of the bell" is a common practice. If your sales team doesn't have a tradition, invent one. Pin the "ace of spades" from a fresh deck of cards to a bulletin board, ring the bell, grab a bottle of champagne and make a toast. The routine doesn't matter: What does matter is that you take a moment to savor the victory. Conversely, if you lose the deal, then take a minute to let out your frustrations with your team—not *on* your team.

Timing of the Sales Cycle

The length of any sales cycle will be affected chiefly by complexity and price. The more complex the problem and the more complex your solution, the longer it will take to close the deal. The more expensive the solution, the more cautious your prospect will be in making a decision. Consider the simple graph shown in the Figure 2.2.

Figure 2.2
Complexity and Price vs. Time and Resources

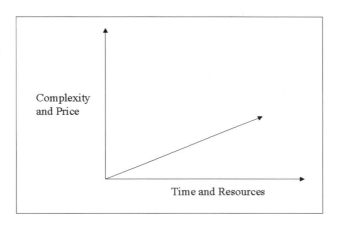

The process from advertising and marketing through to closure represents the complete sales cycle. However, the chief milestones encompass the span from the presentation phase to the negotiations phase. The complex solutions and problems associated with these two phases are hard to solve. This level of difficulty means that it will take more time to complete these phases. Increased time also means increased resource requirements, with you, the sales consultant, serving as the main resource.

You will want to keep track of the amount of time spent on any given account. This will help you to develop a methodology for estimating the amount of time and resources that will be needed from a technical perspective to close future deals. No methodology is perfect, but some broad-brush estimates based upon experience are better than just plain guessing. We will discuss time tracking and analysis in more detail in Chapter 18, "Productivity Enhancers and Time Management."

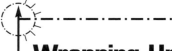

Wrapping Up

In this chapter, we have given you an overview of the basic technical sales process. The most important things for you to remember is that you must be involved in the majority of tasks in each sales cycle and that you are critical to the success of your sales team. Keep your focus on the sales process and you will be a valuable contributor.

In the next two chapters, we look at the environment in which you operate—the Technology Life Cycle and its effect on you and your prospect, and the different types of buyers in a sales opportunity.

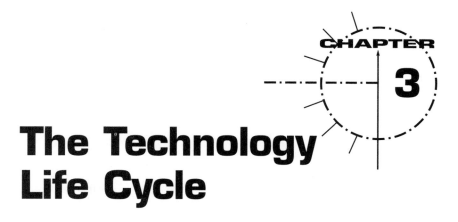

The Technology Life Cycle

With the continual addition of new products and ideas, it seems that technology is moving forward in a relentless march. Nonetheless, the introduction and acceptance of new technology does follow established patterns.

Improvements in technology tend to be absorbed by the marketplace according to an adoption schedule commonly referred to as the Technology Life Cycle. The relative position of your product and technology along this curve can have a fairly dramatic effect on how you, as the sales consultant, represent the product. In this chapter, we will introduce you to the Technology Life Cycle and take you through the process of identifying which sales consulting techniques best fit the position of your product at various stages.

Evolutionary and Revolutionary Change

A prospect's attitudes about technology are governed, to a large degree, by the type of change required for the adoption of that technology. Products that require customers to make wholesale changes in the manner in which they operate are said to be *revolutionary* products. As with other revolutions, the new solution "overthrows" the old one. Conversely, products that do not require prospects to modify their behavior significantly in order to take advantage of the product are considered to be *evolutionary*. Evolutionary products can be integrated into the prospect's existing infrastructure and can offer incremental improvements without the disruption that is caused by revolutionary products.

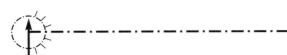

In order to understand the difference between these two types of products, let's examine two different types of new technology and their effects on a prospect:

- 56KB PCMCIA modem cards vs. 28.8 PCMCIA modem cards
- Desktop Linux operating system vs. Windows NT on the desktop

In the first example, we are comparing a new 56KB modem to an existing 28.8 modem. Both products use the same PCMCIA port on your laptop PC and both make use of the exact same set of software programs. You can remove the 28.8 modem and replace it with a 56KB modem without much effort at all. In fact, the 56KB modem is nothing more than a new-and-improved version of the same technology that you have been using all along. The new modem is an example of an *evolutionary* improvement in technology. Prospects will be able to take advantage of the new modem without difficulty.

The change from a Windows NT desktop to a Linux desktop, however, may not be such an easy migration. While Linux might offer some real advantages to the customer, it probably will require some changes throughout the prospect's computing infrastructure. Many popular desktop applications may not run under Linux, and even simple, routine tasks such as backup and recovery might need to be changed. This is an example of a *revolutionary* change. The benefits and advantages to the prospect of switching from Windows NT to Linux must be so strong as to justify the additional work and behavior modification that will be required to make the change.

The Technology Life Cycle

Although these two examples are representative of the real world, they are at opposite ends of the spectrum. In many cases, technology products will fall somewhere between these two extremes. This is exactly what makes it so difficult for you as a sales consultant.

The difference between these two types of products has to do with where they exist in terms of acceptance by the overall market. A popular model for understanding the market acceptance process of new technology is the Technology Life Cycle, which is essentially a bell curve. The bell curve compares the rate of adoption of technology over time, as shown in Figure 3.1.

Figure 3.1
Technology
Life Cycle

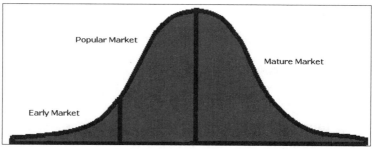

Technology products generally follow this model from left to right. Products are initially introduced to highly technical *Early Market prospects,* who are more receptive to revolutionary changes at the outset of a market.

These prospects gain an interest in your product as a means to outflank the competition. One of the most important features of these prospects is that they are more interested in the gain offered by a new technology than in the disruption that using this new technology may cause. They will put up with problems like insufficient documentation, product quality issues, or a lack of reference accounts in order to get that leading-edge advantage.

Many niche-market products will never grow beyond this segment of the life cycle. There is no inherent promise that any given product will achieve mainstream acceptance. Products that do not grow beyond the early market may find themselves a home in a small vertical marketplace, or they will ultimately fade away.

If the product segment becomes widely known and accepted by the general market, it begins to gain momentum. At this point, the *Popular Market* sees mainstream value in your technology and begins widespread deployment. Products become more legitimate as they become more stable and as multiple competitors emerge. This, in turn, causes more discussion and recognition, and a set of recognized features becomes standard. The Internet economy has been filled with products that have made it to the Popular Market stage of the life cycle. As of this writing, e-commerce business-to-business applications and portals are currently two of the hottest technologies in the Popular Market stage.

The last part of the curve is reserved for those products that make it past the Popular Market stage. In the last part of the curve, the highly skeptical and price-sensitive *Mature Market* appears. Although, as technologists, we may disdain the old-fashioned attitudes of members of the Mature Market, this group brings an enormous purchasing power to the table. Product categories that make it to the Mature Market can enjoy long revenue streams. It is often difficult to know whether a given product is going to make it to the Mature Market phase of the life cycle. Some very prominent technologies, such as Internet "push" technology, died out long before they reached the Mature Market. The phenomenon of "Internet time" has radically compressed this "make or break period." As a result, some of yesterday's Popular Market products are today's casualties.

Once a technology has become something of a standard, you can be assured that it will live on into the Mature Market. Relational database engines are clearly at this stage of the life cycle, as are Web browsers.

We have adapted the Technology Life Cycle model to better reflect its effect on the sales consulting job. After all, you are focused on selling to the field, as opposed to being focused on the overall management of your company. At the field sales level, the life cycle is more a framework for positioning and selling your product.

The full Technology Life Cycle model is more complex when it is applied to a given technology market as a whole. Should you wish to study the life cycle model in more detail, there are a number of excellent resources available for a deeper study of the Technology Life Cycle.

Figure 3.2
Sales consultant's guide to the Technology Life Cycle

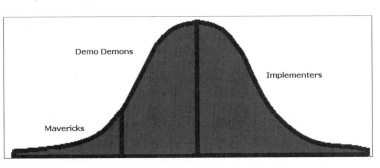

As shown in Figure 3.2, sales consultants follow a similar curve for representing technology. Sales consultants who enjoy working with the latest and greatest technology are what we call *Mavericks*. Mavericks tend to appreciate technology for technology's sake and are generally astute enough to understand the elegance of the architecture and clever engineering that has gone into the design of a product. They can visualize how a technical innovation can be used as a weapon for outpacing traditional solutions to business processes. *Demo Demons,* by contrast, tend to take a less optimistic view of technology. When a product reaches the Popular Market stage of the life cycle, there will generally be a huge market demand for products of its type. Sales consultants in this market place spend the majority of their time pitching the product to prospects— which is why we have given them the moniker, "Demo Demons." Demo Demons are comfortable working with the latest "hot technology" and can assimilate new products quickly and easily. *Implementers* are those sales consultants who are most comfortable working with more mature, stable technology. They differ from their compatriots in that they enjoy mastering a given technological product in its entirety (and they believe the only products worth considering are those that have achieved Mature Market status).

On a personal level, you will fall somewhere on this curve. Your own position on the Technology Life Cycle will determine your fit with your product, the marketplace, and your buyer. The very fact that you have chosen to work as a sales consultant means that you are amenable to changes in technology. However, the degree to which you embrace technology on a personal level will greatly affect the way in which you present technological solutions to your prospects.

The closer the match between your product's position and your personal position, the better the fit.

You will find that you will be much more comfortable selling and supporting technology solutions that match your own personal position on the Life Cycle. Consider the following table:

Table 4.1
Life Cycle Matrix

SC Type/ Life Cycle Position	Early Market	Popular Market	Mature Market
Maverick	÷+		
Demo Demon		÷+	
Implementer			÷+

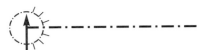

The columns across the top of the matrix represent the position of your product in the marketplace, and each row represents your own personal technology adoption position. There are a series of checkmarks diagonally down the center of the chart that mark the "sweet spot" between you and your product. In cases where your personal preferences intersect the current positioning of your product, the match is perfect. Essentially, this means that you are representing a product that is in the exact phase of the cycle in which your skills and interests are strongest.

In these cases, your personal viewpoint on the advantages of your product tends to match those of your prospective buyers. This makes it much easier for your prospects to understand the feature/benefit pitch, since *your* vision and your *prospect's* vision are likely to be a one-to-one match.

As you move in either direction by a single square, the match between you and your product becomes more tenuous. You will have a tendency to be either "too technical" or "not technical enough," and it will be harder for you to connect with your prospects. This is not to say that it is necessarily time for you to move on, as any one company may have several products that are in different phases of the life cycle. However, it *may* be time for you to start working with a new product within the same organization that better fits your own personal positioning within the Technology Life Cycle.

Determining your own personal positioning on the life cycle model is crucial if you are to become comfortable with your ideal role as a sales consultant.

Sales Consultant "Types"

In the following sections, we are going to take a more detailed look at each basic sales consultant "type," comparing and contrasting each type with the Life Cycle segments.

Maverick Sales Consultant

Mavericks are the purest technologists. They buy technology long before it becomes popular and apply existing technology in new and different ways. Mavericks are quick to immerse themselves in the details of a high-technology product and are not afraid to take things apart and put them back together. Mavericks are the types who build their own robots from a kit—and they lose interest in robots when everyone else has them! In order to assess your fit as a Maverick, ask yourself the following questions:

- Did you have a cell phone and pager long before they were in vogue?
- Did you hook your voice mail up to your pager?
- Do you own an MP3 player?
- Do you read industry specifications in detail?
- Did you write your own EJB server?
- Did you wire your house with Ethernet?

Mavericks enjoy technology for technology's sake. Since they are not afraid of technology, they are perfectly comfortable fixing problems themselves. They don't need a strong technical support organization behind them and can work independently. Mavericks are best paired with technology that is in the Early Market stage. From a sales-consulting perspective, Mavericks aren't concerned if the product does not demo well. They are so comfortable with the technology that they are happy to build things from scratch, right in front of the prospect.

In the following sections, we'll look at how Mavericks match up with the various phases of the Technology Life Cycle.

Mavericks and the Early Market

Early Market buyers are more apt to pursue technology for technology's sake, often well in advance of the development of a large marketplace for a given product. Likewise, sales consultants who are Mavericks are cut from the same mold. They are the first to jump on board with a company that has no marketing, no formal technical support organization, and a product that is still under development.

As of this writing, technology such as Wireless Markup Language is in the Early Market stage.

Mavericks have a tendency to be less "sales oriented." Therefore, they match the buying patterns of the Early Market. Mavericks give straight answers and are not afraid to "sling code" themselves to address weaknesses. Yet, Mavericks can see the vision of how this technology can benefit the market as a whole—and they can translate this vision into an enthusiasm for their technology. If you are a Maverick, you have both an appreciation for elegant technology and architecture and are well schooled in technical details. You may not always be able to answer technical questions immediately, but you will certainly understand the questions and the reasoning behind them. You will be comfortable serving as the first line of defense for support issues, and the engineering organization within your own company has respect for your technical skills.

Mavericks and Popular or Mature Markets

As a sales consultant selling into these market cycles, you may very well be less than satisfied. As your company entered the Popular and Mature Market segments of the life cycle, it has added many sales reps and new sales consultants to deal with increased business. Part of what makes you tick as a Maverick sales consultant is being the "first on the block" to make use of a new technology. You probably do not find it as enjoyable working with technology that everyone else is using. It's an interesting twist of fate. In the early days, you were eager to have the market broadly embrace your technology—and now that it has, you are already envisioning the future.

> Examples of this phenomenon abound in the real world. The sales consultants who were absolute stars in the early going become increasingly disillusioned and underutilized as the market develops. The sales reps begin to look for Demo Demons, so the Mavericks either move into engineering or leave the company altogether.

Since your skills and the prospect's needs are no longer a match, you are faced with two choices. Either start looking for the "next big thing" that can benefit from your skills, or realign yourself with a new part of the product or offering from your company.

> Take the example of the database product. At this point in the marketplace, relational databases are clearly in the Mature Market stage. As a sales consultant for a database vendor, you are very unlikely to be challenged if you come from the Maverick camp. What you *can* do is focus on the leading edge of the mature technology. For example, you can say that the next "big thing" in database technology is the use of XML for cross-application integration. Relational databases may be in the late market, but using XML with the database is still in its early days. You can leverage your long investment in databases while evangelizing a new category where you can still add value.

During the transitional period from the Early Market to the Popular Market, Mavericks can be leveraged to help new sales consultants get up to speed. However, once a market boom hits, the company can often better leverage a Maverick's skills on new products or platforms. If a company does not have another highly technical product line available for the Mavericks, defections are likely to occur.

Demo Demon Sales Consultants

Demo Demons are adept at "riding the next wave." They tend to be adaptable professionals by nature and can master the basics of new technologies quickly and efficiently. Demo Demons aren't as likely to build their own robots, but if you show them how your robot works, they'll be able to "demo it" in a heartbeat. They don't have to fully embrace a certain technology in order to talk about it; nor do they have a burning urge to master technology. In order to assess your fit as a Demo Demon, ask yourself the following questions:

- Are you content to learn new technology without mastering it?
- Do you enjoy working with the hottest technology trends?
- Are you able to learn new technology skills quickly?
- Are you perfectly happy leaving your laptop at the office over the weekend?
- Can you master demo scripts quickly and easily?
- You couldn't care less about the "Easter eggs" inside the new version of Microsoft Excel?

Demo Demons enjoy being sales consultants for many reasons, including the fact that they get to travel and are not stuck in an office all day long. Technology comes relatively easy to them, but they aren't overly focused on it. They can memorize a demo script quickly and easily, but they are not necessarily going to be "gung-ho" about diving down into the details of a product. In short, Demo Demons are comfortable users of technology, but they don't live and die by technology alone. In the following sections, we'll look at how Demo Demons match up with the various phases of the Technology Life Cycle.

Demo Demons and the Early Market

Demo Demons and the Early Market are a less than comfortable fit. While Demo Demons cannot for the life of them understand why anyone would want to know how the internals of the product work, Early Market prospects cannot understand why you would *not* want to know. Early

Market prospects will have a lot of questions, because the product category is somewhat immature. Demo Demons have enough experience to cover the basics—but they are not as eager to dive into the details. They tend to be savvy enough to "sell" around issues but are less comfortable tackling the heavy lifting.

This mismatch is generally temporary, because the company will start to attract more mainstream prospects as the market moves into the Popular Market stage. As a sales consultant, you might find yourself a little outside of your element, but this will change as the market moves forward.

Demo Demons and the Popular Market

Once the Popular Market develops for your product, the market has started to take off. In this situation, Demo Demons are the perfect match for the positioning of the product in the marketplace. Demo Demons sales consultants are slightly ahead of the market, but they are ready for the "next big thing" just as it begins to gain momentum.

As of this writing, technology such as Customer Relationship Management is in the Popular Market stage.

Experienced sales consultants from the Demo Demon category are the perfect warriors for riding the heady growth days of market explosion. If you have worked in the past as a sales consultant in the Popular Market, you know exactly how the game is played. The learning process is much simpler. All you need to do is to master the demo and the key product differentiation messages and then hit the streets.

If this is your first experience in pre-sales, you are in for one wild ride. The company probably won't have time to give you a whole lot of training, so you will have to learn on your feet. The good news is that you will have many opportunities to practice your craft, but you'll have to be careful to avoid developing bad habits at this stage. One particular problem for Demo Demons sales consultants is remembering the need to work the installed base. Customer references will be more critical to the Popular Market buyer, yet the nature of the Demo Demon lends itself to "seek and destroy" missions. As a Demo Demon, you'll have to make a concerted effort to keep an eye on your established customers during this phase of the market cycle.

Winning the Popular Market is critical to the long-term success of the company; large installed bases are critical for the Mature Market.

Demo Demons and the Mature Market

By the time the market matures, Demo Demons are likely beginning to lose interest in the product category. Many Demo Demons can see themselves as sales reps. The transition to the Mature Market is often the time at which they make the jump. As a sales consultant, you will find yourself dragged down by the slower pace and longer sales cycles. Mature buyers want to buy products from the leading vendors. They expect to be able to get good support, and they are more price-sensitive. Demo Demons are adept at giving the "killer demo," but many Mature Market buyers want a presentation that features less technology and more details about market share, standards support, and customer service. Mature buyers will generally conduct longer evaluations, which plays better to the skills of the Implementers.

Implementers

Implementers are the steadiest of all the sales consultant types. They tend to remain loyal to a given technology over a longer period of time and they are generally well organized. They enjoy technology, but they are not obsessed with the "next big thing." Implementers are satisfied to master one technology fully rather than jump around between products. Implementers will still be playing around with the "robot" long after other sales consultants have all but forgotten it. In order to assess your fit as an Implementer, ask yourself the following questions:

- Do you continue to "fiddle" around with more mature technology—such as relational databases?

- Do you read technical manuals from cover to cover?

- Do you understand technology in detail but don't feel compelled to explain every little detail?

- Do you enjoy seeing prospects leverage your technology into a production application?

Implementers enjoy being sales consultants because they get to work with technology without the same constrictions they would have as development engineers. They can continue to master new aspects of their product irrespective of the market position of the product. They tend to stay with the same company for long periods of time, so they are good resources for arcane product knowledge.

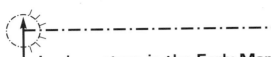

Implementers in the Early Market

Implementers tend to work more methodically than the typical Early Market prospect. They are comfortable with the technical details of a product, but it may have taken them a long time to acquire this knowledge. Implementers will have trouble translating the features of their product into the "solution" as envisioned by the Early Market prospect. They are quick to see the flaws in their own technology as it currently stands.

It is rare to see Implementer sales consultants matched up with an Early Market product. They are highly unlikely to leave a secure position and familiar technology for something new, especially for something that is still at the innovation stage. As a sales consultant, you will want to consider this fact carefully as you consider new job opportunities.

Implementers in the Popular Market

Implementer sales consultants can work the Popular marketplace, although it may not be familiar to them. When Implementers change companies, they tend to move to a company in the *late* phases of the Popular Market. They are not as eager to tackle the go-go-go pace set by the Demo Demons, and they have a stronger need to master their product. This slight mismatch is a very common pairing situation as the product makes the move from one phase to the next. The biggest challenge for the Implementer is to set a fast-enough pace to meet demand in the early going. As the market transitions into the Mature phase, Implementers hit their stride.

Implementers in the Mature Market

The Mature Market prospect is less impressed by fancy technical details and whiz-bang technology. Implementers are the perfect sales consultants for these prospects. This is because Implementers are short on hype, long on product knowledge, and tend to be great at customer support. They know what their customers are doing with the product, and they offer a wealth of technical-support experience. They master *all* aspects of their product and are more likely to be familiar with a sufficient level of detail about industry standards. Implementers are content to explain features in detail, and they are less likely to grow impatient with inexperienced prospects. They enjoy seeing a prospect build solutions with their products over a period of time.

As of this writing, relational databases are in the Mature phase of the Technology Life Cycle.

Mixed Environments

Products exist in just one stage of the Life Cycle at any given time, but you can sometimes get a mix of prospect personalities *within* a single sales cycle. While the buying philosophy for a company as a whole is usually set at a high level, it is common to have some of the technical decision-makers coming from different ends of the Life Cycle. Ideally, as the sales consultant, you will be working at the appropriate stage for your own skills and technological outlook.

For example, if you come from the Demo Demon sales consultant camp, you are probably working a product that has moved into the Popular or Mature marketplaces. Unfortunately, some of the technicians from the prospect's side of the table will not necessarily match up perfectly. Consider this example from the real world:

> It's late 2000, and you're working for a database vendor. Your job is to present the latest and greatest database solution to a new prospect.

Relational databases are clearly in the category of Mature at this point in the marketplace, at least for first-time purchases. A prospect looking at an RDBMS for the first time at this point is clearly a Mature buyer. Simple, right? Not necessarily. Consider the following modification:

> While presenting to this customer, one member of the technology team starts asking about XML (Extended Markup Language) interfaces in detail.

XML is at the early stage of the marketplace. You may not be able to address all of the questions about XML, and XML may not even be on your personal radar screen.

It is tempting to ignore evaluators who are outside the life cycle. Resist this temptation.

Prospects *as an organization* will buy within their Technology Life Cycle class, but individual evaluators outside the cycle may still have a serious influence on the deal. When all is said and done, the actual answers to the XML questions may have no impact on the deal either way. However, the manner in which you, the sales consultant, address the questions and show respect for the "innovative" requirements will definitely have an effect on how the Innovator feels about you and your product.

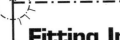

Fitting In

One of the most difficult decisions that you will have to make in your career as a sales consultant is deciding when it is time for a change. When you find yourself no longer fitting in with your current product and position, you have some choices:

- Find another company
- Move to promote another product within your current company
- Take another role within your company
- Alter your outlook

The first choice you might think of is the option to change companies. This is probably the most common choice for new sales consultants who have jumped into the game with companies that do not match their own position in the life cycle. If you have never worked as a sales consultant before, the whole concept of the life cycle may be new to you. Even if you are an experienced sales consultant, you might find that changing companies is the right move. We have found this to be especially true among Demo Demons, who are more comfortable working as hired guns than other types.

But changing companies is not your only option in today's market. Many companies have multiple products in development, in all phases of the life cycle. If you are not a good fit for one product, you might be a better fit for one of the other products that the company has in the pipeline. This is a more common solution if you are a Maverick working in a Mature marketplace. You might have more trouble moving between products within smaller companies that are in the *early* stages of marketing. Larger companies are more likely to have several products in the life cycle, while start-up companies most often are focused on a single stage.

You can always move out of the sales consulting ranks, even if the move is only temporary. Some sales consultants who have spent many years as Mavericks make the decision to move into product management, competitive intelligence, or engineering as their product matures. The skills that you have developed as a sales consultant are still valuable in these other roles, and the change in position may allow you to continue as a contributor as the market matures. The most difficult adjustment that you can make is to change your fundamental outlook on the life cycle. It is very hard to move backward in the curve (from Implementer to Maverick), but it is possible. It is much more likely that you will make the move forward in the curve over time. Your personal situation may dictate that you change your focus over time, and you may end up changing your focus to suit the changes in your life.

Wrapping Up

Deciding where you fit on the Technology Life Cycle scale is an exercise in self-discovery. It is incredibly tempting to place yourself in the position that you *want* to be in, rather than the position that you *are* in. Can you discipline yourself to move from one category to another? Sure, but it is unlikely that you will be able to move from one end of the life cycle to the other. Being a member of one category versus being at another is neither a positive nor a negative. You are what you are.

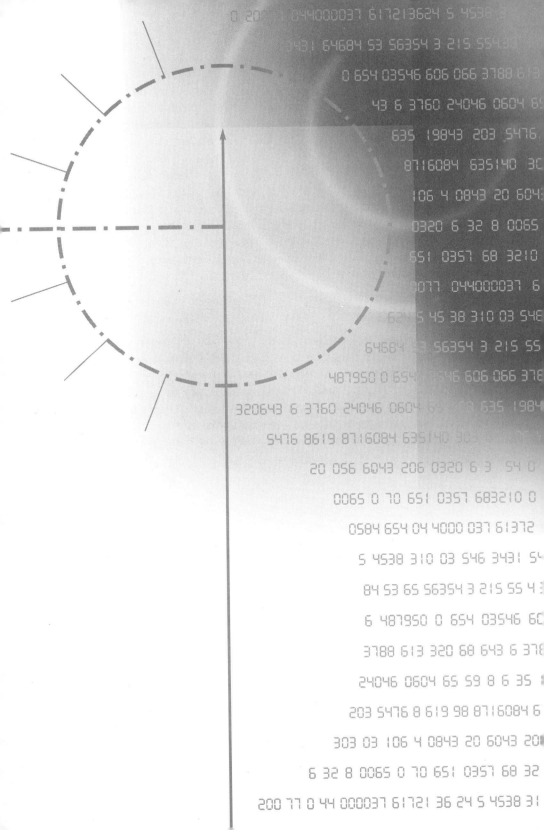

CHAPTER 4

Understanding the Buyer

Throughout this book, we discuss the object of your sales effort—the prospect or customer—as if referring to a single entity. You and your sales team are trying to sell your product to a single organization, not an individual. But, in fact, there are several different entities that you have to sell to in any given sales opportunity.

This chapter will introduce you to the different roles that exist as part of your prospect's evaluation team. Once these roles are examined, we will look at how they relate to the Technology Life Cycle, which was discussed in Chapter 3. Finally, we will discuss common pitfalls that you may encounter in dealing with the different members of your prospect's organization.

Prospect Roles

In any sales cycle, three different roles work together to determine the winner of the cycle. These three roles—played by the technical buyer, the economic buyer, and the end user—all have a part to play in the selection of a product or service.

We call these different parts of your prospect's organizations *roles,* because each may be occupied by one or more people. In most sales of any significant size, these roles are, in fact, filled by different people.

If one person alone claims to play more than one role in an evaluation for a large purchase, the person may be misrepresenting himself or herself.

Each role within the sales process carries its own wide span of responsibility. If your contact blithely assures you that he or she is the economic buyer *and* the technical evaluator for a large sale, this person may very well be trying to hide the identity of one or both of these people from you.

Keep in mind that these positions are simply roles—there might not necessarily be actual individuals who hold these titles in your prospect's organization. Your prospect might not even call on this conceptual framework to describe the different people involved in a purchase; the prospect may instead be referring to a committee acting as the technical buyer. Nonetheless, since each of these roles requires a different approach from your team, you should be aware of the different types of buyers and should be able to ascribe these roles to one or more individuals at your target account.

The Technical Buyer

The primary purpose of the technical buyer is to evaluate the technical merits of your product or service. The technical buyer will be interested not only in these features of your product, but also in the architecture, resource utilization, and ongoing management and maintenance that your product requires.

In most cases, the technical buyer makes a purchase recommendation based on the results of a technical evaluation. He or she may recommend a single offering or a group of vendors whose solutions are acceptable. Frequently, the result of a technical evaluation is a ranking of the available products or services.

It is likely that you will spend most of your time with the technical buyer. This is not a bad thing. You probably share a basic appreciation for technology, and this shared appreciation can act as the basis for your relationship. Focus your efforts on building a solid professional

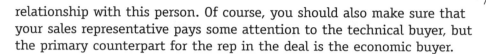

relationship with this person. Of course, you should also make sure that your sales representative pays some attention to the technical buyer, but the primary counterpart for the rep in the deal is the economic buyer.

With many accounts, the technical buyer does not have the task of selecting the ultimate winner of a sales competition. This job is left to the economic buyer, who is described below. However, since the economic buyer is normally less familiar with the technology than the technical buyer, the technical buyer does have the ability to *prevent* you from winning the deal. Needless to say, you can't win a deal if you have been eliminated from consideration by the technical buyer.

Even if the technical buyer does not make the final decision in a sales cycle, his or her seal of approval is an integral part of the sales cycle. There is also a good chance that the technical buyer will continue to interact with your product and your company after the acquisition. Establishing a good relationship with an account is a key to follow-up sales. If these reasons have not convinced you to treat technical buyers with the respect they deserve, the following maxim should satisfy you:

Never neglect the technical buyer, since he or she may sense this neglect and be offended.

Even if your company is able to close business by concentrating its selling efforts on the economic buyer, it does not pay to ignore the technical buyer.

The technical buyer will also be evaluating the technical merits of your sales team. In this sense, you—as the primary technical contact for your team—will have to establish your credibility with him or her in order to win the deal. If the technical buyer believes your team does not comprehend its own technology or that of the environment in which it exists, you may leave the impression that your offering is also not technically up to snuff.

Many companies have their technical hotshots acting as technical buyers. These hotshots may be less experienced team members, both in terms of their time with the company and in their overall life experience and maturity. They will vary in their reactions to you. These younger folks may regard you as a peer, as an older and respected guru, or as a challenge to their feelings of competence. No matter what the relationship, you should make sure that the technical buyer feels comfortable in your presence.

The Economic Buyer

The definition of an economic buyer is fairly straightforward: They are the ones who "sign the checks," whether literally or through giving the approval that is necessary for the funds to be released.

In many companies, the person ultimately responsible for the delivery of payment is someone in accounts payable who is not directly involved with the sales cycle.

But when we speak of the economic buyer, we refer to the person who will be responsible for the final step in the sales cycle—the purchase of your product or services.

In this sense, the economic buyer is always the final authority in a sale. Nonetheless, the economic buyer is not always an *active* participant in the sales process, especially your part of the sales process. Instead, the sales representative is more likely to work with the economic buyer than you are, since your sales rep is usually the person who handles the financial issues of a deal.

Because the economic buyer is responsible for releasing the company's funds, his position is usually more senior than that of the technical buyer. The economic buyer focuses on the benefits that your offering can deliver at a high level.

Economic buyers are more interested in the benefits of your product or service as they apply to their own business affairs. Although economic buyers may be much less familiar with the details of technology, they are almost certainly more familiar with the needs and problems of their own line of business than the technical buyer might be.

And, of course, it goes without saying that the economic buyer is much more interested in the cost of your solution than the technical buyer. In fact, since the economic buyer is more likely to be somewhat removed from the day-to-day operations of the IT department, economic buyers have a distinct tendency to focus on the acquisition price of your offering.

Depending on the structure of your target account, the ongoing costs of support and maintenance may be figured into a different budget or handled from a different cost center than the initial purchase. This can make the economic buyer even less concerned with these issues.

Microsoft is a master at keeping the price of acquiring software low, and its success has forced other vendors to follow its lead. Economic buyers have a tendency to simply look at this initial acquisition cost, which, in Mature Market or commodity market spaces, can be the determining factor in selecting a vendor, regardless of subsequent ongoing costs.

The End User

The end user can sometimes be the forgotten member of the evaluation team. You may not normally consider end users as a part of the sales cycle, but they are the ones who will eventually benefit from all this great technology you are selling. Depending on the type of technology you offer, you may not even be able to define the end user adequately. For instance, if you are selling a database or a set of development tools, is the end user the IT staff or the members of the company who will use the data and applications created *by* the IT staff?

Some products are marketed directly at end users. Products like spreadsheets, word processors and business intelligence tools are designed specifically for end users. In such cases, the end user is actually serving in two capacities—as both an end user and as the technical buyer.

However, the end user is the recipient of all benefits of technology. Your fancy products and services are not the only way to save money or improve products for a company. End users who are made more effective and efficient will also deliver those benefits. Because of this, end users will always play a role in delivering on the promise of your offering. For these reasons, you should consider end users as one of the buyers in a sales cycle.

This doesn't mean a representative of the end user community will be sitting at the table during product demonstrations and chalk talks. But getting a buy-in from the eventual users of technology is good policy on the part of your prospect's company.

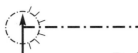

It is a wise company that involves end users in a purchase decision.

To make the most effective case for your offering when speaking with end users, you have to focus on features. Take a practical standpoint. You must build a bridge from the technical features and their benefits, back to the practical realities of the end users' day-to-day jobs. This exercise can be tricky, but it is well worth the effort. Keep in mind that the end users with whom you directly interact are usually the leaders of a large group of end users—the happy, or irate, townspeople storming the gates of the IT castle. It is very nice having this group become vocal supporters of your products.

End users are frequently suspicious of IT staff and management decisions—for good reason, since they are primarily the ones who suffer the ill effects of a poor choice by these keepers of the computing department. Consequently, most IT departments will be glad to make their end users happy by choosing a particular product or service.

Reach out to end users, if you can, without upsetting your technical and economic buyers.

It is quite likely that you may not have any end users represented on the evaluation team. Still, if you think that your offering can appeal to this group even though they are not part of the prospect team, you can probe to find out the type of benefits they seek from the purchase. A good IT department will be aware that they are servicing the needs of the users and will appreciate your interest.

But IT departments may have their own reasons for keeping end users out of an evaluation. Never push them on this subject if you sense resistance.

If your product does not appeal directly to end users, it will still no doubt be used by a group of people who are responsible for ensuring the happiness of end users. You can make your direct contact look good if he can satisfy the expectations of their end user community. When the end users receive the benefits of the wonderful products and technology you have sold to their company, they will look to their internal people who were responsible for this brilliant decision. If you can convince the other buyers involved in the sale of this, they will be more likely to help you to make contact with their own end users. You should never push this particular point too hard, though, so as to not set up a negative reaction from your direct contacts.

It is rare to find end users in control of the final vendor selection, but it is quite common for the economic buyer or technical buyer to consult with them on a choice at some point in the sales cycle. Since this consultation may not include you, or may take place before the sales cycle formally begins or after it ends, you should still endeavor to make sure that the wishes of this type of buyer are somehow satisfied.

How Each Type of Buyer Approaches Your Product

Different types of buyers approach sales situations with a number of styles. Observe the questions that three types of buyers might ask when they consider the fictional SuperServer application server product:

*The **technical buyer** would want to know what platforms SuperServer runs on, whether SuperServer uses operating system processes or threads, and what version of the Java Virtual Machine is used. He or she would also want to know what avenues are available for support.*

*The **economic buyer** would want to know if the pricing is based per client, per server, or on the type of hardware, and if there is a discount on subsequent licenses. He or she would also want to know how much support avenues cost.*

*The **end user** would want to know if SuperServer will help to keep applications from slowing down at 4:30 every afternoon. He or she would not really care about support issues, since they will most likely never interact with technical support directly.*

You can certainly address all of these issues in the course of the sales cycle. But which ones should you emphasize the most and which the least? The best way to determine the answer to this question is to determine which of these types of buyers is going to be most responsible for the purchase decision.

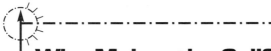

Who Makes the Call?

While it is worthwhile to understand the different roles that make up an evaluation team, you and your sales team really need to know who the final decision maker is for an account.

Under most circumstances, you will have to satisfy at least the desires of the technical buyer and the economic buyer. You will not be able to win a deal if you have lost the evaluation stage for either of these buyers.

However, there is a big difference between passing muster with the technical buyer and the economic buyer and being the sole winner with either of them. It is not at all uncommon for the eventual winner of a sales cycle to be among the top finishers in the technical evaluation and the financial evaluation, but not have the superior product for either category.

Although both buyers must approve of your company as a vendor, one of these parties will typically be more influential in the final selection process. The order of precedence for these two roles has to do with several factors. These factors include the internal politics of the account, the personal authority and negotiating skills of the individuals in their roles, and the place that your product falls in the Technology Life Cycle, which we will discuss later in this chapter.

In all cases, since the authority to purchase your product is the key to a successful sale, you should assemble a profile of the account as soon as you can.

You should determine the identity of the different buyers and their relationship as early in the sales cycle as possible.

Because of the importance of these players, you and your sales rep should make a review of the players and their roles a standard part of every post-interaction review. Keep in mind that your initial impressions of these buyers may not be entirely accurate, so you should continually ascertain which members of the prospect's organization fill which roles.

Working with the Buyers

We mentioned earlier in this chapter that you cannot afford to avoid any of the individual buyer roles participating in the sales cycle. You are primarily interested in the real buyer, but you cannot ignore the others. Although there may be just one person who has the final "Yes" in a deal, there are many others who can say "No" to your company.

At the same time, you should, along with your sales rep and the rest of your team, be aware of the relative importance of each buyer in the final decision. Knowing these factors can help guide the way you divide up resources in the account.

It is possible that each buyer will demand a large amount of attention— more than your team can possibly devote to each. By understanding exactly how the buyers collaborate in reaching a purchase decision, you can help to gain the maximum leverage from your efforts.

Let's say that you have been asked to perform a demo in front of thirty end user representatives. You may even have been asked to perform multiple demos, in effect training end users to use your product, as part of your sales effort. To properly evaluate whether this potentially enormous drain on your time is worthwhile, you should understand where end users will influence this purchase decision.

The same principle applies to an extensive technical evaluation or trial period or to a request for a dramatic discount on your product, service, or maintenance contract. When your account deals with vendors who are competing for their business, it is very easy (and tempting) for them to ask the world of you. Your answer should depend on your analysis of the dynamics of the purchase decision.

One final word on the relationship between the buyers. The buyer role played by an individual or group at your target account is one of the primary determinants of their influence in the sales cycle. But the buyer role—whether played by an individual or a group—is not the only determinant of influence. Although the technical buyer approves the technology, the economic buyer signs the check, and the end user works with the product after purchase, their relationships and influence on the sale are determined by interpersonal factors.

As with all group interactions, there is a dynamic to the interpersonal relationships in a group which can affect the influence of any individual. For instance, an economic buyer may be respected as a technical authority, so his or her vision of your technology could mediate or override the decision of the technical buyer. The technical buyer could be an eloquent supporter who can sway the others. A representative of the end users could be someone as highly placed as the CEO but might very well be the type of CEO who lets subordinates make independent decisions.

You will have the greatest chance of success if you try to please all the buyers in an account.

The Technology Adoption Cycle and the Classes of Buyers

Earlier in this chapter, we briefly discussed how to determine who the "real" buyer is in a sales situation. And you may have noticed that we didn't give you a foolproof way to determine the answer to this problem.

There is a simple reason for this. Just as every account you will ever work on raises a different set of issues, so are there an almost infinite number of relationships among the different types of buyers. The importance of different types of buyers in an account is, logically, related to the stage that your product is at in the Technology Life Cycle. These stages were the subject of Chapter 3.

Early Market Prospects

The Early Market segment of the Technology Life Cycle is the first segment. This stage has the smallest revenue potential. Vendors whose products fall in this category are typically newcomers to a market.

Real Buyer

In this Early Market phase, the technical buyer holds the lion's share of responsibility for making a final purchase selection. Since the technology itself is new, there are few, if any, standards to follow, so most companies realize that it takes a strong technology evaluator to make the best decisions.

Role of Others

The influence of the economic buyer of products at the Early Market stage is much more likely to have been established before you entered the picture. The economic buyer will set a budget for acquiring some new technology, but there are not likely to be many pricing standards or comparisons for the economic buyer to follow. You may be called upon to assist the technical buyer in the preparation of cost-benefit analysis documents that will be used to justify the purchase for the economic buyer.

End users normally have less influence at this stage of the market, but this is not always true. Early Market products can sometimes cause a major disruption for end users. While the technical buyers can envision the longer-term benefits of the new technology, the end users may feel that they have taken a step backwards.

> This was particularly true in the early days of enterprise resource planning applications. Many end users were very comfortable using their existing applications—and the change to these enterprise-class applications caused significant changes and challenges for these end users. As a sales consultant selling into these Early Markets, you will want to consider the impact of your product on the daily lives of the end users. This is a subject that is often overlooked by the technical buyer. You can help make the transition more palatable by keeping the end user in mind at this stage of the game.

To understand the workings at the different stages of the Technology Life Cycle, we can look at a market that both authors were involved in—the market for client/server development tools from the late 1980s on.

> In the Early Market phase of this cycle, any development tool that could work in a graphical environment was a candidate. This included true client/server development tools, such as SQL Windows, screen-scraper technology such as Easel, and even object-oriented languages such as Actor. None of these products shared much in common, aside from their ability to run on Windows or OS/2.

Popular Market

The Popular Market segment of the Technology Life Cycle is the second segment. This stage is the first phase of the life cycle that is open to a wider audience.

At this stage in the market, there are usually only a handful of realistic competitors, and all of these competitors offer the basic features and benefits of the technology.

Real Buyer

The Early Majority market segment involves all of the buyers. The importance of the technical buyer is somewhat reduced, since a wide range of technical features does not exist in the vendor choices. The real revenue opportunities begin at this stage. Dollar amounts are usually bigger, so the economic buyer has a larger role to play. The Early Majority is also where technologically advanced end users become aware of the market area, so they may now have some voice in the selection. These end users may even have been the first to champion your product category within their organization.

—·—·—

> End users have been the strongest voice in the business intelligence space, for example. In many cases, these end users were talented line managers who could see the value of analyzing data at the departmental level. Several of the more successful business intelligence companies were able to spot this trend early on and they were very successful selling directly to the end users. IT generally served as the technical buyer in these deals—but the real decision-making was handled by the end users themselves.

—·—·—

If you have not crossed into the Popular Market phase as one of the market leaders, you will find this market phase very dispiriting, as you continually win evaluations and lose deals or find yourself shut out of opportunities. As the influence of the economic buyer and end user increases, the need to be perceived as a market leader becomes much more powerful, closing off smaller companies regardless of the soundness of their solutions.

Role of Others

Usually all three types of buyers—the technical buyer, the economic buyer and the end user—are involved at this phase of the Technology Life Cycle. All three buyers tend to be concerned with buying from established vendors, particularly the economic buyers. It is during this stage of the market that three classes of products tend to emerge:

- Business market leader
- Technology leader
- Price leader

The biggest vendor in the game is the business market leader. It has captured the most customers and is viewed as the company that represents the overall market for their product category. The business market leader is viewed as the safe buy for the economic buyer, the technical buyer and the end user. The technology leader is the company that is widely regarded as having the best overall product from a technical perspective. Prospects that have strong technical buyers will tend to gravitate towards the technology leader. The last company in the list is the price leader. The price leader does not necessarily have the best technical product, and it does not enjoy the market-leading position of the business market leader. The price leader's biggest advantage is its low price—and it will tend to be the favored vendor by prospects with very strong economic buyers.

Mature Market

The Mature segment of the Technology Life Cycle is the final segment. It is the phase with the largest overall revenue potential. The technology itself is somewhat old news at this point, and there are usually no more than three viable vendors in this market segment. The bulk of each product's features and benefits are very similar at this stage.

Real Buyer

The buyer with all the power in this market segment is the economic buyer. Not only are all the offerings at this stage of the cycle similar, but the technology has also often been around long enough so that awareness of the essential benefits of the products and services has bubbled up to the less technical members of a prospect's organization.

There is also strong general awareness of products in this category, so end users often have some say in the selection. End users may not know much about technology, but they often do have a basic awareness of the marketplace. If the evaluation team picks a product from outside the mainstream of the segment, they risk attracting the wrath of end users should any part of the system fail. Regardless of the reason for the failure, their outsider choice of a product will act as a "blame magnet," and they will have to accept responsibility for causing the failure.

Role of Others

The importance of the technical buyer sometimes fades into the background at this point. His or her opinion may come into play, but in many cases, the technical buyer's opinion is secondary. In fact, since the technology is well established, the role of the technical buyer may be assigned to the same person who acts as the economic buyer. Peripheral factors, such as contract terms and availability and quality of support, come into play at this segment of the cycle. The serious technical buyer is likely to be working on the "next hot technology" at this point in the game.

As we pointed out in Chapter 3, however, many products do not fall into a single phase of the Technology Life Cycle. Even established products are continually coming out with new releases whose features at least flirt with the requirements of Early Market and Popular Market prospects. At the same time, virtually all technology products these days, even the most radical new ideas, are built on a foundation of existing technology. The Internet, as we know it, would never have flourished had it not been for the established communication infrastructure provided by the TCP/IP protocol.

This mixing of phases makes it all the more difficult to simply place your offering in a market segment and identify the real buyers for a product. Although we feel the guidelines outlined in this section can contribute valuable insights to your sales team, you cannot use them in place of your usual investigative work.

The Transitional Evaluation Team

We believe that the Technology Life Cycle, and your product's place in it, have a significant effect on the way different buyers in an account operate and interact. But not every account will conform to these predictions.

In fact, you may find that the personalities and roles in your prospect's evaluation team are not consistent with your definitions. As we observed in Chapter 3, you may have an Early Market prospect who is assigned as the economic buyer for a Mature Market product, or a Mature Market end user in charge of the technical evaluation of your Early Market technology. We call these situations *transitional* evaluation teams, because the personalities on the evaluation team create disconnects for you in the sales cycle.

— · — · —

Consider the situation in which the economic buyer is balking at purchasing your relational database software in favor of an object-oriented database. Normally, you would expect the technical buyer to be the person in favor of using an object-oriented database—not the economic buyer.

— · — · —

Why Does This Type of Mismatch Happen?

Transitional teams result from problems with *scheduling, standard assignments, political considerations,* and *personal technology preferences.*

- **Scheduling**—Some evaluations may take an extended period of time or must be conducted over a specific period of time. The ideal individual to make the decision may not be available.

- **Standard assignment**—In some companies, personnel are assigned to evaluation teams according to a pre-established schedule. Some employees spend all of their time evaluating products. Since most companies buy technology from a range of companies over their Technology Life Cycles, the evaluator who might be less ideal for your product may be right for other products.

- **Political considerations**—Some companies, and some of their employees, find being on an evaluation team rewarding. Others find it to be punishment. In either case, the perception of the role of the evaluation team will cause the role of the evaluator to be used as part of a larger political scheme. Another political consideration has to do with the eventual deployment of the product or use of the service. An ambitious senior executive may want to control the use of the final purchase.

Prospects are people just like you, and they have their own personal views on the Technology Life Cycle. You might find an economic buyer who is a closet Maverick and loves technology for technology's sake. While this person's company might take more of a Mature Market stand in regard to technology, this Maverick may personally favor innovation. You will find it helpful to take notice of each buyer's personal style in order to look for clues as to where they fit in on the technology adoption cycle on an individual basis.

Why Should You Care?

Why should you care if your prospect has a mix of life cycle types on their evaluation team?

**A transitional evaluation team
can spell trouble.**

A variety of problems can crop up in your sales cycle if you are subjected to a mismatch on the evaluation team:

- **Increased resource commitments**—If you have a Mature Market buyer evaluating your Early Market product, you will have to devote a lot of time educating him or her, not only about your product but about the market arena in general.

- **Win the battle and lose the war**—This outcome occurs as part of a tacit conspiracy between you and a member of a transitional evaluation team. Let's say you are a Maverick, always explaining the big picture in your usual charismatic way. When you find a like-minded soul on the evaluation team, you can't help but tend to focus your efforts on him or her. After all, this person gets it! But this mind-meld will only serve to obscure the fact that even though you and your technical contact are in the same boat, that boat doesn't float to a successful conclusion of a deal. You may find yourself at the end of the sales cycle with a confused look on your face.

Winning the technical evaluation and losing the deal is still losing.

- **The organization of the evaluation team may be a smoke screen for other problems in the deal**—The problems we have been discussing up to now have centered around a transitional evaluation team that is not aware that its members are, philosophically, diametrically opposed to each other. For instance, if you hope for an initial sale that will eventually lead to your product being declared a corporate standard and the evaluation team does not seem to consist of the right type of people, you may be much less likely to be able to leverage the current sale into a larger commitment.

- **Your competitors have the right people on their evaluation team**—Oops. This means that you have the wrong type of people on your evaluation team. You have a Mature Market product, yet you have representatives from the Advanced Technology group on your evaluation team. Meanwhile, there is a different evaluation team for your competitor, and it includes the vice president of the business division and the company controller. Not a good sign.

In these situations, as with other danger signs in accounts, your sales team may choose to proceed with the sales cycle. But now you can be fully aware of the potential for increased resources or the decreased possibility of a sale as you make your evaluation of your chances in a deal.

Wrapping Up

In this chapter, you learned about the different types of buyers who no doubt will be a part of the evaluation team at your prospect's organization.

In the rest of this book, we will mainly be considering the prospect in its singular nature. That is, we will no longer spend a lot of time talking about technical buyers, economic buyers, and end users. However, you should keep these different categories in mind at every stage in a sales cycle, to help you and your sales team make the best decisions for your actions in the account.

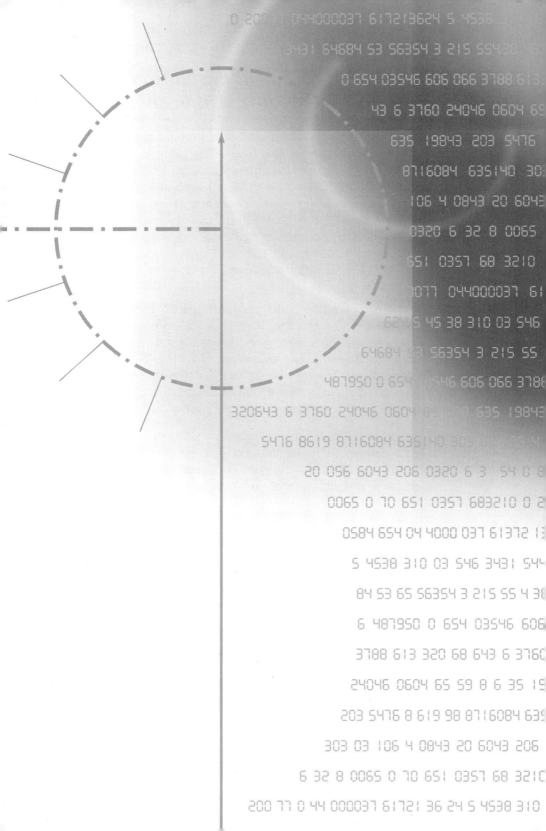

Working with People

If you chose to become a sales consultant, you are probably the type of person who likes to tackle problems. You think analytically and approach problems as obstacles to be surmounted with a logical plan of attack. At least this is true for technical problems.

Dealing with other human beings is another story. People have a nasty habit of having their own unpredictable sets of reactions to your interventions. Because of this, you may feel that the field of human interaction is too soft to merit spending time addressing in a structured manner. In contrast to the way in which you approach technical issues, your dealings with other people are more of a catch-as-catch-can pursuit. But, as with your technical abilities, your interactions with other people can benefit as much, if not more, from a bit of analysis.

This chapter will not give you any magical keys to make the public as easy to deal with as a technical problem. But this chapter should give you some insights into the way you can most effectively relate to others. And even though we focus on your dealings with your prospects and customers, much of the information in this chapter applies to anyone with whom you interact. You may even find that our advice will be useful in your life outside of work. Even though the suggestions are specifically aimed at the relationships you establish with the public in your job as a sales consultant, these guidelines form the basis for most successful social interactions.

This chapter will deal with the basic issues of communication in your job. But we will continue to discuss communication with your prospects and customers throughout the remainder of this book.

Foundations of a Professional Relationship

We all know the characteristics of a good professional relationship. When you have a good relationship with your customers, they respect you and relate with a familiarity that makes interaction easy. We have all had this kind of relationship with some people in our professional lives, and all of us have had relationships that did not live up to this standard. What are the attributes that must be in place to establish a good professional relationship?

Credibility

For a sales consultant, credibility is the most important attribute for a good professional relationship. Credibility is the quality that makes your audience believe what you say. Your credibility is like a fortune delivered to you by your audience. They give you the coins of their belief, which you can spend to get them to accept the things you say. If you establish credibility with your prospects and customers, they will look at you as a trusted peer or valued advisor. If, however, you do not establish credibility, your audience will not even pay attention to what you say. Clearly, credibility is the key to creating effective professional relationships.

Your credibility is your most important asset.

How do you go about establishing credibility? You can establish credibility as an expert in your product throughout the process of explaining and demonstrating your company's offerings. After all, you should know more than your prospects do about your own products, since you are being brought into a sales situation specifically because of your advanced technical knowledge. If you are uncertain about your own depth of knowledge, you can stick to the areas of your product with which you are most familiar.

—·—·—

If you are working with an established customer, they may know more than you about your own products. In this scenario, you should not try to pretend that you know more than your customer, since this could damage your credibility, as explained later in this section.

—·—·—

You can gain even more credibility if you demonstrate that you are an expert about your area technology in general—not just your software. You can accomplish this by giving an overview of your product's positioning in the market or by discussing some of the issues behind the motivations to acquire a product like yours. You can sometimes even establish your credibility as an expert by making an offhand remark that demonstrates your intimacy with the market and technology.

Once you have established credibility in the more general context of your marketplace, you will be able to influence your audience on a broader level. For example, you can position your solution in the overall context of the industry, or, more specifically, with regard to the competition. If you and your competition are both offering a picture of the customers' needs and the marketplace, your customer will likely accept the view of the person who has created a higher degree of credibility.

You can also establish your credibility as a trusted advisor. You can convince customers of your ability to offer appropriate and realistic advice by demonstrating your ability to listen carefully to their concerns and then responding appropriately to them. Once you establish your credibility as an advisor, your customers will want you as a member of their team—but this can happen only if they purchase your product. With credibility, you will find yourself in a position of influence with your customer, which you can use to help complete your sale.

It is easy to know when you have established credibility as a trusted advisor. When the customer starts spontaneously asking your advice on how to handle different situations, this is a sure sign that your advice is valued. After all, there is no reason for customers to treat you as anything other than a source of information about your own product if they see you merely as a technical representative of your company. But once they start bringing you into their problem solving process, you know they respect your opinions and overall knowledge.

To establish credibility, you have to appear confident. When you can address issues with an air of confidence, the implication is that you are displaying merely the surface of a deep ocean of knowledge, rather than being just an inch-deep pond. At the same time, you must be genuine. If customers catch you bluffing on a topic, they will deflate your balloon of false confidence and let the air out of your credibility.

If you don't know an answer, admit this to the user and promise to research the topic and get back to them. Do not feel that you have to answer all questions immediately to establish and maintain your

credibility. In fact, it is often much more impressive to work out an answer in front of your audience, since this will demonstrate your problem-solving ability and help you to form a connection with the customer, who no doubt has to puzzle through problems in his or her everyday work.

Your credibility makes it possible for you to have a more fruitful relationship with your customer. The customer will look to you for detailed knowledge of your product and its uses. Without credibility, you cannot fulfill this vital role.

Rapport

Credibility, by itself, will not enable you to work successfully with the prospects and customers. You have to add the magic elixir called *rapport*.

Rapport is also easy to recognize when it exists. When you establish a rapport with a prospect, you have established a basis for an easy flow of communication between the two of you. Rapport is based on making a positive connection with your prospect—the same type of positive connection that you have with your friends.

> Although rapport in a professional relationship is *like* the connection you have with your friends, it is not the same thing. You should not share personal information or confidences with the public in the way that you share with your friends. A professional relationship is different and more circumspect. It lacks the more open give-and-take that you have with your friends.

Establishing rapport enables you to create a connection with your audience. It is important to establish this connection before you move on to the more challenging task of actually communicating with your prospect. If you take a few moments to establish the connection and begin the process of building rapport, you will find it much easier not only to communicate with your prospect, but also to convince them of your important points.

How do you go about making this connection?

You establish rapport by making a connection between yourself as a person and your audience.

This tip may seem self-evident—except for the three little words "as a person." Rapport is a connection based not on your position as a representative of your particular company, but on your standing as an individual and fellow member of the human race. You establish rapport by finding some way to connect your life with the lives of those people in your audience.

There are many ways to do this. If, for example, you are dealing with a group of people, it makes sense to begin your first interaction with a little small talk. You can mention the weather, a noncontroversial sports event, or a local attraction.

This type of small talk can help break the ice and give you clues about the interests of your audience. If you mention an event or a topic and your audience responds positively, be sure to follow up on their comments. You can also mention an upcoming trade show or an ongoing debate within the industry of your audience. If you receive an encouraging response, you can ask questions to learn more about their thoughts and feelings on a particular topic.

This type of interaction serves two valuable purposes. First, it gets your audience used to answering your questions. Later in your interactions, when you ask questions that focus more directly on your sales efforts, they will be more likely to continue their established relationship with you by answering those questions.

Second, you are expressing an interest in your audience. You are focusing on *them*, and this is always flattering. In seeking out information about your audience's interests, you help them establish a connection with you.

You can judge how well you are doing in your effort to establish rapport by listening and watching your audience. Are they responding with additional information or merely giving you brief answers to be polite? Are they leaning forward when they speak to you, or are they leaning back and folding their arms across their chests, as if physically pulling away from you? Indeed, are they *actually* physically pulling away from you? Don't laugh—we've had this happen to us.

Usually, the mere fact that you are making an effort to establish a connection with your audience goes a long way toward making that rapport a reality. Remember, it is not only more comfortable for you once you have established rapport with your audience; it is also more comfortable for them. Similarly, a lack of rapport can indicate that something is amiss in your sales cycle.

As part of a sales cycle, I was performing a benchmark for a customer. A benchmark is a test of the speed of a particular piece of hardware or software. Since some of the tasks of this particular benchmark took as long as thirty minutes, and since I was running the benchmark live, I was very interested in creating a rapport with the prospects. Thirty minutes can seem like an eternity if you are just sitting around waiting for a test to complete.

I began trying to establish a rapport by mentioning the New York Giants football team, who were at that time in the NFL playoffs and doing great. "How about those Giants?" I ventured—to which the key prospect, a bit of a cold fish, responded, "I don't like football."

"Uh, how about those Knicks," I said, changing the topic to the local professional basketball team. "I don't like basketball," he replied, just as coldly.

At this point, it was getting a little chilly in the room, and the other members of the prospect team were getting a little uncomfortable with my obviously unsuccessful attempts.

I asked the prospect if there was any sport that he *did* like. He replied, "I enjoy watching my son swim." I quickly responded, "Hey, how about that Mark Spitz?"—causing everyone in the room to laugh at my desperate attempt to make a connection using the name of an Olympic swimmer.

Not only did we win the benchmark, but I was also able to convince this difficult personality to accept a slight bending of the rules for the benchmark in our favor. The rapport established between the customer and our sales team helped them to understand why the rule change was necessary, even though it benefited our product.

You can never have too much rapport, just as some people believe you can never be too thin or too rich. It is very important to establish a connection with your prospect at the beginning of your interaction, be it one to one, on the phone, or at a trade show. But rapport entails a commitment. You can't just take a minute or two to connect with your audience and then proceed to ignore them the rest of the time. Occasionally, you will have to reach back and reconfirm the connection. You can accomplish this by working in references or questions about the topics you used for establishing rapport into your subsequent interactions. Continually look to expand the basis for that rapport.

For instance, perhaps your connection with your prospect was first based on your mutual interest in a local sports team. You might mention the outcome of their most recent game the next time you talk to your prospect. Or if you began a conversation around a particular issue connected with his industry and subsequently read an article about the issue, you might ask if your audience saw the article. If they haven't, they will usually be grateful to get a source for more information. If they have, you can chat about the article, thus deepening the connection.

A lack of rapport will make interaction with the customer more difficult. Rapport makes your relationship with the customer easy. The comfortable give-and-take that is the hallmark of good rapport with a customer makes communication a pleasure and will trigger the exchange of more valuable information. A customer may not always buy from the sales team that has the best rapport with him, but a lack of rapport can stand in the way of your sales team getting the vital information it needs for closing a deal.

Trust

Trust is both the ultimate attribute of a professional relationship and the one that is the most difficult to establish. When a prospect trusts you, the entire character of your interaction changes. You become an advisor, a true consultant, rather than someone whom the prospect must guard against. In a sales cycle, trust gives you an enormous amount of influence.

How do you create an atmosphere of trust in your professional relationships? Trust—unlike credibility or rapport—can only be built up over a period of time. Because of our inherent human nature, trust is much less likely to be granted to you than credibility or rapport. Most of us tend to believe, as well as to like, our fellow men and women in the starting stages of relationships. However, an equally large percentage of us are hesitant to immediately trust the other member in any relationship—especially when they are part of a sales team.

Trust is not the same as credibility. You can be credible—that is, believable—but not trustworthy. And it is certainly possible to establish a rapport with your audience but still not be trusted. Many prospects, in fact, will regard your sales rep as someone who may be telling the truth but who should not receive their ultimate trust. It is not at all uncommon for a prospect to ask you to confirm a statement by a sales rep. You, as the sales consultant, are more likely to be trusted simply because of your position.

Trust is not simply granted. It is earned. You earn someone's trust by being credible and reliable over a period of time. Because of this, it may be difficult to reap the full benefits of establishing a trusting relationship early in the sales cycle, when it can do you the most good. However, don't take this slow process as a reason to neglect the stages that build trust. One of your primary goals is to turn prospects into long-term customers. A long-term customer relationship almost always includes the element of trust.

> Trust is built up over time and repeated interactions. You can increase opportunities to create a trusting relationship with your prospect by increasing your number of interactions with them. I often try to speed the trust-building relationship by using a little trick.
>
> Sometimes a prospect asks a "hard" question, one that even an experienced and competent sales consultant might not readily know how to answer. I make it a point to express some confusion over the best answer and then I promise the prospect that I will call in a few days with the answer.
>
> I then call back the next day with a fully thought out and researched answer—which I knew the day before! But by indicating that I will call them back, and then following through on my promise even earlier than I originally promised, I am able to take another step in building a level of trust between us.
>
> The prospect's response to my call also gives me a feeling for how the sales cycle is proceeding. If we have a pleasant chat, not only is this a good sign, but I am often also able to get more information on the prospect's needs and wants or on how the competition is doing. If the prospect does not take my call or does not bother to return a message, it is usually a sign that something is amiss.

Credibility makes a relationship with your customer possible. Rapport makes the relationship easy. Establishing trust with your customer makes the relationship sustainable over time. If your customer trusts you, you will be included in their ongoing plans. Trust is the key factor that enables you to turn a prospect into your customer.

Telling the Truth

Credibility, rapport, and trust are precious commodities that underpin the overall success of a professional relationship. But you can destroy all of them in an instant by lying to your customer. If your customers cannot believe you, they cannot trust you. If your customers suspect that you are spinning tales, your credibility will disappear. And no one likes a liar, so your rapport will be seriously damaged if you are not honest with your customers.

Never lie to a customer.

Telling lies in a professional relationship is a losing game. Your customer may not be aware of whether you have told the truth or not, but the consequences of lying are so severe that it is not worth taking the chance. Even if your customer does not immediately know that you have lied, he or she may discover it later, in conversations with your peers or through your competition.

This doesn't mean that you have to be brutally honest about everything, including the weaknesses of your product. Present your views, making sure that you add the appropriate precautions. It is quite easy to say "I have heard" or "I understand" instead of stating definitive facts. If the information that follows this type of caveat turns out to be incorrect, you can always thank the customer for clearing up your mistake. This resolution to a situation is preferable to being perceived as a source of misinformation.

You should make it obvious to your audience that you are concerned with the truth in every sense. If you have made a particularly important claim, under the mistaken impression that it was correct, you should then make a point of contacting the customer to explain the mistake. Everyone makes mistakes, every day, so you may very well improve your rapport with your customer at the same time that you convince him or her of your deep concern for the truth. Your actions will both increase the trust your customer has in you and add to your credibility.

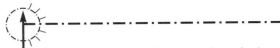

Being honest solidifies the foundations of a professional relationship. Lying destroys these foundations. There is too much at stake to ever jeopardize your relationship by lying to a customer.

Your Personal Style

All right. You have to establish a good professional relationship with your audience. How should you go about doing this?

There are countless ways to establish and maintain professional relationships. And there is one constant that runs through all of them:

You can only establish a good relationship by being yourself.

Your audience will have a sixth sense for detecting insincerity—and they will not like it.

— . — . —

> A colleague of mine had what came across as a very insincere style. He always seemed to be listening too hard or showing exaggerated body language. Although this gentleman was an excellent sales consultant in many ways—he was intelligent, quick, and responsive—his manner made it harder for him to establish a good professional relationship with his customers. These drawbacks tended to extend the sales cycle in some situations.

— . — . —

We firmly believe that everyone is unique, and that each of you reading this book will be able to develop a personal style that naturally reflects your true self. But for those of you just starting out in positions calling for extensive interaction with an audience, it is worthwhile to mention some strengths and weaknesses associated with personality types commonly found in sales consultants.

We have identified a few personal styles that occur frequently in sales consultants:

- **The colleague**—who shares a group of experiences with the audience. You address your audience easily as a group of peers.
- **The no-nonsense technician**—who bases his or her style on knowledge of the product. This type of style does not necessarily mix in a lot of humor.

- **The visionary**—who always keeps the big picture in mind. This type of style is particularly effective in the early stages of a technology market, where the best is yet to come.

- **The dynamo**—whose personal force sweeps up a room. However, a dynamo has to make sure that he or she does not leave his audience behind.

Many of you no doubt possess some aspects of each of these personal styles—or even take on different styles in different situations. But by understanding your basic personal style, you can present yourself in a much more genuine way. As your display more of your true nature, your relationships with your prospects and customers will become even better.

Using Your Personal Style

Although we are all different, all of us have a similar goal as sales consultants. We try to convey our product in the best light to convince prospects to become our customers. To understand how different personal styles can achieve the same end, let's look at how each personality type described above might use its style to accomplish a task.

We will look at a common situation: how to establish the fact that your product or service is a proven solution to the customer's problem.

A colleague might approach this issue by talking about his or her personal experience with other customers. A technician might give a brief history of the problem, highlighting the technical barriers and the various attempts to overcome them. A visionary might show how the customer's problem is part of a larger issue and then point out how his or her solution will perfectly counteract the overriding problem. And a dynamo might simply sweep the prospect along with assurances that "everyone" uses his products for this type of problem—citing, of course, some relevant references.

Each of these approaches is valid, and none of them is actually "wrong." Most of us have traces of more than one personality type in our makeup. However, you may find yourself feeling more comfortable with just one or two of them. Your preferences should be a tip-off to what your own personal style is.

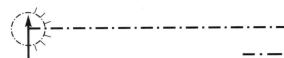

Whatever your style, always remember to be genuine. You cannot establish a true connection with your customer if you are not true to yourself. When you feel comfortable with the image you present, your confidence shows. When you attempt to present an insincere façade, it is much more difficult to establish trust, rapport, and credibility with the prospect.

Mistakes

When you respond to an audience in a genuine way, you are exposing yourself as a human being. And, like all human beings, you are fallible. At some point in your interactions with your prospect, you will make a mistake. Rest easy. This happens to everyone.

Realizing that you are fallible should take some of the pressure off your presentations. You don't have to be perfect all the time. In this book, we give you the guidelines to help you become the best sales consultant you can be. But there will be times when you will stray from these guidelines, based on the situation you find yourself in, because you will misjudge a situation, or because you make a less than optimal decision. There are very few mistakes that can't be forgiven, especially if you admit your mistake to your customer.

Forgiveness can be given if you admit to your mistake.

An apology can go a long way toward establishing a good relationship. Don't let your embarrassment or pride stand in the way of your success in working with a customer. The ability to admit a mistake should be a component of every sales consultant's approach. Your readiness to admit your own failings can, and should, be used as a way to establish greater credibility, rapport, and trust with your audience.

An ounce of forgiveness can result in tons of gratitude and rapport. Even if you don't feel you have to apologize for a mistake, it always helps—especially with those people you work with every day, such as your sales reps.

Finally, remember that a mistake is a misstep—as viewed by your prospect. You may have presented the right information but did it in a way that turned out to be a mistake. Even if you are technically correct, you can still make a mistake in the way you communicate. It is always the best course of action to err on the side of caution and make amends for any perceived mistake.

Enhancing Communication

Success in a sales situation is predicated on facilitating communication with your customer. If you have a good relationship with your customer, you will find it much easier to communicate with him or her. Strong lines of communication will make the task of solving your customers' problems much easier to accomplish, and more pleasant, too.

You build your channels of communication through interacting with your customer. As a vendor, you will, of course, have some established patterns of communication. You will present to your customer and will respond to customer requests. But it is helpful to establish other avenues of communication, usually around casual topics outside the established boundaries of the sales situation. If your customer finds it easy to talk to you, he or she will be willing to share more information as a by-product of the communication process.

Let the customer guide you to better communication.

The way to establish a wider span of communication is to find subjects that your customer enjoys talking about outside of the sales situation. But you can't force someone to talk about something that only you enjoy. Just because you spend every waking hour trying to find new ways to enhance your 1966 GTO coupe does not mean that your customer has the slightest interest in the car. Excessive focus on such topics will cause the customer to turn off your attempts at communication. The results may continue into more formal sales communications.

You can discover a likely topic for casual conversation in a number of ways. Start out by making small talk about general subjects that most people care about, as suggested above to establish rapport. These types of topics could include the location of the business, the good features of your customer's neighborhood, or topics of general interest. You can bring up these topics as asides, to see how the customer reacts. You can also do a little intelligence work by looking around the person's office to discover evidence of interests, such as in pictures on their desk or walls.

The key to establishing a conversation is to watch the customer's reaction. Find a conversational gambit that he responds to. Even something as simple as a comment on the weather may elicit a comment from your customer that will lead to an area of interest. He or she might mention gardening or an outdoor activity. Your challenge is to pick up on your customer's enthusiasm and draw him or her out on the subject.

Most customers want to be your friend.

Remember, the more communication, the better the rapport. The more communication, the more information you will gather about your customer. You will learn the way the person thinks and the particulars of his or her problem. And the more information you have, the better you will be able to position your products and solutions to meet the customer's needs.

We always make it a point to ensure that there will be communication with the customer outside the established face-to-face times of sales meetings. In order to accomplish this, we keep track of questions the customer has that will require investigation and follow-up. It is a good practice to keep records of these types of questions in a visible place such as on a whiteboard, flip chart, or pad. Using this approach delivers two key benefits: It lets the customer see that you take questions seriously, and it lets you deal with questions rapidly and professionally.

Rather than fumble around for an answer that you aren't sure of, you can simply add the question to a list that you will deal with later.

Review the list of questions at the end of your meeting. Schedule a time to get back to the customer with the answers. By following through in the specified time, you establish your responsiveness. Your reliability will enhance the trust your customer has in you and your company.

Communicating with Your Customer

As we have mentioned, communicating with your customer is not only a way for gathering information, but it is also one of the most important means for establishing a good relationship. Although communications with your customer are very similar to any communicating you do in your everyday life, there are some small differences that you should observe.

In normal conversations, there is a give-and-take between the parties. Depending on your particular style, you may find yourself listening a little more or talking a little more, but the distribution of speech will be somewhat evenly divided. By contrast, when you give a chalk talk or do a demonstration, *you* are on stage, dominating the conversation and occasionally fielding questions from your audience. You are fully in control. It can be very fulfilling to have most of the attention of the audience directed toward you as the star of the show. However, when you finish your formal presentation, you have to remember to refocus the attention on the real star of the show—your customer.

The analogy of the sales presentation as a show is appropriate in more ways than one. When you go to a show, you may or may not be interested in paying attention to the stage. You may have other things on your mind, or the show might not turn out to be exactly what you were anticipating. It is your choice whether or not to focus on the stage.

The same applies to your customers and prospects in a sales situation. They may not want to pay attention to what you have to say, especially at the beginning of your presentation. It is up to you to gain their attention by reading cues from their reactions.

You can also grab the attention of your audience by amusing, intriguing, or surprising them with something you do or say at the beginning of your presentation. You can engage them early on by asking them to introduce themselves or by asking a question. Although in a perfect world you could expect to be given the attention of your audience, we live in a slightly more complex environment.

You may earn the attention of your audience.

This maxim emphasizes that you *may* earn the attention of your audience. However, you also might not have the attention of the entire group at all times. It might be hard to get everyone in a group to pay attention to your presentation. We have always tried to draw in the people who do not seem to be involved, but you need to do this in a gentle and unintrusive manner. Don't go overboard trying to get the attention of a single recalcitrant listener. In the process, you might lose the attention of the rest of the group.

You should also try to avoid the opposite error of presenting to a single person in a group. Other people in the audience will sense what you are doing and may resent being left out. Even if you have determined that there is a single decision maker in your audience, it is rude to ignore the others.

Remember, just as each of you has your own personal style, each of your customers has his or her own style. It may not be easy to find a way to shape your interactions so that your styles complement each other, but finding the right balance will be a tremendous aid in making the sale and even more important in turning a prospect into your customer.

Keeping Their Attention

It is vitally important to keep your audience involved, but it is difficult to keep them involved during a lecture. Even if you are a fascinating speaker, most people's attention will occasionally drift. You shouldn't be offended by this—it's a fact of life. It is better to see the attention of your audience wandering than to be speaking to people who can sleep with their eyes open. At least the former group will give you visual cues of their inattention.

Everyone's attention will eventually drift.

You can help keep people's attention by getting them involved with your presentation. Bring up issues that are specific to their situation on occasion. Doing so will change the tenor of your talk from a speech to more of an interaction.

You can also get your audience involved by asking them questions. Asking questions changes the format of a presentation from a listening-only session to one of give-and-take. But this technique will only work if the questions lead to an exchange with the audience. If you ask a rhetorical question and do not pay attention to the answer, you have not only neglected to change the format, but you also may have alienated your audience by not listening to them. If you do not listen to their responses and acknowledge them, why should they listen to you?

Drifting off is a natural function. It is extremely difficult for anyone to pay rapt attention to anyone else for very long. In fact, studies have shown that most people can't pay attention to a single type of presentation for more than twenty-five minutes.

You can have some control over your audience's attention if you break up your presentation. Shift from a straight lecture to a chalk talk or demo, moving from one place in the room to another. Or ask your prospect a question or two to break up the monotony. It makes sense to *plan* some of these types of breaks in advance.

Remember, it is inevitable that people's attention will drift throughout your presentation, even in the best of circumstances. You can counteract this reality by being sure to mention the most important points in your presentation several times, in several different ways, so that each person will have several chances to hear and understand these points.

Humor

Humor is one of the best ways to keep people's attention. A joke is a kind of side step in the onward march of your presentation. It can help convince people to pay attention to you (they might miss something funny) or to bring their attention back to the presentation if they have drifted away as the rest of the audience responds to your humor.

A broad range of topics can be the subject of humor. You always have the old standards—the weather and such. If your repertoire of jokes includes some that are relevant to your product or your customer's area of business, they should be easy to work into your presentation.

I used to have a few jokes that fit in at particular places in my standard demo. The places where I would put jokes were very strategic. A joke, as much as anything, breaks up the potential monotony of a technical presentation. By telling a joke, you vary the tempo and tone of your communication, which helps to get your audience's attention.

In this sense, it doesn't really matter if a joke itself is really very funny. Even comedians sometimes get their biggest laughs from quips they make after a joke bombs, like Jay Leno on "The Tonight Show." An important part of humor is its unpredictability, so while your audience holds its breath as you "fail" with a joke, you can take advantage of their moment of uncertainty by directly noting that failure with a remark. Your remark will release the tension of the moment and bring on a laugh—all while building your credibility. After all, you aren't even trying to pass off a bad joke on them. Why, then, would you be lying about your products?

> I personally don't appreciate it when people begin their presentations with a joke. I have found that, as often as not, they take this approach only because they have read somewhere that you should start and end your presentations with a joke—which means I am in for a long period without humor.

By only using a joke at the beginning and end of a presentation, the presenter gives up one of the key virtues of humor—its ability to break up the monotony with its unpredictability.

You should always be true to yourself, so if you feel more comfortable starting off with a joke or quip, by all means do so. But try to weave your attempts at humor into the larger fabric of your presentation, rather than segregating it off by itself.

Not every joke is appropriate for every audience. Telling an inappropriate joke can result in losing an audience's respect and attention. You might also destroy any chance you have of creating an atmosphere of rapport with them. Avoid questionable topics and the inevitable problem areas of politics and religion. Take note that you might encounter other questionable areas when you are unfamiliar with a prospect's ethnic background, morals, or religious beliefs or those of his or her family, significant others, or friends. Of course, as you get to know your prospect or audience better, you will have a better sense of the areas you should avoid. You will also have already built up a connection that will allow the prospect to understand you and your foibles better.

In general, self-deprecating humor is safe. By taking a (gentle) poke at yourself and your own foibles, you humanize yourself to your audience. When you make fun of yourself, you help your audience to relax.

Dealing with a Difficult Audience

There are times when you run into a prospect, customer, or audience member who is what we would classify as "difficult." There are many varieties of difficult customers. Some are overly argumentative, some continually spout the company line of your competition, and some refuse to pay attention to you. Even worse, some customers interfere with their colleagues' ability to pay attention.

If you find that you have one or two difficult members of a larger audience, you should try to discover how these people fit into the overall picture at your prospect's organization. Indeed, you should make it a point to understand the position of everyone who participates in an interaction. You will learn more about all of this in Chapter 8, which covers preparing for sales call.

The prominence of a person in the prospect's organization can influence the way you deal with a problem. If the person is a peripheral member of the team, you can usually acknowledge his or her dissatisfaction in a polite way, and then move on in your effort to win over the more important members of the team. Don't let a single individual interrupt the main thrust of your presentation.

The dynamics of the personal relationships in any group of people are often far more complex than you might expect. For instance, perhaps the difficult member of your audience is a lower-ranking person who nonetheless is very influential with the more powerful members of the organization. Or perhaps the entire group seeks to avoid conflict, and, therefore, usually gives in to the loudest complainer.

Regardless of how insignificant a member of the team appears to be, always treat everyone at your prospect's organization with courtesy and respect. You don't know what goes on after you leave.

If a difficult prospect is a key member of the evaluation team, you will somehow have to deal with him or her more directly. When a customer is being difficult by constantly challenging and arguing with you, don't take the bait. Be willing to discuss the issue and bring up opposing viewpoints, but don't leap into a battle.

Sometimes the prospects that initially seem most difficult can be turned into your strongest supporters. They will challenge you simply to prove their own mettle both to you and to their co-workers. I have always referred to this tactic as "wrestling." Like eager lion cubs, these people just want to tussle around a bit to demonstrate their strength. Once you establish yourself as someone worthy of their respect, you will win them over. Never back down with this type of difficult prospect. Stand your ground, politely, and you may eventually win them over.

Sometimes a prospect is difficult because he or she is taking out unrelated frustrations on you. The person may be having problems with his private life, job, employer, or a specific task. A little empathy can go a long way. And, like a grown lion with a thorn in its paw, such a person will often be grateful to you if you display empathy, and he also may become a supporter over time.

How do you know the source of the difficult customer's manner? You very well may not be able to, but you can at least figure out how to best deal with them. Whenever you try to deal with a difficult customer, pay extra careful attention to his or her responses. If a customer persists in advancing arguments, regardless of your counters, back off. Likewise, you should back off from overly aggressive challenges. No one wins in a war of mutual destruction.

Most important, resist the temptation, strong as it may be, to defeat the difficult customer in a battle he or she started. Even if you are right, you will earn their undying animosity by embarrassing them in front of their co-workers or the other members of the sales team.

Sometimes the most progress in a sales cycle can be made with the ornery customer. This customer may very well see you as a threat to his or her technical leadership in the company. If you give in to this type of person a bit, he or she may begin to accept you as a peer rather than a potential rival. If you acknowledge that there are some valid reasons for the opposing opinion, the customer may start to do the same for you. You can turn a potential loss in a small battle into a way to gain a valuable ally in the war.

View the difficult customer as an opportunity and as an alert to the fact that something may be amiss.

A problem in communicating with your customer can indicate a problem in the sales cycle.

Even when the source of the problem is unresolved personal frustration on the part of the prospect, it makes an enormous difference for you to know the reason behind this frustration. Is it because of a situation in his or her personal life, or has the frustration come about because the customer is ordered to talk to a vendor (you!) whom he or she does not like for some reason? Perhaps the customer is just a curmudgeonly type in general.

Keep in mind that people have an existence outside the scope of your interaction. If you have a cranky member in your audience, that person could very well be cranky about *everything*. It's even possible that he or she is a misanthropic, ornery type who is disliked by everyone at the organization. Even in this situation, it pays to have some patience and to treat the misbehavior gently. If others are in the audience, you will win some small sense of admiration from them by showing restraint.

In all of these cases, by showing a little restraint, you will have taken a potential threat to your sale and turned it around to your advantage. In one sense, by dealing in a professional and adult manner with a troublemaker, you have further established your credibility. In an even more important sense, you will have uncovered an obstacle to your sales effort. If you can work around these with other members of the customer team, you may be able to salvage the sale. However, if you cannot, then you may consider moving on to the next opportunity.

There are situations where, despite your sense of propriety and restraint, you feel compelled to dispute something that was said in a meeting. A prime example occurs when a prospect makes a damaging, but untrue, statement about your product, services, or company.

What do you do when the customer makes an obviously untrue statement? In particular, what do you do when it is an untrue statement that is damaging to your cause? You must be careful handling such situations. First, do not directly confront the individual who has made the statement. The customer made the statement for a reason, and the confrontation will shut off communication before you can get to the reason. It is perfectly acceptable to offer a slightly different opinion, couched with caveats such as "I was pretty sure that...." and encourage the customer to elaborate the reason why he or she made the statement. If the customer was simply misinformed, you can help him or her to understand the basis of the mistaken impression. The customer may be trying to defeat your sales effort, in which case you can find ways to return the focus to the strong points of your solution. The customer may just be a difficult person who is trying to show you up and establish their technical superiority.

If the entire evaluation team believes a damaging falsehood about your product, your chances of success in a sales cycle are significantly diminished. If a misstatement about your product is simply the opinion of one member of the team, you can simply look to the others on the team to help correct the misimpression. If you try to battle it out, your combative nature may turn off other people at your target account who actually could be your allies.

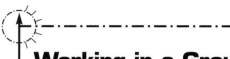

Working in a Group

The above discussion has centered on how to work with individuals. But you will usually be working with a group of people, which presents its own set of issues.

Most groups have their own complex dynamics. Some members are leaders, while some are more hesitant. When you work with a group from your prospect's organization, the dynamics are frequently based on extensive interactions that have nothing to do with you.

As with an individual prospect, you should take your cues on how to interact with a group by paying close attention to these overall dynamics. Listen and observe carefully. It will be very difficult to change the way members of a group of prospects interact with each other, so it is always best to let them take the lead in fitting *you* into *their* group.

You will have to listen in a slightly different way than you do to an individual. Don't just concentrate on the member of the group who is speaking. Check how the other people in the group react to the speaker.

One member of your prospect's team may dominate the conversation. But are the other people in the group listening and tacitly agreeing with this natural leader, or are they shying away from the speaker who may be a controlling bore? The differences between the two types of reaction are vast, and they forecast different ways for you to react.

If your group has a respected leader, you can spend extra time concentrating on him or her. If a blowhard dominates your group, you will gain the loyalty, trust, and affection of the others in the group by helping them to be heard.

And, of course, make sure that *you* are not seen as that dominating blowhard. You may be the most technically competent person at the table, but that doesn't mean that your opinion is more valuable than anyone else's.

Wrapping Up

The perfect relationship with a customer or prospect is one of trusted peer and guide. The customer starts to use you as a resource, rather than as an outsider. When customers begin to ask you how to solve their problems, you know you have established the rapport that can help you to make sales and establish fruitful long-term relationships that can result in additional sales and valuable reference accounts.

The bottom line in all of this, as we have stated before, is simple: People prefer to buy products from their friends. Your ability to establish a good relationship with your customers will have a direct effect on the success of your sales efforts. Make every contact with the public a laboratory for learning more about using your own personal style.

Since communication is the key to a successful sales cycle, we will be returning to the topic of communication again and again throughout the rest of this book, and even returning to some of the techniques and suggestions introduced in this chapter.

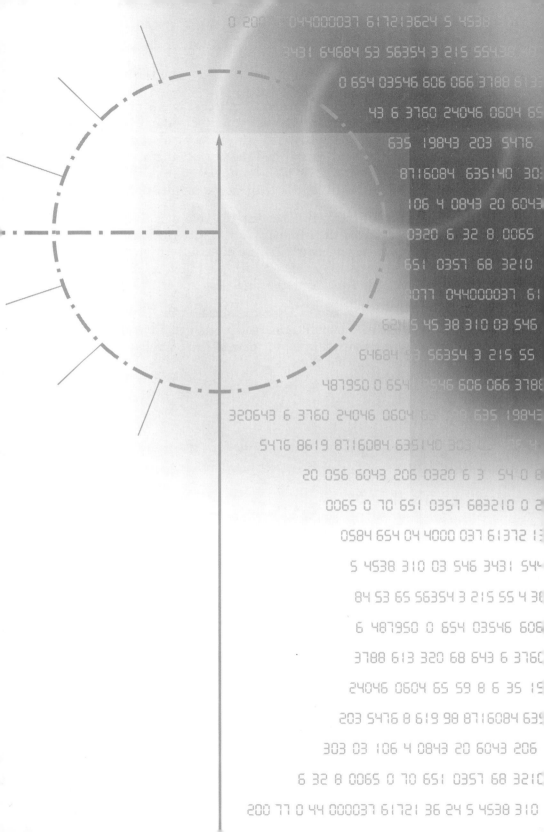

Feature Benefit Selling

As a sales consultant, you will find that one of the keys to positioning and selling technical products successfully is your ability to explain and position the features and benefits of your solution. Most high-tech companies adopt some type of standardized approach to selling their product that is generally centered around solution-selling. Instead of selling products, you try to sell solutions. Nevertheless, as a sales consultant, at some point you will likely find yourself talking about your product's features in detail.

In order to tie these features back into the overall solution, you will need to guide your prospect to benefits that will be obtained from using your product. Often, it is not enough to simply explain product benefits in generic terms. Prospective technical buyers may not have the experience and vision to translate generic product benefits into specific values that apply to their own situations. You may need to help your prospect translate the specific capabilities of your product into tangible benefits that can be applied to his or her own situations. In this chapter, we will take a look at using feature-benefit technical selling techniques.

Features

Many successful companies close sales at a very high level within prospect organizations. In these cases, the sales teams may be able to close a prospect without delving into the details of their product set at all. If your company can close deals through this type of total-solution-selling, it can be an ideal situation from a cost-of-sales perspective.

For example, let's say that you are working as a sales consultant for SuperServer, representing the SuperServer application server product. Your sales team begins working with a prospect who is looking for a complete e-commerce solution for his online bookstore. Ideally, your company would be able to propose a complete solution for the prospect—and this solution might involve pre-packaged e-commerce applications and third-party services. In such a case, your team might be able to close the deal without ever diving into the technical features of SuperServer at all.

Detailed product evaluations and technical presentations take lots of time and resources. If your sales team can avoid competing at this level, it will probably do so. However, at some point in your technical selling career, you will likely have to delve into the detailed capabilities of your product in order to help land a prospect. In these situations, it will be your job to position the features of your product as a solution-set for your prospect's problem.

It becomes your job to help turn product features into benefits for your prospect. The starting point for this process is to learn how to explain and position your product's feature set.

Consider a buyer who is in the market for a new desktop Pentium-class personal computer. This buyer may start by making a list of the features that he or she is looking for. Such a list might include the following items:

- 128 MB of memory
- 56K modem
- 8GB hard disk
- 32x CD-ROM

In essence, the features are driving the technical sale themselves, since the buyer is likely to consider only personal computers that offer these items. When you approach the problem from this angle, it becomes very simple.

But what happens when multiple vendors offer computers configured with the exact components listed above? In such cases, the buyer will make a decision based upon some other factor. Experience tells us that the final sale might be made based upon nonfeature factors such as the relationship between the sales rep and the buyer or the convenience of buying from one manufacturer over another. However, for the purposes of this example and the technical sales process, let's put these additional factors to the side for the moment.

Continuing with this example, assume that three hardware vendors—Dell, Gateway, and ACME—offer machines with the desired list of features. Furthermore, assume that all of these machines are the same price and that the buyer is equally confident in purchasing from any of the three suppliers. The sole differences between each of the machines is a single feature:

- Dell—100MB Zip drive
- Gateway—2GB tape backup system
- ACME—memory transmogrifier

With this extra information, can you figure out which product the prospect is likely to buy? Not necessarily, but you can probably narrow the list down, even if you are not familiar with the various options for personal computers. While the first two machines offer features that might be enticing to a buyer, the ACME machine offers something called a *memory transmogrifier*. The odds are pretty good that you have no idea what a *memory transmogrifier* is used for. And we can assure you that the prospect will not have any idea either, since there is no such thing as a memory transmogrifier. (*Transmogrification* is a real word that, roughly translated, means "to change from one thing into another.") We chose this particular example since we could be sure that you, and our fictional prospect, would have no idea what this feature is.

When the prospect is deciding which personal computer to purchase, the fact that ACME offers a memory transmogrifier probably will not be an incentive to buy it. Since the prospect does not know what the feature is used for, he or she is not likely to find any *value* in having that feature in a computer. In this case, the prospect will likely narrow down the selection to a choice between the Dell and the Gateway. The prospect has to understand what a given feature actually does if he or she is to consider the feature as part of the evaluation process.

Prospects are not likely to make technical buying decisions based upon features that they do not understand.

Our example is somewhat simplistic, because commodity products do not generally justify the expense of having sales consultants around to assist in the technical sale. However, the example is simple enough to be universally applicable for sales consultants, since you will no doubt be familiar with personal computers.

Suppose that you were representing ACME Computer as the technical sales consultant, and further suppose that there *is* such as thing as a "memory transmogrifier." Assume that it is a piece of hardware that automatically copies the memory of the computer to the hard disk while the computer is running. In the event of a system crash, the memory transmogrifier would have the ability to restore the machine to the exact state it was in before the computer crashed. Even unsaved word processing documents would be restored to memory exactly as if the machine had never failed. Now that you understand the feature, you could explain it in simple terms to the prospect.

A prospect must first understand the purpose of a feature before he or she can assign a value to the it.

As technical people, we have a tendency to assume that merely listing the various features of the product is enough to convince the prospect of the features' value. How many times have you recited a list of features as part of your presentation and demonstration *without explaining what the features actually do?*

Feature Blab

The art of listing a bevy of features without ever explaining what they are used for is something we call *feature blab*. Feature blab is one of the more serious problems that you can encounter as a sales consultant, and unfortunately it is a common problem. The features of your product often form the basis for your technical sale. Presenting a feature without verifying that your prospect actually understands what it is used for means that you are just wasting your time—and their time, too. In effect, all you are doing is "blabbing away" about the glorious capabilities of your product. You might just as well be speaking a foreign language.

In fact, you *are* speaking a foreign language. You are communicating in the native "technical tongue" of your product. Do not assume that your prospect can speak your language. Listen to the blab:

> *"... And the Java-Cowboy Application Development environment features a memory transmogrifier. So, you've got that going for you, and that helps."*

Not only are some members of your audience not likely to know what a memory transmogrifier is, but they are also probably afraid to look foolish by admitting that they don't know. So, how are they going to place a value on this feature when they compare it to the various features offered by your competitors' products? The answers are that they can't and they won't. This is especially bad if the "memory transmogrifier" is actually one of the best features of your product. You just pitched your best stuff, and the prospect doesn't know it. Does this sound a little far-fetched to you? It shouldn't. It happens every day.

The first step in the feature-benefit technical selling process is to adequately explain the features of your product.

Once the prospect understands the capabilities of a given feature, he has begun to travel down the path to understanding how this feature can help solve his business problem. The second part of the process is for the prospect to accept a given feature in terms of the benefit that it can provide.

Turning Features into Benefits

Explaining features is only half the battle. The way to win the war is to connect features with their associated benefits. A benefit is a description of how the prospect will profit from your solution. More specifically, a benefit is the individual advantage that the prospect gains from any given feature.

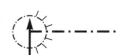

Generic benefits are not enough, because they don't necessarily stick in the prospect's mind as being associated exclusively with your offerings. Your prospect has to be able to attach any given feature to a *specific* benefit that is germane to his or her problem (although there are cases in which benefits are so obvious and universal that they do not need to apply to the *specific* problem of the prospect).

Take, for example, the situation in which you have two cars that are identical in all aspects, except that one is equipped with the new polar-star fuel injection system (the feature). You *explain* that the benefit of the polar-star fuel injector is that the car will get twice the mileage for the same gallon of gas with no reduction in engine speed or power. All other things being equal, your prospect would pick the car with the polar-star fuel injector, right?

Well, maybe. The answer is "yes" when the price of a gallon of gas is $50. But what if the price is only ten cents? The answer is less certain. Sure, if all things were exactly equal, then your technical prospect probably would still buy the car with the polar-star fuel injector. But in real sales situations, products are almost never exactly equal, only similar. The difference is the *expected benefit* that the prospect will get from the features in your product versus those of your competitor's product.

This holds true for both technical products and nontechnical products. Let's say that you are looking for a winter coat, and you are comparing two different winter jackets in a high-end outfitter's store. Both jackets are the same color, but one is wool and the other is made of down. Before you can make a choice between the two coats, you would need to understand that the key *feature* of the down jacket is the down. Furthermore, you would need to understand that the main *benefit* of down is that it has a much higher capacity to keep you warm while being much lighter in weight.

Which jacket do you buy? Take a look at the following table:

Table 6-1
Features must be aligned with benefits.

Buyer	Wool	Down
Big and strong	X	
Tendency to be extra cold		X

The left-hand column lists a simple set of attributes for the individual who is making the selection. The two right-hand columns mark the coat that offers the best benefit for each attribute. The overall problem is the same: You need to buy a winter coat. If you are big and strong, you may not care that a down jacket is lighter. In fact, since you are big and strong, you may not get cold enough to warrant the extra warmth of a down jacket. On the other hand, if you have a tendency to feel cold, you might opt for the down jacket, provided you understand its extra capacity for warmth.

The benefits of the down feature are the extra warmth and lighter weight. These benefits will appeal to you only under these conditions:

- You understand the benefits of down (it is lighter and warmer)
- Lighter weight and greater warmth will help solve your problem in some way

The critical element involves how the benefits *apply* to the buyer. No consumer is going to argue that a fuel injector that uses half the normal amount of fuel is not a benefit, nor that a jacket that is lighter and warmer isn't valuable. The questions are these:

- Will it be valuable to the prospect *specifically*?
- Does your prospect fully *understand* the value?
- How does this benefit *compare* to other benefits offered by competing products?

The good news is that technical selling is never quite as cut-and-dried as the preceding examples. If it were, we would all probably be out of a job! The bad news is that the value that the prospect will assign to a given feature is wholly dependent upon perception of their needs. Your product is going to have an array of features, each of which will offer an array of possible benefits. The key word is *possible*. For any prospect, the benefits of a given feature will be directly related to how *effective* that feature is in solving the prospect's *particular* problem. Each benefit will have an associated value that is unique to the prospect in some fashion.

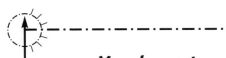

You have to personalize features and benefits in order to maximize their impact.

The more tangible and personal the benefits of your features, the more likely it is that the technical buyer will choose your solution instead of the competitor's. In other words, the buyer will assign higher *value* to features that address his specific problems.

And it is your job to make these features and benefits personal—that is, to make them specific to your prospect's individual situation. The secret to doing this is to gain a firm understanding of your prospect's specific business problem and technical requirements. In the following sections of this book, we will examine methods of interviewing your prospect before you give presentations and demonstrations in order to gather this data. In the qualification meeting, you will learn about your prospect's business problem and technical requirements. During the presentation and demonstration process, you will play back those requirements and connect the features of your product to your prospect's specific problems and explain the benefits of each feature as it relates to each problem.

We have no doubt that your product marketing department will go to great lengths to create a set of presentations and demonstrations that extol the virtues of your product. In general, they have probably identified the right sets of issues, features, and benefits. They may even create presentations that are specific to a set of vertical prospects such as manufacturing, retail, financial services, aerospace, and insurance. What your marketing department cannot do for you, however, is build a custom presentation that relates specifically to the needs of *your* individual prospect. This is your job as part of the sales team.

Personalizing Features and Benefits

When you interview a prospect before making your sales presentation and demonstration, your job is to grasp the business problem and technical requirements. Through the earlier stages of the sales process, you most likely have learned the specific terminologies and business practices for the industry in which your prospect operates.

In most cases, you will be working across a variety of industries unless you are selling a vertical application, such as an accounting system for retail stores. But even if you are selling a standard retail system, you will likely work with different kinds of retailers. After all, grocery stores have different terminologies, practices, and procedures than clothing stores, but they are still both retail operations.

> Technology products and solutions that are focused on a specific group of prospects within a single line of business are typically called "vertical" products. Conversely, products that are targeted to multiple types of companies are considered to be "horizontal" products.

Before you make your presentation to the prospect, you need to create three lists that will contain the following information:

- Major features of your product
- Prospect's business problem and technical requirements
- Ancillary operating facts about the prospect

You should be able to create the first list in your sleep. It's a list of your product's major features and benefits as they are understood by you and your team of sales consultants. The standard sales literature will also contain bullet points that outline the key features of your product as well. The last (and possibly most important source of information) is one that you might commonly overlook—your own installed-base of customers will have developed opinions about the value of your products. They may even be working with the product more closely than you are, and can provide insights that may not have occurred to you.

Use your customer base as a source for insight into the features and benefits of your product.

It is not necessary to gather information from your customers before every sales call, but you should make a practice of checking back with your customers for feature/benefit advice every so often. This is especially important after you have released a new version of a product, since the features and associated benefits are likely to have changed. Combine the data from all three sources (marketing, your sales team, and your customers) into a master list of important product features.

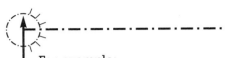

For example:

Assume that you are representing the application server product called "SuperServer," introduced earlier in the book, and that SuperServer has the following major features, which will make our first list:

- Written in Java
- Provides pre-built routines for database access to major relational databases, including XYZ-Db and IEM Dbx
- Includes easy tools for monitoring the performance of applications
- Supports declarative XA-style transactions
- Wizard interface makes it easy for customers to install
- Extensive examples on the CD-ROM shortens the learning curve for new developers

Our second list simply restates the basic business problem that your prospect is trying to solve. It also supplies the technical requirements for your solution. You will have gathered most of this information during the qualification process:

Federated needs to write a new online order entry application to sell its widgets over the Web. Its technical requirements are as follows:

- Must be written in Java
- Plans on using XYZ-Db standard relational database for this project
- Must interface to the JHacker programming tool that the company has standardized on

Our final list—ancillary facts—is tougher to create, since it relies on your intuition and data-gathering skills. During the qualification process, you no doubt will have learned some information about the prospect's business and environment that may be applicable to the features of your product. You will have gathered information about the business climate, the state of the industry, the competition, and the in-house pressures facing your prospect and his or her team.

Another source of ancillary information comes from customers who are in the same industry as your prospect. It does not hurt to check with your network of sales consultants to find out if anyone else has been successful (or unsuccessful) in selling to a similar prospect. All of these elements can play into your feature/benefit presentation.

Through your meetings with Federated, you pull together the following ancillary facts:

- Federated's closest competitors have Web sites up and running already
- The IT department has a number of skilled Java programmers
- Operations lacks experience in managing application server products
- Federated has other applications using the IEM Dbx database

In reality, each of these lists is likely to be longer and more complex, but you needn't make these lists extremely lengthy. An honest, "quick and dirty" list is much better than a formal, overblown document.

In most cases, a primary list of features and benefits would tend to change slightly on a monthly basis in response to new releases of the product and/or feedback from customers. If you are constantly adding and deleting to your list of major features and benefits, you probably need to study your product more carefully to be sure that you understand the major value delivered by your product.

The next step is to blend the lists into a workable table of features and benefits that you can use as a skeleton for framing your presentation and demonstration. The first feature from our example on your list notes that SuperServer is written in Java. Although this is certainly a benefit, it may not be a major benefit for Federated, since it is already *requiring* that the product be written in Java. Therefore, spending time pitching the benefits of a Java-based server is probably not the right choice when working with Federated. However, if Federated had specified that "written in Java" was a nice feature, but not a requirement, and your intelligence told you that some non-Java application server competitors were in the deal, then spending time on the feature/benefits of a Java server might be the right approach. In the example case, you might put Java on your list of features to cover, but you would probably not focus so strongly on this feature and its benefits. Remember: You have a limited amount of time to make your case, so you should not waste it explaining features that are already understood and accepted by the prospect.

Federated plans to build this application using the XYZ-Db database, and SuperServer works with XYZ-Db. Therefore, focusing on SuperServer's integration with XYZ-Db should be part of your approach. This is where the hard work begins, because at this point, all that you have is a single bullet item explaining that you work with XYZ-Db.

A feature of SuperServer is that it works with XYZ-Db. Initially, it appears that the benefit to Federated is that it plans on using XYZ-Db as the database.

But it's not that simple. The fact that SuperServer runs with XYZ-Db is a feature that points to a set of other features, which in turn have specific benefits that can be applied to Federated's situation. Consider Figure 6.1:

Figure 6.1
Features and benefits.

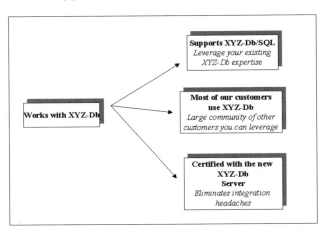

The base feature of SuperServer is that it works with XYZ-Db. But this is just a pointer to a set of more *specific* features and benefits. If you break this basic feature down into a smaller set of sub-features, you can then begin to apply specific benefits that Federated can achieve by using SuperServer. In Table 6.2, we have highlighted three specific features that flow from the base feature and then attached benefits to these procedures.

The final step in the process is to translate these generic benefits into specific benefits that will apply directly to Federated. Consider the following table:

Feature Benefit Selling — Chapter 6

Table 6.2
Translating generic benefits into specific benefits.

Detailed Feature	*Specific* **Benefit for Federated**
Supports the use of XYZ-Db's own version of the SQL language.	*Federated already has built a number of XYZ-Db applications using the SQL programming language. SuperServer will allow you to re-use this expertise directly within the application server. You can save time and resources and get the application into production more quickly.*
XYZ-Db database users represent the largest installed base of SuperServer customers.	*Federated won't have to "break new ground" with SuperServer, as we have many other XYZ-Db customers. Our support site has lots of good tips and code samples using XYZ-Db that you can take advantage of to shorten the learning curve.*
SuperServer is certified to work with the newest release of the XYZ-Db server.	*The fact that SuperServer is certified with the XYZ-Db eliminates any finger-pointing when problems arise. You can be assured that the Java code you write with SuperServer will work with the XYZ-Db database.*

The key is to personalize the benefits into terms that prospects can understand. You must help them apply the benefits to their personal situations in order to solidify the advantages of your product in their minds. You have to remember to couch the benefits into technical terms that apply to their specific situations, and you have to keep the conversation on a technical level. If you cross the line and start wrapping your benefit statements in too much "sales talk," you will damage your credibility with the technical buyer. For example:

Wrong:

SuperServer's Java Virtual Machine is the best, fastest JVM on the market, and you definitely want to work with the best.

Right:

Third-party analysts have rated the Java Virtual Machine in SuperServer as very reliable, and performance tests have proved that the JVM executes code more quickly than other products. These features will help reduce your development time, since you can quickly modify and test code. Your programmers will not have to spend time tracking down failures, so they can concentrate on getting your order-entry application built and deployed.

In the first case, the benefits are not specific enough. Unsubstantiated words like *best* and *fastest* are, by themselves, not credible enough for a sales consultant. That isn't to say that the prospect shouldn't hear the words *best* and *fastest;* it's that they shouldn't hear these words coming from *you.* Your sales rep will handle the "best" and "fastest" part of the discussion. Your job is to handle the technology.

In the second paragraph of the example, we essentially make the same points, but we also offer proof points, and we tie the benefits back to the prospect's own specific situation. Proof points are endorsements or verified statements from credible third parties that validate your technical benefit claims.

A good proof point can nail home the benefits of a feature, but you must be careful which sources you use.

Public resources such as trade magazines, analyst groups (Gartner, Meta, IDC, etc.), or public references are great. But before you use these sources, make sure that they are not also raising concerns about your product. For example, ABC Research may have come out and endorsed the power, speed, and reliability of the SuperServer JVM. That's great. But what if they also go on to say that SuperServer as a company is on shaky ground in a market that is quickly consolidating? Sure, you have nailed home the performance benefit, but you may also have called attention to a serious objection if the prospect looks at the entire ABC Research report.

For the remaining bullet points on your features list, the only other item that scores a direct connection to Federated's needs is the ability to support IEM Dbx. What is not clear is how this feature can *specifically* benefit Federated. Your own research tells you that Federated has other applications that make use of Dbx. Ideally, you would have gotten Federated's technical people to tell you more about the use of Dbx within Federated so that you could build a benefits case around SuperServer's support of IEM Dbx.

However, since you know that SuperServer supports Dbx, and Federated has some Dbx already in place, you can have a benefits dialogue on this topic during your presentation. Base your discussion on the principles of feature/benefit technical selling. For example, you can combine your sketchy knowledge of the use of Dbx with a question that can lead to more benefits:

SuperServer supports Dbx as well as XYZ-Db, and we offer certain features that map specifically to the Dbx database. I noticed that you also use Dbx here at Federated. Do you need to tie into these systems with the new order-entry application? Are you planning on migrating some of these applications over to an application server in the future?

If your prospect warms to the topic, you now have the opportunity to expound on some additional benefits based upon the response that you get. For instance, the prospect may respond to the above question with this answer:

We use Dbx for some of our back-office accounting systems that run on a mainframe. We are trying to move away from the mainframe, but we might want to port some of these applications to UNIX versions of Dbx in the future.

With the use of a simple question, you've received the opening to pull out some additional features that SuperServer offers. You can now tie the features back to the specific applications that your prospect mentioned. You can build a stronger set of benefits and thereby increase the value of your solution to the prospect.

In the best situation, you would already have this information in hand before the presentation. There is no problem improvising, though, based upon your knowledge of SuperServer's Dbx interface and your own experiences.

However, you may not always get the opening from the prospect to delve into these additional features and benefits. Consider the following response to your Dbx question:

Those are old systems. We don't need to interface to them, and we are not going to be using Dbx as a database in the future.

This type of response is your signal to move on. Spending valuable selling time stressing the features of your Dbx interface is not going to score points with the prospect, because he or she has no plans to continue using Dbx. Dbx support may be a feature of your product, but your customer's plans indicate that this particular feature *carries no benefit for him or her*. In such cases, don't belabor the point. Mention the basic feature and move on, as the following example illustrates:

Wrong:

However, you may not be aware that there is some advantage to continuing to work with Dbx. Let me spend a few minutes to explain some of the key Dbx features that we support...

Right:

In case your situation changes, SuperServer does offer specialized interfaces with Dbx. Now, another feature that we offer will have some value to you...

The last two categories of items on your feature/benefit lists do not appear to offer any *specific* benefit at first glance. The list also contains features that you do not support. In the first category, we have the following item:

- Supports declarative XA-style transactions.

Following our feature/benefit rules, you will need to explain the capabilities of this feature to your prospect. The potential customer may not even know what XA-style transactions are good for. Your explanation must include specific benefits that can be applied to Federated's own situation:

SuperServer supports XA-style transactions, which is an industry standard for performing data transactions. In Federated's case, you would never want to take an order for a customer without also marking the items in order-entry as being "sold." Transactions are used to ensure that all parts of the operation are performed as a logical group. Because this is so common, a standards group has defined a technique, called XA, for this process. SuperServer is built to make use of this XA standard without requiring any low-level coding. Your developers will be able to create your order-entry transactions using business terms, and SuperServer will translate these transactions into XA-standard transactions without any additional work on your part. This will save your programmers time and effort and will help you to get the application into production faster.

Notice how the feature is explained in terms that your prospect will understand, in the context of his own application needs. We referenced a "standards body" to reinforce the viability of the feature and we tied the description of the feature to the proposed order-entry systems application. We also associated the benefits with one of Federated's own stated requirements (to get the application up and running quickly). It is much more likely that Federated's technical decision-makers will consider XA-style transaction support to be a desirable feature now that they can see how it can benefit their specific situation.

There is one more threshold you need to cross in order to cement the feature in the prospect's mind and that is acceptance of the benefit. We'll get into this shortly.

Before we do, however, we need to cover the issue of those requirements that your product does not support. If you look back at Federated's list, you will note that it wants a product that will integrate with "the JHacker application development tool." Since SuperServer does not support JHacker directly, this requirement becomes an objection, a reason not to buy your product. Chapter 12 covers objections, and the best ways to handle them, in depth. The process of integrating your three feature/benefit lists will help you to identify possible objections and allow you to develop a strategy for dealing with them.

FBA: Feature, Benefit, and Acceptance of the Benefit

The final step in the feature/benefit selling process is to get your prospect to acknowledge the value of the feature and benefit. We call this *accepting the benefit*. This topic forms the third leg of the feature/benefit triangle.

Technical selling means FBA: Feature, Benefit, Acceptance of the Benefit.

When your prospect accepts the benefit, he or she forms a sort of "mental" contract with you, implicitly stating that you have sold him or her on the advantages of a certain feature. This makes it harder for your prospect to select a competitor's solution. The more mental bonds you create, the harder it will be for your prospect to buy somebody else's product.

Consider the description that we used above to explain the value of the SuperServer JVM:

> *Third-party analysts have rated the Java Virtual Machine in SuperServer as being very reliable, and performance tests have proved that the JVM executes code quicker than other products. These features will help reduce your development time, since you can quickly modify and test code. Your programmers will not have to spend time tracking down failures, so they can concentrate on getting your order-entry application built and deployed.*

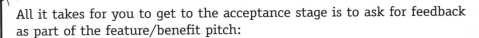

All it takes for you to get to the acceptance stage is to ask for feedback as part of the feature/benefit pitch:

If I am not mistaken, one of Federated's goals is to get its order-entry application into production by the end of next quarter. Do you think the SuperServer JVM feature can reduce your cycle times and let your programmers develop applications more rapidly?

If you have tied the benefit closely to Federated's needs by personalizing it, then you will probably get the response that you want. Don't be afraid to poll several of the technical evaluators for feedback by asking open-ended acceptance questions, such as these:

- *Do you think that the increased reliability of the SuperServer JVM will help your systems administrators to remain productive, Bob?*
- *As a programmer, Lisa, is it useful for you to be able to test code more often by taking advantage of the fast JVM?*

You may be thinking, as you read this example, that it would be difficult for someone to answer negatively to this type of question. And you are right in surmising that an affirmative reply does not necessarily mean a full-fledged endorsement of the benefit.

Even this type of closed question can elicit a variety of positive responses, from enthusiastic support to grudging acknowledgment. All you really need to do with this question is to get the prospect to acknowledge that he or she understands the point you presented. While reaffirming the acceptance may sound a bit forced on your part, your sales rep can use the temperature of the response as a entry to the discussion. Now the rep can begin to do some heavy-lifting sales work.

Get several respondents involved and concentrate on getting them to give you some feedback. In the best cases, they will warm to your benefit statement. In the worst cases, they will raise some objections. But they are going to have these objections whether they raise them or not, and the only way you can deal with them is to get them on the table.

Acceptance statements give you the pros and cons that your sales rep will need to bring the deal to a close. Keep the discussion technical, and if you are not comfortable asking for acceptance, give your sales representative the opportunity to "jump in" and ask for it. Ideally, however, you alone will want to get the acceptance from your prospect, because technical people will feel more comfortable agreeing to statements from you, the sales consultant. Technical people are less likely to agree with a sales rep because it makes them feel like they are being "sold."

Wrapping Up

The key to getting your features and advantages across is FBA selling—feature, benefit, and acceptance of the benefit. Prospects cannot value features that they do not understand, and they will value benefits that are tied closely to their unique situations and problems. Avoid harping on features that you personally like if they do not match up with the needs of your prospect. Make sure that you close the explanation of any feature with an acceptance. At the end of the day, you will have a firm road map from which to conclude the technical selling process.

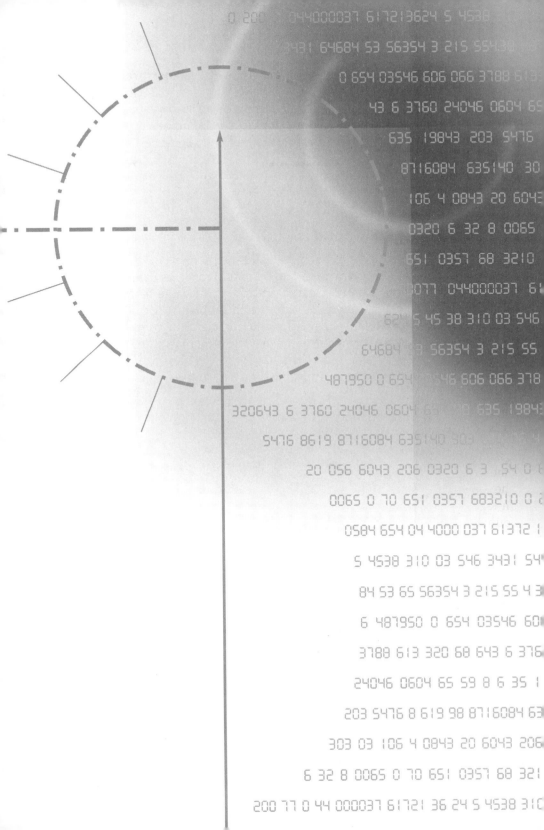

CHAPTER 7

Mastering the Demo

The product demonstration is often the ultimate event in the technical selling process. The demo sets the stage for the remaining phases of the evaluation. You will find it difficult to recover from a poor product demonstration. Conversely, an outstanding demo can, virtually by itself, make you the front-runner for the remainder of the evaluation.

Being the front-runner is a lot like being the champion in a heavyweight title fight. The onus is on the challenger to knock out the champ, while the champion is likely to win any decision that "goes to the cards." Your job is to get yourself into the front-runner's seat with an outstanding production demonstration.

Some facets of the sales consultant's job may not come easily to you. Other sales consultants may be flashier or more charismatic. But everyone can learn to give a great demo. This chapter will help you to lay the groundwork for delivering a great product demonstration.

Mastering the Demo by Mastering Your Solution

The first step in giving a powerful product demonstration is to attain mastery of your own solution. While it is difficult to technically qualify a prospect without adequate product knowledge, it is almost impossible for you to give a good product demonstration if you yourself lack thorough knowledge of your product.

Some of you may be fortunate enough to work for a company that already has a robust and sparkling demo suite. In such cases, all you have to do is follow a set of written directions to show off your products—and these types of demos can provide an adequate beginning.

But every demo can be improved if you add particular details for each customer. Part of your job in giving the demo is to establish your technical credibility. Although you may be an adequate "demo demon"— someone who can exhibit the features of a product—your competition may be able to flesh out their demos more impressively and thus beat you in this all-important stage of the sales process. By giving a demo with only a cursory knowledge of your product, you partially cede control of the sales cycle to your competition, giving them a chance to win the deal.

You will often be asked to give product demonstrations long before you have a sufficient working knowledge of your product. Why, you ask? The answer is simple: Sales consultants are a scarce resource, and as soon as the company finds itself short-handed, you are going to get the call. And the fact is, once you pitch your first demo, the floodgates are going to open as far as your sales team is concerned. How long you will be given to master the product before being asked to give product demonstrations depends upon the complexity of the product and the type of audience.

For example, as a sales consultant for a vendor selling an e-mail package, you might be expected to handle product demonstrations for end-users after a short training period. However, you might not be as adequately prepared to demo the product to the information technology (IT) department of the same company. IT personnel would be more likely than end-users to ask detailed, functional questions outside your experience base as a new sales consultant.

A winning product demonstration always begins with mastery of your own product.

You rarely will be able to completely control the competence level of the audience. Your audience may be absolutely overwhelmed by the technical details of your product and area of technology, or they may be experienced veterans. Therefore, best practice dictates that you master your own product before you start giving product demonstrations.

Preparation lies at the heart of genius, so mastering your solution will make your demos more effective. As Abraham Lincoln once put it:

If I had eight hours to chop down a tree, I would spend six of them sharpening my ax.

There will be exceptions to this rule, of course, and you can use these exceptions as opportunities to practice your demo. For example, your company may have site license deals with large Fortune 500 organizations. In such cases, the central purchasing department typically will negotiate a fixed-price deal (either by site or by user). Individual business units will have to use your product as their "standard" when they start a new project. It is often customary to give these business units a courtesy demonstration before they purchase the product. In such cases, you might be able to give a satisfactory demonstration without having a solid foundation of product knowledge.

What does mastering your product entail? Are you expected to be able to answer, off the top of your head, every question that every prospect asks? No! Should you commit the entire product reference manual to memory? Not necessarily. As standard operating procedure, you should be able to handle the vast majority of questions about your product. As preparation, start with the simple things that you need to know, and then work your way to the more complicated items. As you follow through this progression, you will eventually come to an inherent understanding of the way your product "thinks." Once you reach this plateau, you will find you can answer questions about your product intuitively.

The first step in mastering your product is to take part in a formal product-training program.

Formal Product Training

When a company hires you as a sales consultant for a product, it is customary that it provide you with some formalized product training. Typically, this training comes in two forms: First, you will be trained in the basic workings and features of the product, just as if you were a customer. Second, once you have mastered these concepts, your company will frequently provide you with sales training for the product set. Ideally, this next training will concentrate more on the features and benefits of your product.

If the company hired you from the ranks of its own customer base, you may be able to skip the formal product training. But formal product training represents only the start of the process. You need to *master* your product in order to give powerful product demonstrations.

Unless you have significant experience with the product as a consultant or customer, you should attend formal product training.

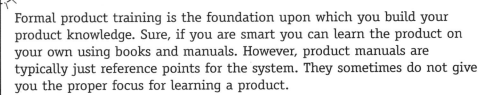

Formal product training is the foundation upon which you build your product knowledge. Sure, if you are smart you can learn the product on your own using books and manuals. However, product manuals are typically just reference points for the system. They sometimes do not give you the proper focus for learning a product.

Formalized product training, especially introductory training, will almost always concentrate on the most *common* tasks and procedures. It will help you to focus on the primary tasks up front. This training will also give you the chance to work through the product with actual *customers* who are at the same point as you are in the learning curve.

You will be able to see how they perceive the product, and you can get a better understanding of how customers plan on using it. In particular, formal product training will provide you the answers to three important questions:

- What kinds of questions do customers have about the product?
- How do customers (and by extension, prospects) plan on using the product?
- What features were important to other customers in selecting your product?

The kinds of questions asked during initial product training are likely to be the types of questions that prospects will ask you during the sales process. Although the context in which the questions will be asked will differ, you can prepare for the sales process by noting these questions and answers now.

Take detailed notes on the questions that customers ask during product training.

Attending product training with real live customers almost allows you to be a "fly on the wall" for a series of demos. However, the answers that the instructors give may not be the same answers that you will need during the actual sales process. Keep in mind that the objective of product training is to transfer product knowledge, while the objective of the selling process is to close a sale.

For example, a prospect might ask the question, "Can SuperServer connect to my legacy IEM Dbx database?"

If SuperServer does not provide a supported interface to the IEM Dbx database, the product trainer may offer some possible workarounds.

However, because the training session is a general course that has *teaching* and not *selling* as its aim, the trainer will probably not spend a lot of time trying to work out an answer to this specific problem. After all, the instructor has other customers in the course to worry about. (Some of these customers may very well have their own innovative answers and workarounds for these questions that they, along with their sales consultants, developed during their sales cycle.)

Conversely, during the sales process you might have to develop a much more thorough answer to this question, including specific examples of how the integration can be accomplished. For the time being, though, the important thing is to capture the question. If one customer is asking this question, then other customers will be asking it, too.

Customers who take the training classes are planning to use your product to solve real-world problems. This information can be incredibly valuable as you learn to position your product. Listen to these customers and find out how they are planning to implement, deploy, and use your product in the real world. You may be surprised at the variety of ways that customers come up with. You can leverage these ideas in sales situations in the future.

> There will be cases where understanding the end uses of your product are relevant. At other times, it will be completely irrelevant. If you are selling software such as a relational database that can be applied to many different problems, it might be useful to see how your customers plan to deploy the product. On the other hand, if you are selling network routers, which are also technology products but ones that serve a more specific task, the data might be less useful.

It is also very important to take the time to informally "interview" the customers in the training course. Find out which features of your product were critical for their decision-making process. After all, these people have made the choice to buy the product that you will be representing. Since they are in training, they are likely to have recently completed the purchasing process, and their experiences in the sales cycle will be fresh in their minds. Here are some key questions to ask:

- What other products did they consider?
- Which features were important to them, and why?

- Have they identified any weaknesses in the product?
- How are they planning to work around these weaknesses?

Most new customers are more than willing to talk with you about their experiences in buying the product, especially if you position yourself as a new employee of the company. Although the customers are not there to answer your sales questions, they are still new to the product and the evaluation process is fresh in their minds. Try to balance your need to gather this data with the customer's need to learn the product while attending training. Don't make a nuisance out of yourself while pursuing this data! After all, this information is more helpful to *you* than it is to the customer. Try not to be intrusive: Start by asking customers individually if they could spare a few minutes during a break to talk with you about their experiences. You might then be able to arrange to take the customer out to lunch or dinner, where you can cover these topics more fully.

The last thing you want to do is to disrupt the customer during training.

You do not want to chase customers around on breaks or hound them for information. At the beginning of the training course, introduce yourself and let the others know your position within the company. Make sure that you get everybody's name right and then get settled into the course. After the first half day or so, you will have the chance to see the customers in action with the trainer. Once you get a handle on the landscape, you can start spending some time with customers at *their* convenience. Use the information that you have gleaned from listening to them ask questions as an entrée to a more detailed discussion. For example:

Wrong:

Hey Susan, I'm new with SuperServer and I was wondering if you would fill me in on your evaluation of SuperServer?

Right:

Susan, I was interested to see that you are planning to use SuperServer to connect to a database back on your mainframe for the new inventory system you are building. Your team seems to have a lot of knowledge and experience. I would love to have the opportunity to spend a few minutes talking about the project at some point this week if it's convenient for you.

Gather as much information as you can from the customer by listening and learning. Because you are not yet directly involved with a customer in a sales situation, this will be the last opportunity for you to see how customers view your product while you still have an unbiased opinion. Later, as you use your own product and serve as a public spokesperson for the technology, you will tend to filter any customer data through your personal experiences. At this early point, however, the customers have been through a sales process with your product, and you have not.

Professional Conduct in a Formal Training Course

Be aware of how you conduct yourself during the training course itself. Although you are new, you are still an ambassador for the technology, and you need to conduct yourself in an appropriate manner. In particular:

Do not grill the instructor as if you are one of the students.

If you have some issues, differences of opinion, or additional questions, take them offline. Grab the instructor at the break and ask if he or she will make a few minutes for you at the end of the day.

The instructor is running the course. You are there to learn. Many new sales consultants think that they are "helping" by constantly interrupting with personal anecdotes and commentary. Ask questions where appropriate, but resist the urge to "add your two cents" at every opportunity. In particular, you want to avoid asking "tough" questions and putting the instructor on the spot.

On the other hand, this does not give you a license to adopt the "not my problem" attitude. Being new and in training does not excuse you from acting as a representative and resource for the company. If customers have problems or ask for help in tracking down an answer, you have some responsibility to help. You are not expected to have the answer at the tip of your fingers, but you are nonetheless expected to help if you can. Normally, the instructor will carry the load during training, but you will find that once customers have your name and number, they will call on you if they have problems in the future. Customers tend to view sales consultants as "free" support resources. You will need to steer the customers to support and consulting for most problems, but you still have to return phone calls and answer e-mail.

In addition to mingling with the customers during product training, you are expected to pay attention, follow the lectures, and complete the lab exercises. Formal training provides the groundwork on which to begin mastering your product.

When Your Company Does Not Offer Formal Training

You may find yourself working for a company that does not have formal product training classes (this is especially true with companies at the Innovation stage of the Technology Life Cycle). If you are new to the sales consulting game and your company does not provide formal product training, you may be in over your head.

The company should at least have computer-based training or a training manual. Experienced sales consultants (or new sales consultants who come from the customer base) can get by without formal training, but this situation is not ideal. Once you have completed the formal product training process, you will be ready to tackle the second phase of the product mastery process: working with the standard demo.

The Demo Pyramid

The process of mastering your own solution forms a series of layered stages, with each stage building upon the previous level. This process is depicted in the pyramid that you see here in Figure 7.1.

Figure 7.1
The Demo
Pyramid.

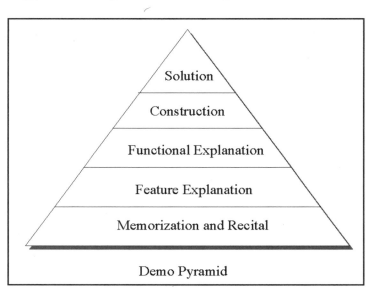

Solution

Construction

Functional Explanation

Feature Explanation

Memorization and Recital

Demo Pyramid

The figure is depicted as a pyramid for two reasons. First, each level of the pyramid builds on previous levels, with the highest level of mastery being the ability to demonstrate and sell the complete solution that matches the prospect's requirements. Second, in keeping with the "many are called, few are closed" theme mentioned earlier in this book, you will find that fewer and fewer sales consultants make it to the next higher level in the chain. In the following sections, we look at each layer in detail.

Memorization and Recital

Mastering technology requires a structured plan. Unless you have a skeleton from which to work, you will never be sure that you are hitting all of the important points. For a sales consultant, the first level is the *standard demo kit*. And the first level of the hierarchy calls for rote memorization of the standard demo script.

> If your company does not have a standard demo kit, you should create your own or ask a more senior sales consultant for his or hers.

The product demo kit is typically composed of three parts: the script, data, and some examples of your product at work. The standard demo is typically included with the product kit itself (in fact, when you install the product you can often install the demo at the same time). The product demonstration script is much like a screenplay or movie script. It provides a flow for you to follow in demonstrating your product, along with the appropriate "story" that follows the demonstration. Most companies already have a demonstration script, which you can follow.

If you were to ask most experienced sales consultants, they would tell you that the average demo kit is almost universally bad. The script is usually built around a fictitious "company" and the premise of the company is almost always some hokey scenario that rarely models the real world. So what? The important thing to remember at this point is that you have been given a place to start.

> There are certainly exceptions to the "hokey" rule, but they are few and far between. Many companies have focused on the age-old employee/department demo, even though this type is universally shunned by sales consultants. Some companies show occasional creative flair, but the standard item is pretty dull stuff. I have yet to work for a company

that had a really decent demo. Don't worry about this. Use any material you have as a framework for learning about the product. We'll worry about improving the demo scenario in the next chapter.

You will be selling two basic types of technical products—hardware and software—or offering service and support for these two types of products. If you are selling hardware, it will have switches and knobs, and if you are selling software, it will have some kind of user interface. Both types of products require the same first step in achieving mastery.

The first step to mastering your product is to make sure that you know what each and every knob, screen element, and button is used for. Start with the part of your product that is typically demonstrated for the user. Then, move outward to the more obscure features and functions. In the sections that follow, we will concentrate on using a software application as an example; however, the same basic principles apply to hardware products (in fact, many hardware products have software components).

There are certainly exceptions to this rule about mastering each element. For example, certain classes of hardware products may not have a "demo" in the traditional software vein. In such cases, there is still usually a script of features and instructions on how to show them off. The script, in effect, becomes the demo. Nonetheless, you will probably find that the slide presentation and the chalk talk, which we will discuss later, will be the place for reviewing much of the material that you would cover in a typical software demo.

On the opposite side of the spectrum are products such as enterprise resource planning software, or ERP systems. These product offerings are so large that they almost always provide a large number of individual demo scripts to match the various subsystems they offer (such as general ledger, purchasing, inventory, or maintenance). If you are selling application software that has many different modules, you should start with a single module and work your way up. There is not much call for a sales consultant who can only demonstrate the first couple of screens of twenty different modules. Focus on a subset first, and then work your way through the rest.

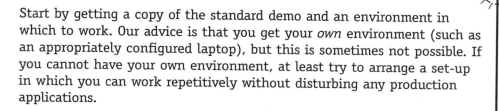

Start by getting a copy of the standard demo and an environment in which to work. Our advice is that you get your *own* environment (such as an appropriately configured laptop), but this is sometimes not possible. If you cannot have your own environment, at least try to arrange a set-up in which you can work repetitively without disturbing any production applications.

> It helps to be creative in some cases. I represented an asset management software package that provided a module for managing a shop-floor inventory using robotic cranes that picked parts for work orders. The cranes were three stories tall and cost millions of dollars, so it was not possible to "demo" the inventory piece. However, it turned out that the crane manufacturer had a piece of software that "simulated" the movement of the robots. I plugged this simulator into the back end of the demo, and thus was able to practice showing how the cranes worked without actually moving the cranes themselves.

To make our point in this chapter, we will use a simple case in which you represent a company that sells an application for tracking the timecards of employees, called TimeKard Plus. Such an application makes a good reference point, since it probably has a relatively small number of screens (not more than twenty-five) and panels.

Although you have gone through product training, it is unlikely that you have internalized all of the critical information about your products. Training provides a foundation to build on and gives you the basic skill set to work with the demo without getting lost. The next milestone is to take the demo script and memorize the flow. The flow is extremely important, since your prospect is much more likely to understand the totality of your offering if the structure of the demo reinforces the structure of the product.

The flow of the demo should reflect the structure and key benefits of your products or services.

In this sense, the flow of the demo is almost more important than the content of the individual steps.

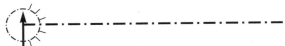

The memorization process should be taken in two passes.

- First, memorize the flow, physical steps, and keystrokes
- Then, memorize the technical "sales" pitch

Start by memorizing the flow of the demo and the various physical hands-on steps necessary to follow the flow.

In the example of the TimeKard Plus product, the demo script might start out by showing how an employee would enter time into the system. Next, it might show the prospect how to run timecard reports and add new employees to the system. Finally, the script would end with some sample management reports displaying charts and graphs of employee data.

Basically, the script is simple, and you would probably only need to exhibit about a dozen screens and reports. Don't worry about remembering the descriptions that accompany the keystrokes—just work on memorizing the order of the panels and the keystrokes themselves. Work through the panels until you feel comfortable showing off all of the tasks in the demo without any mistakes, and without having to look at the demo script.

Once you have the keystrokes down, you can start memorizing the "pitch" that accompanies the process flow. Most demo scripts include some descriptive texts to use along with each panel and screen that you show.

Returning to the TimeKard Plus example, the script might offer the following description:

> On this first panel, you can see where the employee can enter his or her employee number into the data entry screen. Then, TimeKard Plus automatically timestamps the entry. You will notice that this panel allows the employee to scan in a bar-coded badge as well. The date and time can be set remotely from a central computer....

If you have read through the chapter on feature-benefit selling, you will probably notice that the preceding description lacks any specific tie-ins from features to benefits. Many times, the standard demo script will only cover features. At this point, this does not matter, because you are simply trying to *memorize* a flow and a *standard* sales pitch. Once you get the foundation down, you can start folding *prospect requirements* and *benefit* statements into your demo dialogue.

You may feel ready to start giving demos at this point, but even the simplest demo needs more than just adherence to a script. In addition to the standard set of panels that *appear* in the demo script, there are additional capabilities on the screens and panels that are not part of the demo script. You will need to be cognizant of what these features do before embarking on a demo.

Feature Explanation

In most cases, your product-marketing department has put together a demonstration script for the base capabilities of your product. As a starting point, it does not matter if the demo script is particularly good, so long as it touches the major *features* of the product. But on each panel, menu, or report there are features that are not discussed in the demo script. Up until this point, you have comfortably ignored these features for the most part. Unfortunately, in the real world, your prospects will not necessarily ignore these additional features.

Take the screen shot of the fictitious TimeKard Plus system shown in Figure 7.2 as an example.

Figure 7.2
The logon form for TimeKard Plus.

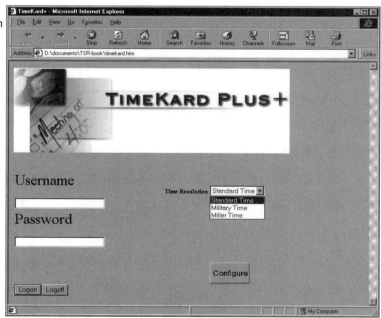

The screen shot is a standard logon form for the application, and we can use it to illustrate two important demo points. In all probability, the demo script for TimeKard will include a short discussion about logging onto the system. The script would probably describe logging onto the system using the user name and password. Notice the "Time Resolution" field, which has three choices. As part of the demo script, you might talk about selecting either "standard time" or "military time." In the screen shot, however, there is a third option called "Miller Time." Maybe the demo script does not mention "Miller Time" per se, since it is rarely used. Here's the first demo mastery *gotcha*:

Never show an option in a demo if you do not know what it is used for.

A prospect is bound to ask you what "Miller Time" is used for, and you are going to be in trouble if you do not have an answer. What kind of trouble? Credibility trouble—that's what kind. The prospect is going to lose confidence in your technical knowledge if you cannot answer a simple question about your own product's features. This situation is very different from not knowing if a certain feature of your product will work as a solution to the prospect's business problem. In the "Miller Time" case, you would be showing a lack of basic functional knowledge about your own product. The situation is compounded because you show ignorance using your own hand-picked demo. This kind of trouble is especially destructive if it happens within an early panel of your demo. You may not even be past the first screen and you have already lost some of your audience's confidence.

In this second level of the demonstration, you have to know what each option is used for, even if you aren't going to talk about it.

If you look closely at the figure once again, you will notice a button at the bottom of the screen. Unlike the "Time Resolution" element, which you probably have included in your demo script, the "Configure" button may not even be part of the demo. Maybe it is used for a special function that is only accessed in rare cases. It does not matter. If you are going to show this panel in a demo, then you'd better know what this button is used for. We guarantee you that some prospect at some time will ask about it.

> Some prospects will try to undercut the effectiveness of your demonstration by asking you just these kinds of questions about somewhat obscure features. This type of prospect may have an ulterior motive in mind, such as undermining your credibility with other members of the evaluation team. Don't cede control to them by "fudging" an answer about a feature shown on a demo screen.

The difference between the two cases outlined above ("Miller Time" and the "Configure" button) is subtle, but important. In the first example, the feature is shown as part of the standard demo script in an indirect fashion. You might need to talk about the difference between "standard time" and "military time" in order to point out the advantage of TimeKard's ability to support both formats. "Miller Time" is lumped in with these other two options and you will end up drawing attention to this feature by virtue of the fact that you are showing the other two options.

In the second case, you might not have any cause to draw attention to the "Configure" button at all. However, simply because it appears on the screen, you will need to have an idea about its meaning. Sometimes, large groups of features are hidden behind a single option such as this. For example, what if the "Configure" button was used to display a menu of dozens of configuration options? Would you need to know what all of these sub-options were? Not necessarily. As long as you have a reasonable explanation of the "Configure" function itself, you would not need to dive into all of the elements below the button at this point.

For example, consider this typical discussion between a prospect and a sales consultant:

Prospect: *What is that "Configure" button used for?*

Sales Consultant: *We have built a lot of specialized entry points into TimeKard that can be used to manage the way in which the software is run. For example, you can change the working directory of the program, the fonts that are used to display the fields, and even the color scheme. This is more of an advanced feature of the product, and it might help you to see the base product in action before we talk about the configuration settings. I'll continue with the demonstration and we can come back to the configuration button later.*

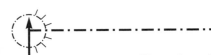

This strategy will work as long as you do not actually dive into the panels behind the "Configure" button. If you show the panels themselves, then you have to be prepared to talk about them in detail as well. Level Two in the demo pyramid is all about mastering the "features" list for the demo script. For each panel (or menu, or screen, or knob, or button) used in the demo script, you need to make sure that you know the function of every ancillary function. You may find you need to talk with technical support, consulting, or other sales consultants to get the information you need. In the end, the extra effort will be worth the time because, eventually, a prospect will start digging into the details on a screen.

> I always find it helpful both to print out screen shots of the various panels in the demo and to make notes on the back of the pages. I put numbers on the screen print to designate each function, and then write a short definition of it next to the number on the back of the printout. Writing it down helps me to cement the knowledge in my head, and the physical printouts are easy to carry around. When I have a spare few minutes over a cup of coffee, I can pull out the sheets and study for a little while.

In our discussion of the "Configure" button, we mentioned a hypothetical situation in which this single button leads to a variety of additional choices. If you were to click on the button, your prospect—and quite possibly you—could rapidly become lost in the details. This is a great reason for you to have a conversational knowledge of all the options on your panels. You can avoid unpleasant surprises in which you may lose your audience's attention.

The phenomenon of "too many features" also brings up the second major *gotcha* in mastering your demo: It is very tempting to load up your demo with extra information about these little features as you learn them.

Just because you know what a given feature is used for doesn't mean that the feature is worth mentioning in a demo.

From the standpoint of mastering the demo, be sure that you know the use for each element in the demo, whether you plan on showing the feature or not. Most demo scripts are not perfect, and as you gain experience with a product, you might replace the standard with your own demo. In the meantime, the demo script provides the basic framework for your presentation, and the fact that neither the "Miller Time" option nor the "Configure" button appear in the script is significant. It is important that you know what these options are used for, but unless the feature becomes relevant to the needs of the prospect, it is probably not germane to mention it during the demo. (We'll talk more about the relevance of a given feature in the next chapter.)

When you have fully mastered your product, you will be ready to answer *functional* questions such as, "How do I make the product do this, or that?" At this point, however, and at this level of the demo pyramid, the key is for you to master the *features*. As you gain experience with the product, you will learn to translate features into functions, and apply new functional problems to your product's feature set, which represents the third level of demo mastery.

Although you can begin giving demonstrations to prospects when you have reached Level Two of the demo pyramid—feature explanation—you will be much more valuable to your sales team when you have reached Level Three—functional explanation.

Functional Explanation

From features come functions. At the next level of the demo pyramid, you will begin to master the *functions* of the product. Functions are the "how-to" capabilities of your offering. Your product is loaded with features, and by using these features your prospect can accomplish tasks. Thus far in the demo process, you have been following a standard script, and for the most part, this script has emphasized the "sweet spots" of your product. After all, marketing does not build a demonstration that emphasizes *negatives*; marketing concentrates instead on the *strengths*.

The scripted demo provides you with a skeleton upon which to build, but it is only part of the story. In the real world, it is unlikely that your prospects will only want to see those features that are covered by the demonstration script. In fact, they are more likely to ask functional—as opposed to feature—questions. At Level Three of the pyramid, you will start to tackle functions instead of features. Functions can be difficult to master, however, because there will rarely be a "script" for you to follow.

Consider the following example of a "functional explanation" for the TimeKard Plus system:

> **Prospect:** *How do I transfer my time and attendance data from TimeKard Plus into Microsoft Excel for further analysis?*

Sales Consultant: *Great question. Take a look here at the interface menu. TimeKard Plus has the ability to export data in a wide variety of formats, including a direct link into spreadsheets. We give you two choices. You can either output the data into an Excel file format, which you can then copy to another machine or even e-mail to other locations. We also give you the choice of loading the data directly into Excel, in which case TimeKard Plus will even start up Excel for you. Notice that TimeKard Plus also gives you a panel of choices so you can control which records are included in the export operation. Let me show you by selecting the "Export All" menu choice....*

In this example, the prospect is interested in finding out *how your software can solve a functional problem*. This is an example of a functional question. The functional part of the problem is the question; and the answer to the question is somewhere within the feature set of your solution. Answering functional questions is all about matching problems to solutions.

All functional explanations are spurred by a "How do I..." question.

As you take prospects through the demo, they will inevitably begin to ask questions that are outside of the demo script. If you have qualified the prospect carefully enough, you should be able to anticipate these types of questions. No matter how prepared you are, however, new functional questions will always arise during the actual demo.

Two types of functional questions arise from the demo:

- Functional tangents
- Technical requirements

Functional tangents are questions that spring from a feature shown in your demo. For example, you might mention the "data exporting" capabilities of TimeKard in your demo. This reference may trigger your prospect to ask a specific question about data exporting. These types of questions flow naturally from the features that you have shown.

Functional tangents can be very important to your sales cycle because they often spur your prospect to view your technology in a new way. Technical requirements, by contrast, do not necessarily spring from your demo, since these are functional requirements that the prospect has developed as part of his or her own decision-making process. You should have discovered most of the technical requirements during the qualification meeting, but new requirements frequently appear during the demo.

As you may have already noticed, functional questions tend to spring from real-world issues. If your background is related to the business area of your product, or to the arena in which your prospect will use your product, it might be easy for you to anticipate functional questions. But if you do not have direct experience in your product's business area, there are five key resources that you can use for researching functional questions:

- Product training
- Customer visits
- User groups
- Sales consultants
- Technical support

Product training is the first stop on your path to functional enlightenment. A formal training course covers a much larger area than the demo can expose. Use training materials to develop lists of functional capabilities for your product. Earlier, we suggested that you interview other customers during training to get valuable insight into their use of the product. This data can now be applied to your list of functional capabilities.

You can take this training to another level by arranging to spend time with one of your local customers. Work with your sales team to identify suitable customers, and then spend a day with them to see how they use the product. This will give you insight about how a specific customer uses the product in a given situation.

The best venue for getting a more broad-based overview of the product is through the *user groups*. Local user groups tend to focus on local issues, and you can learn a great deal through working with these teams of users. Of course, you will also have to contribute something with your attendance at the user group. In Chapter 14, "Working the Installed Base and Alternative Sales Channels," we will provide you with more details about working with user groups. At this point, for the purposes of mastering your demo, you can look to the user group as a source for good "How-do-I" questions.

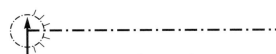

Customers may be your best sources for functional requirements, but your fellow *sales consultants* can provide great insight about the kinds of questions that prospects are likely to ask. You will get the best leverage out of your fellow sales consultants if you have reached Level Two of the demo pyramid.

How can you expect to mine for functional nuggets if you do not even have the flow of the demo under your belt? Master Levels One and Two, and then arrange for a meeting with a small team of your sales consultant colleagues. Walk through the standard demo together. As you review each panel and feature, compare the types of questions and problems that arise from prospect situations. Build a complete list of questions and explanations to use as a base, and be sure to send copies to your managers and marketing department. You are likely to find many common issues, and these should be added to the standard demo script to help new sales consultants get up to speed.

As an added source of functional questions, you can look at the *technical support* logs for customers in your area. The telephone technical support group generally keeps detailed records of the questions that customers ask, typically taking common questions and answers and rolling them into "frequently-asked-questions" (FAQ) documents. You can blend these documents with the information from your other sources.

As you build up a library of functional knowledge, you will need to learn how and when to apply this information. Just because you know "how" to do something with the product does not make this knowledge either valuable or applicable to any given prospect. Functional explanations do not necessarily apply to each and every customer universally.

Take the "data-export" question, for example. Many customers may have a need to export their data into Excel. It may be worthwhile expanding the contents of your demo script to include this new "feature" (and associated function). However, if you have a prospect who asks about exporting the timecard data back to his or her Digital PDP/11-70 (circa 1978) computer, the answer might be different. You might research the issue as part of the technical requirements, but you shouldn't add this discussion to the standard demo script.

As you begin to build up your library of functional explanations, you will move on to Level Four of the demo pyramid—construction.

Construction

At a certain point in your demo training, you will reach the milestone at which you begin to build your own demo. However, we are not advocating that you drop the corporate demo script in favor of your own complete demo. There is tremendous value in keeping a consistent corporate message, and this message gets diluted if every sales consultant uses his or her own demo. Rather, we are advocating an extension of the standard demonstration platform in two directions:

- Show and tell, instead of just tell
- Personalization

Now that you have completed Level Three of the demo pyramid, you should be able to address most functional questions as they arise during the demo. This does not necessarily mean that you are prepared to actually demonstrate the answer to the functional question. You may instead end up drawing the solution on the whiteboard, or talking about the solution while pointing to the demo screen.

Take the following question as an example:

Prospect: *We have standardized on XYZ-Db as our database platform. Can you use XYZ-Db as the repository for TimeKard Plus data?*

After having mastered Level Three of the pyramid, you should be prepared to address this issue. You might talk about TimeKard's use of Java Database Connectivity (JDBC) drivers that allow TimeKard Plus to use most of the common database engines for storing data. Assume that your standard demo uses IEM Dbx as the database, and further assume that many people have asked you the "XYZ-Db" question during demos. Now that you have arrived at Level Four of the pyramid, you should be able to actually "show" the answer, and not just "tell" it:

Sales Consultant: *Great question. We have lots of customers who use XYZ-Db as their standard database. We run very efficiently on XYZ-Db. In fact, we even use their SQL language to store data in the database. I have a copy of XYZ-Db running on my laptop here as well. Let me start-up XYZ-Db, and then I'll show you how TimeKard Plus can connect to an XYZ-Db database.*

In an ideal world, you would have found out that the prospect had standardized on XYZ-Db during the qualification meeting, and you would

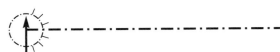

come prepared to "demo" on top of XYZ-Db from the beginning. In such cases, the "show" part of the "show-and-tell" would be set up before the demo even began. Being able to "show" answers is a lot more effective than just being able to talk about the answer.

Although this can be a very powerful technique, it can also be a path to destruction. Many sales consultants become too confident in their own abilities after awhile, and start "winging it" by trying new things on the fly. Beware of this potential pitfall.

Never attempt to demonstrate a feature unless you are sure that it will work.

If you attempt to show off a capability and fail, you have raised an objection in the prospect's mind. It does not matter why it failed; the prospect will only remember the failure. When you construct new "show" elements for your demonstration, make sure that they work before using them with a prospect.

The other type of construction is *personalization*. When you personalize a demo, you replace some of the standard elements with customer-specific information. The most common example of this type of construction is to replace the standard logo within a demo screen with the customer's own corporate logo. Some examples of extensions to the standard demo for different types of products could include these:

- **Routers**—Show a network diagram that includes your router with machines in the prospect's network.

- **ERP Applications**—Add some of the prospect's vendors as standard vendors for a purchasing demo.

- **Business Intelligence**—Build a demonstration cube using data similar to your prospect's line of business (retail, financial services, etc.).

This type of modification to the demo can help the prospect to visualize the solution to problems using your product. However, you must have enough experience with the product to be confident that you will not "break" other parts of the demo by making these changes. Be sure the changes you make do not inadvertently confuse or offend the prospect in some way. Don't do anything that will cause your prospect to think that you can't handle a simple demo. If you can't handle a demo, how can you be trusted to implement the real solution?

As you create extensions to the standard demo, keep the materials easily accessible, if you can. Nothing impresses a prospect quite like your ability to show a feature at work, as soon as the prospect asks about it.

Solution

The last layer of the demo pyramid is the solutions layer. It encompasses two distinct elements:

- Mapping prospect requirements to your solution
- Fluency in associated disciplines

When you combine the elements of the fourth layer of the pyramid with feature-benefit-acceptance selling, you have almost reached the pinnacle of demo heights.

Consider the example answer that we posed earlier to the data-export question:

> **Prospect:** *How do I transfer my time and attendance data from TimeKard Plus into Microsoft Excel for further analysis?*

> **Sales Consultant:** *While we are right here on the interface menu, let me show the export feature of TimeKard Plus. If I am not mistaken, Joe, you have standardized Microsoft Excel as your data analysis tool, right? We give you two choices. You can either output the data into an Excel file format, which you can then copy to another machine or even e-mail to other locations. We also give you the choice of loading the data directly into Excel, in which case TimeKard Plus will even start-up Excel for you. Notice that TimeKard Plus also gives you a panel of choices so you can control which records are included in the export operation. I know you are interested in analyzing weekly trends, so let me select the timecard entries for this week and have TimeKard export them into Excel...As you can see, you can leverage your existing investment in Microsoft Excel, which will lower both your costs and learning curve. Is this the type of interface you were looking for, Joe?*

Notice that the feature is tied to a specific prospect-requirement (integration with Microsoft Excel), and that we confirm this requirement with the prospect. We *show* the capability to move the data to Excel (we don't just talk about it), and we mention some specific benefits and ask the prospect to accept them as valuable. Game, set, and match.

You might not be able to "show" every answer using the product. For example, when demonstrating an asset-management product, I was often asked how to integrate the asset database into pre-existing general ledger applications. The software had a general-ledger extract, but required a rather complicated set of steps to use. In these cases, I would show the main general ledger panel on the laptop, but would go to the whiteboard to "demo" the interface to their system. It worked as a reasonable compromise, especially considering that many of the general ledger systems that we hooked into were running on mainframes. I would even cover any possible objection with a quip like, "I left my mainframe at home today."

One remaining element needs to be mastered before you reach the summit. It is the element that we call *fluency in associated disciplines*. It is quite common for your product to be part of an overall solution that involves several other products. Consider, for example, TimeKard Plus. Many customers would want to use Microsoft Excel to analyze data in the TimeKard application. But you will dilute the value of your demo if you are unfamiliar with Excel, or if you are not able to comfortably move around in Excel to show off the TimeKard data.

To reach the summit, you need to identify the ancillary products and technologies that form the complete solution. Add them to your repertoire. Become familiar enough with them to answer some basic questions and to be able to show off your product, but don't forget to keep the focus on your own solution. Identifying these ancillary products can be difficult, for their range can be very wide indeed. If you are a "purchasing" specialist for an ERP company, for example, you might need to have some expertise in Microsoft Excel, or perhaps in some financial analysis software. You probably would not need to be very experienced with the inner workings of the underlying relational itself. If the prospect wants to look at the database in detail, your company could bring in a database specialist. However, if you work for a very small niche-market ERP vendor, you might find yourself in the position of having to master the database, too.

At this point in the game, having mastered the demo pyramid, you have actually mastered your own solution. You started out trying to perfect the demo, but you have ended up becoming an expert in the product itself along the way.

Wrapping Up

Mastering the demo pyramid is not an easy thing to do, and you will find yourself having to master a new pyramid when you move to a new company. The good news is that mastering the demo is a lot like learning a foreign language—once you have learned one new language, it is always easier to learn another.

The trick is to follow a prescribed game plan. Start by memorizing the basic demo, and then move into the higher levels of the pyramid. The first two levels require the most discipline, and you must force yourself to practice in order to perfect them. The remaining levels of the demo pyramid will come to you as a natural outgrowth of repeatedly performing your demo.

In Chapter 8, we will take you through the process of applying your mastery of the product to the qualification process. Through qualification, you will determine which prospects are a good fit for your solution and which features and functions to highlight in the demo that will follow.

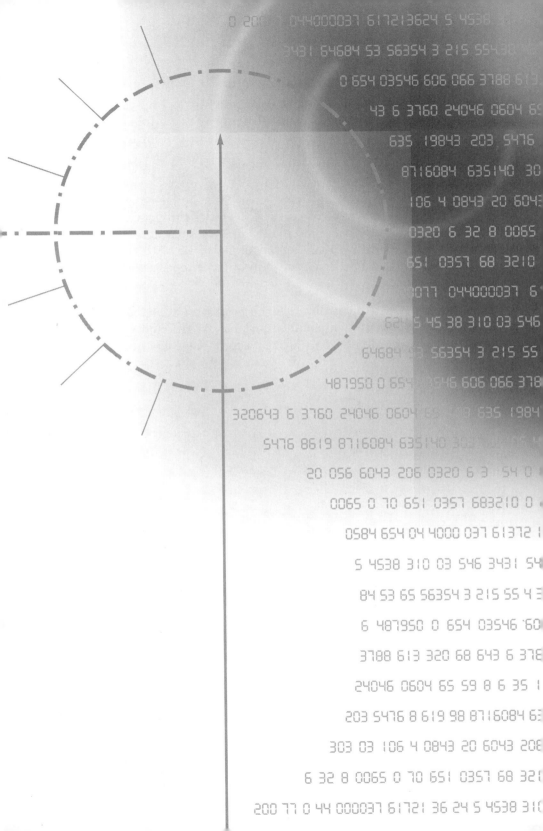

Chapter 8

Qualification and Planning for Presentations and Demonstrations

Among the most critical events in the sales process are the face-to-face meetings that you will have with your prospects. Any enterprise-class technical sale will require direct interaction with the prospect in order to close the deal. Very few prospects are willing to spend hundreds of thousands of dollars for a product without at least seeing some sort of demonstration. However, before you invest in a full presentation and demonstration, you need to determine if your prospect is a good fit from a technical perspective. You also need to have gathered enough information about your prospect to adequately position your solution from a technical perspective. By evaluating the qualifications of your prospect, you will be able to create a plan of action that will give you the maximum amount of control over the sales cycle.

The medium for gathering this information is called the *qualification meeting*.

Your sales representative will take primary responsibility for qualifying prospects, but it will be your job to serve as the eyes and ears in the account on behalf of the rep. As a sales consultant, you can help gather the necessary data to help your sales rep decide whether to pursue a deal with any given prospect. In this chapter, we'll take a look at the overall qualification process from the technical perspective.

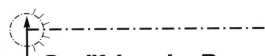

Qualifying the Prospect

Qualification means determining if your prospect has a good possibility of becoming your customer. Qualification is an extremely important part of the sales cycle—its effectiveness will be one of the key factors in the overall success of your sales team. Your sales representative has probably started the qualification process in his or her first contact with the prospect over the telephone. For more inexpensive products or services, or for those with an accelerated sales cycle, most of the qualification process takes place over the phone. But larger or more involved sales will usually call for face-to-face qualification meetings. A direct meeting, especially early in the sales cycle, carries its own particular challenges. This chapter will help you to understand how best to handle these meetings. It's up to your sales representative to decide whether the qualification process requires a direct meeting with the prospect. If there are no direct meetings scheduled, your rep, and possibly you, will conduct the process over the telephone. But the greater the opportunity, the more likely it is that the sales rep will schedule some type of face-to-face qualification meeting.

Qualification Meetings

Before investing significant resources, a good sales representative will attempt to qualify a prospect as a likely fit as a customer. Sales reps use the qualification meeting to ask questions and provide basic information to the prospect in order to determine if there is any basis for a deal. The sales team has a limited amount of time and resources, and its goal is to maximize revenue. Your sales rep will use the qualification meeting to determine where a given prospect belongs in the sales cycle. Prospects who are ready to make a decision and have allocated time and money for a solution are the types of prospects that the sales team is looking for.

One of your primary tasks during the qualification meeting is to listen. The goal of the meeting is to get the prospect talking. And what do people like talking about most? You guessed it—their hobbies, their interests, their opinions, and, in a nutshell, themselves. You are in an ideal position to find out these personal things about the prospect (especially if the meeting is taking place in the prospect's own office). The focus of the conversation is between the sales rep and the prospect, so you are free to notice the personal details. Even if you don't directly engage in that much give-and-take with the prospect, you can still learn his or her personal style and store up details about interests.

In their offices, people display family photos, diplomas, certificates of achievement, desk mementos, and so on. Notice these details and write about them in your notes. Prospects will also pepper informal conversations with critical pieces of data about their own division or business unit, revealing information about sales targets or growth plans. These little nuggets come in handy later on in helping to tear down any walls of mistrust between the prospect and the sales team. This data-gathering process needs to be accomplished with a certain practiced smoothness. On one hand, you should not simply ignore the conversation and work away like a court transcriber. On the other hand, the focus of the qualification meeting is not on you as a sales consultant, so you can gather personal data while still remaining "checked in" to the meeting itself.

Keep quiet during these meetings. Avoid offering unsolicited opinions and talking just to hear yourself talk. Remember, you are the "technical expert." A certain reserved, quiet demeanor is appropriate for these initial meetings. It's the sales rep's job to talk here—your role is to listen. The overall conversation will flow more smoothly if you and your rep are not both trying to respond to the customer. Later on in the sales cycle, you will be on "center stage."

During the qualification meeting, the sales representative tries to acquire basic information such as the following, the details of which we explain in the next sections of this chapter:

- Bulldozer/BMW assessment
- Competition
- Budget/Timeframe
- Problem definition
- Solution set
- Technical requirements
- Decision process

The Bulldozer/BMW Assessment

When deciding whether to pursue a deal, the first step in the process is to make a Bulldozer/BMW assessment. Is the prospect looking to buy the type of product that you are selling? We call this process the "Bulldozer/BMW assessment" in light of the following example: If you want to move a ton of dirt, you buy a bulldozer. On the other hand, if you want to drive fast, you buy a BMW. Although the two products share some

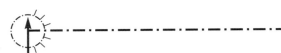

characteristics (both have engines and steering mechanisms, both are used for transportation, both can carry), they are not interchangeable.

The sales rep will often conduct a basic qualification over the phone before visiting the prospect and may even handle the first qualification meeting without involving sales consultant resources. This is particularly true during the Bulldozer/BMW assessment. All technical products have a basic set of capabilities, and the first step in any qualification process is to figure out if the basic needs of the prospect match the feature set of your product. This type of analysis is a very high-level comparison of needs to features. It is used for eliminating prospects who are not looking for what you sell.

In most cases, the sales rep will have enough experience to make a basic decision by himself or herself. But if your product is particularly complicated or sophisticated, the sales rep may want to set up a face-to-face meeting in order to make the Bulldozer/BMW decision. This is particularly true when the prospect is not sure what to look for. Sometimes, prospects will evaluate BMWs because they don't even know that Bulldozers exist. This is true in the Internet age, where the lines between product categories are less clear.

Competition

An angle that the sales representative will use to make the Bulldozer/BMW decision is to find out which other products the prospect is considering. To carry on with our metaphor, if the prospect is looking at John Deere, Komatsu, International Harvester, and Porsche, then you know that there is a problem—especially if you are selling the Porsche. Why is the prospect looking at two entirely different types of products? The situation does not bode well for your success in a deal (see Chapter 16, "Eight Challenging Prospects" for more information on this topic).

Budget

If the deal seems at all possible, the sales representative will try to discover if the prospect has received budget approval for the purchase and the overall timeframe for the deal. It is not your job to deal with the monetary aspects of a deal. However, the following is always true:

No money, no deal.

It sounds almost too simple, doesn't it? But your sales team has to make sure that there is money to spend, and it needs to learn *when* it can be spent. You may find that your prospect has a deadline—such as the end of this fiscal year. Or you may learn that the prospect will not have the money until a particular time, such as the *next* fiscal year. Either of these facts will have a great effect on the timing of the rest of the activities in your sales cycle.

And what if there is *no* money? Usually, you will politely walk away from the table, thanking your lucky stars you had this qualification meeting before devoting any more resources to this unattainable deal. But there may be times when your sales rep may decide to continue the sales process, even if the money is not readily apparent. Perhaps the deal is important enough for you to wait for the available budget. Perhaps the deal is with a significant company with whom your rep wants to begin a relationship.

The sales rep ultimately determines the qualification of a prospect.

Problem Definition

As you might have noticed, the sales representative may not have needed your help before reaching this point in the qualification process. Now, however, he or she may need your guidance in helping with the problem statement and, later, with the solution set, technical requirements, and the decision process.

The *problem statement* is a succinct definition of the business problem that the prospect is trying to solve with your product.

Technical selling starts with a simple definition of the business problem to be solved. The sales representative will help the prospect to define the problem in simple business terms. For example, the prospect sells widgets and needs to process orders 50 percent faster or needs to increase sales by 20 percent. The stated business problem will not necessarily have any direct correlation to the product that you represent.

It is critical for you as the sales consultant to create a firm definition of the business problem that the prospect is trying to solve. Why? By our very nature, sales consultants are technical people, and we love details; consequently, we often tend to focus on them to the exclusion of the big picture. The problem definition becomes the means by which you can focus your attention back on the bigger picture.

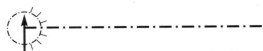

This is also where you can finally nail down the Bulldozer/BMW decision on whether to proceed with the sales process. As part of the qualification process, the sales rep will be trying to wrangle the solution set out of the prospect. The problem statement is the foundation for determining the best solution set.

Getting to the problem statement is not always an easy process, but it is critical in deciding whether or not to proceed with a given prospect. I often found it useful to try to summarize my understanding of the problem statement for the prospect toward the end of the qualification meeting, to be sure that I understood the problem correctly. It's impossible to propose a solution if you don't know what the problem is. Sometimes, it helps to think of yourself as a doctor. Your doctor needs to know what is wrong with you before he or she can prescribe a treatment.

The Solution Set

The *solution set* is the array of possible solutions that the prospect is considering in order to solve a business problem. The solution set may involve both competitive products as well as solutions that do not normally appear in most of your sales opportunities.

For example, assume that the prospect has the stated business problem of "improving inventory control by acquiring a new inventory system." The solution set can include such diverse products as relational databases, application development tools, and pre-packaged software solutions. The definition of the solution set combined with the problem statement forms the building blocks for your technical sale.

As you can tell from our description of the elements of the qualification meeting, the basic process at work in this meeting is more *discovery* than *presentation*. The goal is to extract information from the prospect; therefore, you should concentrate on gathering data as opposed to offering data. Let the prospect ramble on about his or her needs, goals, and requirements. You will value this data when you begin to present your solution.

Technical Requirements

The final two elements of the qualification meeting are the *technical requirements* and the *decision process*. At this point, you should have concrete ideas about the business problem to be solved and the solution set. In many cases, the sales rep will have this information in hand before the face-to-face meeting with the prospect. The first part of the meeting will have been spent reviewing this information.

The technical requirements are the specific solution details that the prospect will use to make the technical decision on a product solution. Notice that we did not say the *decision*; we specifically said the *technical* decision. Prospects select a vendor for many different reasons, and decisions are not always technical. Your job as a sales consultant, however, is to make the technical sale in cooperation with the sales representative.

The overall sales process is going to be easier if the prospect views your product as the best solution to his or her problem. The battle plan for technical selling is the *planning triangle*, which is covered later in this chapter. The battle plan is drawn up based on information gleaned in the qualification meeting. This plan is executed with the presentation and demonstration.

The technical requirements are the specific product features and functions that the prospect will use as the yardstick for selecting one product over another. Technical requirements can involve low-level functions such as "the database must be able to store 10 gigabytes of data in a single table." Technical requirements can also be business functions that are part of the solution—for example, "the order entry system must be able to automatically calculate reorder points daily." In the first case, we are truly talking bits and bytes, but in the second, we mean higher-level business functions that could be implemented in many different ways. Both are examples of technical requirements.

In any case, you should try to get a specific list of requirements on paper for a deal. Don't get too obsessed with this list. Prospects may not always have a clear set of technical requirements early on in the sales cycle. As they begin to work with each of the vendors to schedule presentations and demonstrations, the list of technical requirements will begin to solidify. It is ideal if the prospect already knows what he is looking for— but this will not always be the case.

Prospects who cannot outline their requirements may not know their requirements.

You also should not be surprised if the technical requirements change or evolve over the course of the sales cycle.

You may receive only a partial list of the technical requirements during the qualification meeting—and some of the requirements will change over the course of the sales cycle.

One of the side tasks to accomplish during a qualification meeting is to find a "coach" for the sale. A coach is a member of the prospect's team who favors you and your solution. Such a person can help to guide you through the sales process. Your sales rep will identify a coach from the sales side, and you will need to develop a coach for the technical side

A coach is a terrific asset, but you may not find one at this stage in the sales cycle. Many times, technical people will not be attending these sessions. In such cases, there will be just three of you—the lead-member of the prospect team, your sales rep, and you—conducting the qualification session. You still need to concentrate on building the list of technical requirements. If the prospect is highly organized, he or she may have a checklist or another document that describes the features and functions he is looking for.

If the prospect has a technical requirements document, be sure you have a copy to work from.

If the prospect has taken time to make a list of desirable and required features, you need to make sure that you have a copy of that list. This document is different from a request for information (RFI) or a request for proposals (RFP), either of which are typically bulked up with extraneous questions and requirements (see Chapter 13, "Responding to RFIs"). This list will be short, but it will contain the key elements that the prospect is using to evaluate the technical solution. If the prospect does not have a written document, you will have to gather the data by listening and asking questions. The trick is to ask questions without giving away too much data and without raising objections.

For example, your product runs on Windows NT and UNIX, but has not yet been ported to Linux. The prospect tells you that he or she would like a product that runs on both UNIX and Linux as part of the technical requirements. Jot this information down in your notes, but do not point out the fact that you do not yet support the Linux platform. If your sales rep is unaware of the issue, you can review it with him or her later on. At this point, all you need to worry about is capturing the data.

The technical requirements will form the core of the forthcoming product presentation and demonstration. You need to understand the prospect's requirements in order to proceed.

> *Make sure you thoroughly understand the technical requirements as described by the prospect before proceeding to a product presentation or demonstration.*

Let's say the prospect states, "The product must support the use of an embedded flux-capacitor." If you do not know what a flux capacitor is, you have two choices: First, you can ask the prospect directly, though you risk exposing your ignorance. Since you are not in presentation mode, this is less likely to be a problem—you can ask questions more easily in this discussion forum than you can when you are running the show as a presenter.

You can also research the issue off-line if you are confident that you have the contacts and resources to find the answer. Our personal bias is to ask, especially if the question is specific to the prospect's line of business. Once you understand the issue, you can always do additional research on the topic and drop these facts into the demonstration and presentation later on.

After you understand any particular technical requirement, you then need to figure out just how important this requirement is to the overall evaluation process. This is known as *establishing priorities* for the technical requirements. By establishing priorities, you will get a better

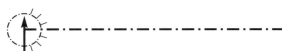

idea both of how well your product stacks up against the competition and of your chances of winning the technical evaluation later on. It is important that you establish priorities for each of the major technical requirements. A common mistake is to ask your prospect about priorities only when the technical requirement is something that your product cannot meet.

For example, you diligently take notes and ask questions as your prospect describes the technical requirements for a new inventory system. You don't bother asking about priorities for features until the prospect mentions that the company wants the software to run on Linux. However, at the moment, your product only supports NT. Suddenly asking, "How important is that to the overall solution?" is tantamount to saying: "We don't support Linux right now."

Ask about priorities as you go along. Sometimes, the prospect's response to the priority question will even provide you with additional data. Continuing with this example, assume that you run on Linux as well as NT, but that more of your installed base is using NT. Asking the prospect to prioritize the platform requirement might lend him or her to describe a particular enthusiasm for Linux. This response, in turn, will allow you to better prepare for the presentation and demonstration process by gathering together some Linux-specific feature points.

Each technical requirement must include a priority.

Part of your job at this point in the process is to make some judgments about the real importance of various requirements, based on the prospect's descriptions. We have been in many sales situations in which the prospect gave everything a high priority, but the supporting data told a different story. You can often gain additional insight into the prospect's technical requirements by asking ancillary questions about the technical environment. By applying these answers to the technical requirements, you can begin to gain a truer picture of the technical requirements process.

For example:

> **Sales Consultant:** *Joe, it sounds as if you are looking for a solution that supports both NT and Linux. Can you give me an idea which types of applications you are running on these platforms at the moment?*

If the prospect insisted that the software support both NT and Linux, but they themselves were only using NT, you would have to question whether Linux was truly an important platform for them. It might well be important—maybe this application will be the pilot program for Linux. On the other hand, it may be a signal that Linux just isn't as important as it initially appears to be.

Decision Process

The final item in the qualification meeting is to understand the *decision process*. The sales rep will typically drive this issue on his or her own. The decision process is composed of the steps that the prospect plans to use in selecting one vendor and solution over another.

The decision process will often be unclear until the initial product presentation and demonstration have been completed. Vendors will often fall out of contention after these milestones, and this will affect the decision-making process. (You will learn more about the decision process in Chapter 11 on managing evaluations.) The relevance of this topic at this stage of the sales process is that it typically is the last element of the qualification meeting. At this point, the sales representative tries to get some commitment to the buying process and brings the qualification event to a close.

A satisfactory conclusion for a qualification meeting still does not necessarily mean that your company will proceed through a sales cycle with the prospect. At this point, what you have in hand are the facts to make an informed decision about moving forward. The qualification meeting is generally conducted with a subset of the people involved in the overall decision process. The next step in the sales process will almost always be a presentation and demonstration, and it is important to know who else from the prospect's side of the table will take part in this next event.

Let's say that you are selling an application product such as a general ledger application. You may be a guru about the ins and outs of general ledgers, but you may not be as skilled with information technology issues. If the IT staff is not going to be involved with the upcoming demonstration, then this may not be a problem. However, if IT plans to show up for the next meeting, you may need to bring additional resources along in order to answer questions.

There will always be additional people dropping into the deal later on. Nonetheless, it is important to avoid as many surprises as possible by getting as much information as you can during the qualification stage.

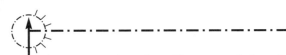

As we mentioned earlier, one of the challenges that you will face in the qualification meeting is to gather data without raising objections to your solution.

You will learn all about handling objections in Chapter 12, when we will be addressing objections from the prospect's side of the table. During the qualification process, the prospect will not necessarily have any specific objections to your proposed solution. But you need to avoid introducing objections yourself. Consider the following example:

> *You are representing a Java application development tool for building enterprise-class applications. During the qualification meeting, the prospect describes a technical requirement that the product be able to "debug" Java code at the server level. Your product does not support server-side debugging. What should you do?*

The qualification meeting is not the primary sales event for your prospect, but it *is* the primary data-gathering event. At this point in the case described directly above, you have no idea how important Java debugging on the server is to the overall solution. If the prospect demands the requirement as part of a list of technical features, then your response should be to take note of this for private discussion with your sales partner later on.

Do not create an issue in your prospect's mind by pointing out the fact that your product does not support a particular feature.

If the prospect asks you directly whether you support this feature, then you need to finesse the issue. Finessing is the art of saying "yes" to a complicated question, and the art of the finesse is covered in more detail in Chapter 13.

Does this mean that you should lie to the prospect? The answer to that question is an emphatic *no*. In most cases, your company will be able to provide you with a technical answer to key issues that require more detailed explanations. The qualification meeting is not the proper venue for addressing these issues. The presentation and demonstration events are more appropriate times and places to provide these detailed responses. In most cases, your company will have a strategy for addressing technical issues that allows you to provide a "yes" answer for the purposes of the qualification meeting.

The primary focus of the qualification meeting is for *you* to gather information—not the customer. After the meeting, your sales team may decide, based on the information that comes out, not to pursue the sale. But this is the sales team's decision. You should not allow a prospect to rule you out at this early stage. At this point in a sales opportunity, you should at least be in control of your own actions and scheduling.

Some serious technical hurdles can be loosely addressed in the qualification meeting.

For example, the prospect has a requirement that your product run under Linux as well as some other commercial UNIX platforms. Your product does not run on those platforms, so how do you defuse the issue for the time being?

Assuming that your sales partner does not take the lead to address the issue, it may fall to you to do so. You can address the issue in a positive manner without getting into the specifics. Finesse your answer with a line like the following:

> *"We are always adding support for additional platforms. I will have to check with our release management team to make sure that we support Linux."*

It is not unreasonable for you to "not know" whether Linux is supported, and checking back with your release management team is an appropriate response. The key is to address the issue at that moment and then move on to gather more data.

Why not just give the prospect the straight answer right now? The answer is that you haven't even begun the real selling process yet. Once you organize the requirements according to their proper weighting, you may find that this individual requirement isn't all that important. The prospect may decide that your product is the perfect solution and that the company is willing to live without support for the missing feature. Since you have not even started the presentation and demonstration process, your prospect hasn't had the opportunity to see the benefits of your offering. *The key is to avoid introducing a problem before the sales process has moved into high gear.* This does not mean that you should ignore the issue, however. Once you have finished the qualification meeting, you will need to address any lingering problems with your sales rep during the debriefing session.

Qualification Meeting Debriefing

The net result of your attendance at a qualification meeting should be well-organized pages of notes based on your discussion. The three critical items in your notes are the *business problem,* the *solution set,* and the *technical requirements.*

The *business problem* will ultimately form the backbone for your presentation and demonstration, as it is the foundation for the needs of the prospect. The *solution set* determines what other products are in contention for the deal and helps you to frame the relative strengths and weaknesses of your product in the overall decision process. Finally, the *technical requirements* are the features and functions that the prospect considers critical for any proposed solution. These three elements will form the backbone of your presentation and demonstration in the later stages of the sales cycle.

For the time being, the key point for you to remember is that you will need to have a firm grasp of all three aspects of the sale before you proceed to the presentation and demonstration phase.

While the data is fresh in your mind, it is time to review this information with your sales rep. This way, you can be sure that you both agree on the data that you have gathered. Your first job is to frame three key pieces of data for your sales partner:

- Technical match-up
- Sweet spot
- Showstoppers

The combination of the business problem and the technical requirements form the basis of the overall technical match-up for each sales situation. You know the nature of the problem that the prospect is trying to solve; you have a basic feeling for the technical requirements of the solution; and you know the capabilities of your product. Put all three of these elements together and you have a basic feeling as to how well you stack up.

The technical match-up is your "gut-check" estimate as to whether the prospect is a fit for your product. You pull this estimate together in two easy steps:

First, jot down the major *technical* advantages of your product. You can cull this list from three sources: the marketing department, your customers, and your own experiences. Don't use the same list for every prospect; instead, take five minutes after the qualification meeting while the essence of the prospect's problem is still fresh in your mind. In the back of your mind, consider how product marketing positions the product, how other customers in similar situations view your product, and how you would use your product to solve the prospect's problem if your roles were reversed.

For example: Let's say that you represent a Web development tool vendor. After considering the combination of marketing, customers, and your own experiences, you jot down the following list of basic technical advantages that your product offers:

- Runs on multiple UNIX operating systems and NT; portable
- Has the fastest transaction processing performance
- Has powerful utilities for experienced database administrators
- Supports extensive personalization
- Supports data replication techniques
- Uses less memory on small server machines
- Connects to many popular RDBMS engines

The second step in the process is to compare this list with the business problem and technical requirements that you developed during the qualification meeting.

Continuing with the example, consider the Table 8.1.

Table 8.1
Business Problem Comparison Table.

Business Problem	Prospect needs to replace an aging inventory control system with a Web-based application in order to improve efficiency.
Solution Set	Prospect has special application requirements that preclude buying "off the shelf," and has decided to write the application himself or herself using a relational database and a Web development tool.
Key Technical Requirements	Support for heavy transaction processing loads, support for multiple UNIX platforms, leverage SQL skills of their existing programmers, HTML development tools integrated with database.

Compare your list with the features listed in the table. You will notice that some of your major advantages do not necessarily line up with your prospect's stated technical requirements. Both of the lists include the requirement to support heavy transaction loads and the need to run on several varieties of UNIX. However, several of your advantages—such as small memory footprint and data replication—are missing from your client's list. Furthermore, the prospect identifies a requirement to have an embedded HTML page builder with the development tool. Your product may offer such a tool, but the fact that you did not include this item on your list may mean that it is not one of the best features of the product. Although a comparison of both lists indicates a pretty good fit between what you do best and the requirements for the technical solution, it is not a perfect match.

The comparison between your basic strengths and the prospect's stated technical requirements forms the basis for the technical match-up.

When two lists match nearly perfectly (they are never absolutely perfect), you have hit your technical *sweet spot*. We've borrowed this term from baseball—it refers to the part of the bat that is perfect for hitting the ball. Players will tell you that when you hit the ball with the sweet-spot, you can be sure that the ball will travel a long way. You can apply this concept to your technical sale. When your major features closely match the prospect's requirements, you have the makings of a deal. Does this mean that you don't have any selling to do? *No*. You are still going to have to sell, but the prospect is going to be receptive to the selling process.

The opposite of this situation is the *showstopper*. We call it a showstopper because, quite literally, the situation stops the show. A showstopper occurs when your product lacks a feature that the prospect has unequivocally identified as being crucial to the solution. Here is an example:

> *The customer has emphatically stated that the general ledger application must run on Linux. Your product doesn't run on Linux.*

The first step in dealing with a showstopper is to tell the sales rep about it during the qualification debriefing. Sometimes the showstopper will not require any more research or discussion. Your job is to identify the issue and then offer alternatives to the sales rep. Be truthful about the practicality of these alternatives.

Take the example described above. Even if your general ledger package does not run on Linux, it may instead run in a standard Web browser. One solution is to pitch the browser as an alternative. Normally in these cases, the sales rep will pitch the solution to the prospect before the presentation and demonstration phase. In most cases, the prospect does not even know about the showstopper; your rep will want to be sure that the issue is on the table before proceeding. Sometimes the workaround will be acceptable, sometimes it won't be. But it is not up to you to make the final call. Your job is to arm the sales rep with possible solutions, and it is the sales rep's job to decide whether to proceed.

> ### *In the end, it is the sales rep who has the responsibility to make the final call about whether to proceed with a sales opportunity.*

When you are working with an experienced sales rep, you will find that most situations fall somewhere between sweet spots and showstoppers. As your sales team matures and becomes more familiar with your product set, your qualification calls will hit the mark more often than not. Experienced sales reps will work the phones before even *scheduling* the qualification meeting.

The qualification process is designed with two goals in mind. The first goal is to provide you with the data to build a powerful presentation and demonstration for the next phase of the sales process. You will learn more about applying your qualification knowledge to the sales process in later chapters. The second goal is to maximize the effectiveness of your collective sales time. You need to spend time and resources on deals that you are likely to win. In order to understand this goal better, we will now take a look at the "costs" for your time.

Activity-Based Costing

Common sense tells you that traveling to a prospect's site to give a demonstration is one of the most costly things that you will do. Typically, it takes at least a day of your time, involving travel costs to get to the prospect's location. If you factor in your fully burdened salary and benefits, you will no doubt agree that face-to-face meetings are expensive. You may find it worth your while to calculate just how expensive these events can be. Assume that you make $80,000 a year and

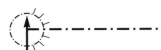

that your benefits and other costs (office, computer, etc.) are worth another $40,000. If you work forty hours per week for fifty weeks a year, it costs your company $60 per hour to keep you employed. Table 10.2 lists the costs for you to visit a prospect for a meeting and demonstration.

Table 10.2
Costs for visiting a prospect.

Cost	Amount
Fully burdened salary for one day's time	$480
Round-trip airplane flight (Newark to Chicago)	$1,070
Hotel	$150
Meals	$75
Miscellaneous (parking, tolls, etc.)	$25

The total cost for this trip would be $1,800—a lot of money.

But the problem with this calculation is that it is just dead wrong. Sure, the travel costs are about right, but the major problem with this example is that you are using your salary and benefits as the basis for the calculation of your hourly rate. You need to start looking at your job from the opposite perspective—from the sales perspective. Let's assume for the purposes of argument that you are partnered with a single sales representative, and that this rep has a yearly quota of $1,200,000. You work the same forty hours per week for fifty weeks per year. This yields the following calculation:

$$\$1,200,000 \text{ revenue} \div 40 \text{ hours/week} \div 50 \text{ weeks/year} = \$600 \text{ Revenue/Hour}$$

or

$$\text{Yearly quota} \div \text{number of hours/week} \div \text{number of weeks/year} = \text{revenue/hour}$$

Each hour of your time is expected to generate $600 in revenue. In fact, this calculation is probably on the low side, since your company probably expects you to spend a certain amount of your time on nonsales-related activities such as professional development. However, for the purposes of estimating the costs of your time, this estimate is close enough. If you replace the salary cost in the preceding table with the new value of $4,800 ($600/hour for eight hours) you will find that the cost for a one-day meeting is a whopping $6,120—and that the biggest single expense is the allocation of your time.

Sure, we're taking some mathematical license here, since it does not cost your company $4,800 for a day of your time (and mathematical purists could argue that the sales revenue is actually split between you and the sales representative). However, the company does expect you and your sales partner to generate $1,200,000 worth of sales revenue by the end of the year. Therefore, think of this mythical hourly rate as your opportunity cost for each activity that you undertake. Looking at it from this perspective gives you a better picture of just how expensive it is to spend an entire day working with your prospect. Does this mean that it is not a good idea to spend a day in this way? No. What it does mean is that you need to maximize the effectiveness of the time that you spend working with your prospects.

Wrapping Up

One of the key ingredients to a successful technical sale is to be able to match the capabilities of your product to the needs of the prospect. To make sure that you are spending your valuable sales time wisely, it is always better to get the requirements in advance.

In the next chapter, we will turn to the process of presenting data to the prospect in the form of product presentations. The information that you gather in the qualification process will be the framework that you will use to pitch your solution.

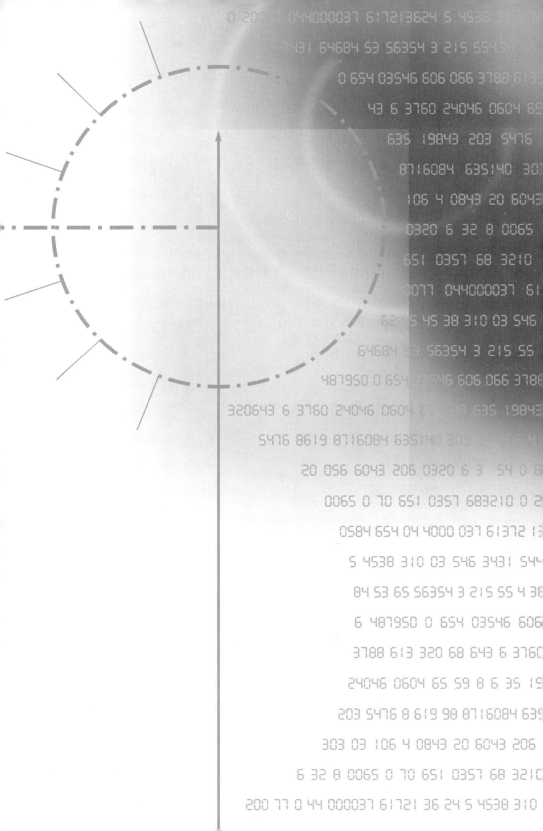

Making Effective Technical Sales Presentations

The largest single slice of your time as a sales consultant is likely to be spent making presentations. An effective presentation can set the stage for a successful product sale, so it is critical that you learn this skill. Many of the principles for presentations apply to product demonstrations as well, but demonstrations are important enough that we will deal with them in more detail in the next chapter.

Pre-Meeting Planning

You will need to complete two main tasks before embarking on a presentation or demonstration with a prospect. As you learned in Chapter 8, on qualification and planning, the very first component of a successful sales effort is to get a firm grasp on your prospect's needs. There is no way to decide accurately how to position your solution unless you have studied the prospect's business problem and technical requirements. From these requirements, you can build your feature/benefit lists, which will control the flow and content of your technical presentation.

In Chapter 7, we discussed the second task on your pre-meeting checklist: mastering your solution. As you learned, you not only need to know your own product "cold," but you also need to gather any ancillary information that might help to sell the complete "solution." You will often visit prospects who work in entirely different lines of business, even if you are selling in a vertical marketplace. Once you have merged your qualifications data with your feature/benefit lists, you will undoubtedly find gaps in the solution. As discussed in the previous chapter, be sure to fill in these gaps to create a complete solution before embarking on your presentation and demonstration.

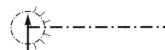

As we also discussed earlier in this book, the technical sales consultant faces three main phases of selling, while the sales rep has several additional milestones. The first phase is the *qualifications* process. The second phase is the *presentation and demonstration* stage (in Hollywood parlance, the presentation and demonstration stage means *"showtime!"*). The last phase of the technical process is the *evaluation* phase, but you can never reach this phase without qualifying properly and making an effective presentation/demonstration.

Agenda

An effective presentation and demonstration must have a formal agenda for the meeting. A formal agenda accomplishes two purposes: It allows you to properly schedule the inevitably limited time for the presentation, and it enables you to make sure that your time estimates are in line with the customer's expectations. A formal agenda can help you to gain and keep control of at least this portion of the sales cycle.

Sure, there will be times when you have to give a quick demo later on in the sales cycle to a new group or a new player in an ongoing deal. In such cases, there may not be time to create a formal agenda, but you should still start your presentation with a brief description.

In all presentations, start by telling your audience what they are going to hear.

When you provide an outline of the general flow of a presentation for an audience, they will have less trouble keeping on track during the course of the presentation, even if their attention occasionally wanders.

For the more formal group presentation, you need to have an agenda that includes the following items:

- Attendees
- Items
- Facilities

Attendees

The first item lists the attendees at the meeting. You may never actually receive a complete list of people, however, since turnout frequently changes. But you and the sales rep need to wrangle a list of probable attendees from the meeting's sponsor. The meeting sponsor is the person on the prospect's side of the deal who is chartered with setting up the meeting and working you through the sales process. Sometimes, this person is also your "coach" in the deal, but in most cases, the person's job is to herd the vendors through the evaluation.

The attendance list should include at least the name and title of each attendee. There will be a mix of technical and nontechnical types; accordingly, divide them between yourself and the sales rep. Ideally, you should get permission from the meeting sponsor to call the technical people from this list in advance. Use the guise of "reviewing the agenda" when you call them. If you can have a quick conversation on the phone with the technicians before the meeting takes place, you are likely to obtain interesting data about technical requirements and evaluation criteria. You can also make sure that everyone's expectations have been set properly. Like a good trial lawyer, you want to avoid surprises.

> As the sales consultant representing asset management software, I was often involved in large, complex deals that sometimes took more than a year to close. We often had to spend an entire day making slide presentations to "set the stage" for the demonstrations to come several weeks later. By calling around to the technical team in advance, I was able to avoid many ugly confrontations by letting them know that the first meeting would not include a product demonstration. The pre-meeting phone call provided me with the opportunity to set expectations properly.

There is no guarantee that the people on the attendee list will actually show up. In addition, there often will be new players who show up at the meeting who were not on the list. That's OK. The more you know up front, the easier it will be to add people to your list and the more likely it is that you will have a successful demonstration event.

Items

The items list contains the individual components of the meeting that are agreed to by the sales rep and the meeting sponsor. A typical items list might look like this:

- Overview of prospect's business and statement of the problem—9:00–9:45
- Slide presentation describing the company and marketplace of the product—9:45–10:15

- Slide presentation, product architecture, and overview—10:15–10:45
- Break 10:45—10:55
- Product demonstration—10:55–11:40

Critical items that the prospect wants to see covered:

- Service, training and support options 11:40–11:50
- Wrap-up, Q&A—11:50–12:00

The preceding list is an example; it will not suit every situation. Complex products such as enterprise resource planning (ERP) or customer relationship management software (CRM) often require multi-day meetings with extensive agenda items. The more complex situations will require specialized sections for individual groups of prospect team members from such functional areas as purchasing, accounting, and manufacturing. The specific list of items on the agenda will vary accordingly with the type of product and its complexity. The important things for you to do are to create a schedule of tasks to be accomplished in the allotted time and to gain agreement on these tasks with the prospect. Your sales rep will use the agenda items to continue to qualify the prospect, and you can use the agenda to plot out your demonstration strategy.

The timings noted in the agenda are there for your benefit. In the sample agenda shown above, you will know in advance that you need to move into the demo by 10:55 if you want to accomplish everything you have planned.

There is one agenda item in our sample that bears special mention: the break. It is unrealistic to expect people to sit and listen to your captivating presentation without answering nature's call, stretching or perform other important physical functions. By explicitly noting when a break will occur, you allow people in the meeting to pace themselves, rather than be faced with the unpleasant situation where one person after another leaves the meeting. You may end up with a partial quorum for many minutes as the parade slowly passes through. If you don't plan for breaks, you may lose a vital part of your control over the demonstration process.

The foundation for the product demonstration is contained in the feature/benefit list that you created as part of the qualification process. And, more importantly, the agenda should include any items that your prospect has identified as *critical* to the product demonstration. You will find there will be things that the prospect absolutely wants to see during the production demonstration. This is part of the negotiation process between your sales rep and the prospect, but you will undoubtedly have some say in this negotiation. We'll delve into this issue later on, but for the purposes of this portion of the discussion, it is important to document the game plan for the demonstration in order to set the expectations between you and the prospect.

Facilities

One small, but critical, part of the agenda consists of the facilities that you require in order to give your presentation and demonstration. Always include this topic in the agenda discussions with your prospect. This item is often overlooked, but the sales process can start off on the wrong foot if it is not looked after properly. The facilities include things like the size of the room, projection devices, and power and network access. Ideally, you will create your own "cheat-sheet" of facilities requirements so that you will always have it near. It is bad practice to agree to an agenda and then have to go back to make changes because the facilities do not support the items that you agreed to in the agenda.

Despite assurances from your prospect that everything is in order, it is best that you put together your own "bag of tricks." A good bag of tricks has all the things that you will need to make your presentation work, including:

- A power strip (with an extension cord)
- Network adapter cables
- A variety of projector cable adapters
- A telephone extension cable
- Whiteboard pens, several colors
- A laser pen-light
- An external mouse and pad
- Floppy disks
- Velcro strips

There are likely to be other items that are specific to your product. By all means, you should feel free to add to this list. Whatever you do, keep your bag of tricks neat and well organized, and use the Velcro strips to keep all the wiring organized. It doesn't help to have the right equipment and then have to root around to find what you are looking for.

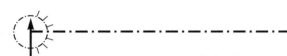

Two items are not part of the bag of tricks, but, of course, are critical to the presentation and demonstration. The first item is your laptop computer. Even if you are not selling software, you are most likely giving presentations using a laptop computer. Your company will provide you with one, so you probably won't have much say about the brand or configuration. The second item is a projector. Your company will have to decide whether or not to provide you with a projector to go with your laptop.

You do not have any real control over the projection device the prospect will provide you. It is always better to control your own destiny, and having a quality projection device often allows you to give a much more professional presentation than you could if you had to rely on whatever equipment the prospect may (or may not) have. Since a proper projection device can make or break a presentation, we recommend that your company pay the cost to provide you with a lightweight, quality projection device.

First Things First

The success of your presentation can often be assured in the first fifteen minutes of the meeting, long before any of the formal presentations. Ideally, you will have had a chance to meet most of the key players either through the face-to-face qualifications meeting or through telephone conversations. New players will almost always be in the room for the presentation, but the key is to try to meet the technical decision-makers before the presentation meeting.

The most important task to accomplish at the start of the meeting is to introduce yourself to all of the people in the room individually. Get all of their names. In most cases, you will not have the chance to remember everyone's name during personal introductions, but there will be time for this during the formal around-the-table introductions.

You want to be in the presentation room, completely set up and ready to go, fifteen minutes before the scheduled start of the meeting.

When the sales rep sets the meeting, make sure that he or she has arranged with the meeting's sponsor to gain access to the presentation room at least a half hour before it begins. You will need some time to set up your equipment (laptop, projector, etc.) before the crowd begins to wander in. Also, the casual time before the formal start of the meeting gives you an excellent opportunity to meet the attendees in person.

You cannot meet the attendees if you are busy fiddling around with your equipment.

Once you are set up and ready to go, you can mingle with the people as they wander in for the start of the meeting. People tend to straggle into meetings, so being in the appointed room early provides an excellent opportunity to get a few moments with each of the attendees individually. It is important that you try to greet as many of them as you can personally. People are more likely to warm up to your presentation once they have gotten to know you. A personal greeting will get the ball rolling in the right direction. Ideally, you want to get a business card from everyone, but do not push the issue or browbeat anyone into giving you a card if he or she is reluctant.

Once you have received as many business cards as possible, you can use them to replicate the positions of everyone around the room. This way, you can quickly glance down at your cards to respond to people by name. It's even nicer if you can just remember their name, but most people will appreciate your attempt to know their names, even if you can't memorize them.

Sometimes, the people you meet will have unusual names. Make sure that you know the correct pronunciation of each name, writing it down if you have to. There is no shame in not being able to pronounce someone's name correctly at first glance. I have found that people are more than willing to help you pronounce their names properly if you ask politely.

One cardinal sin to avoid is using a nickname unless the person asks you to do so. For example, if you are introduced to an attendee and are given a business card with the first name of "Susan," do not assume that you should start calling this person "Sue." It is better practice to ask politely what she prefers to be called.

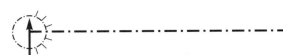

There are different levels of formality for different situations and for different people in the same situation. For instance, older people may not appreciate being called by their first names by someone much younger, and executives may feel that being called by a less formal name shows disrespect. It is always better to start by calling someone by a more formal name, such as "Mr. Smith," than simply assuming that the person would like to be called "Bob" (especially if his name is not Bob but Robert).

Once the meeting starts, the sales rep will take the helm and run the meeting. One of the first things that he or she will do is to present the agenda and introduce the sales team.

Allow the sales rep to introduce you and give a short description of your background.

Create a suitable biography that accurately captures your experiences, and let the sales rep introduce you using this biography. You can add to the description when you complete the introduction, but it is easier—and more appropriate—for the sales rep to "brag" about your accomplishments than it would be for you to do the same.

This is especially true if you have some special accomplishments in your background such as patents, published works, or awards. Though it is unseemly for you to call yourself "award-winning," there is good reason for the sales rep to do so. Technical accomplishments help to establish your "bona fides," and it is useful for your prospect to have this information. The sales rep can easily communicate this information without losing any credibility.

Once you have introduced yourselves, the sales rep will have the members of the prospect team introduce themselves as well. This is a critical step in the presentation process. Make sure that you write down everyone's name, and try to jot them down in the order in which the people are sitting. If you have already arranged their business cards, you can add information on a supplemental piece of paper or on the card itself. This way, you will have a seating chart that you can refer to when you wish to call people by name.

After the introductions, it's time to get the proverbial ball rolling.

Types of Presentations

You will no doubt find yourself working within different presentation frameworks in your career as a sales consultant. There are two basic types of presentations:

- PowerPoint presentation
- Chalk talks

Many sales presentations will entail both forms of presentations—a chalk talk followed by a PowerPoint presentation or vice versa.

Sales consulting as we know it today really came into its own in the 1980s. Although both computer hardware and software have been around longer than that, the advent of the minicomputer helped to spawn the modern era of technical selling. The ability either to connect to a remote computer or to carry the computer to the customer ushered in the explosion of technical selling. This power curve has accelerated even more with the birth of the Internet. However, despite the rapid growth in technical selling, the start of the presentation process is still referred to as the venerable slide show (although it rarely involves actual slides).

PowerPoint Presentation

In the early days of technical selling, the basic product presentation was given using 35mm slides. The presentation thus became known as the *slide show*. The transition to personal computers and color printers allowed the product presentation to migrate from slides to overhead transparencies and finally to presentation software such as Microsoft PowerPoint. Today, the vast majority of product presentations are made electronically and are run from your computer desktop. Regardless of which medium you use, however, the presentation is still essentially a slide show. Hereafter, we will use the terms *slide show* and *PowerPoint presentation* interchangeably to refer to this task.

The slide show presentation forms the core of the first part of the presentation portion of a meeting with a prospect. Your corporate marketing department creates the materials for your slide show presentation. You will find that the content of the presentation follows a fairly standard format. Every slide presentation will cover the following basic elements:

- Company information
- Market data
- Architecture

- Product description
- Service offerings

One core element of all slide shows is the company information section, which presents the relevant financial data for your company. Your sales partner will always give this portion of the presentation, but its size and position in the program will vary according to your company's position in the marketplace.

The key element in the company information is normally the market data, which presents the size and growth of the marketplace along with overall competitive positioning. These slides will generally include graphs from companies such as International Data Corporation, Gartner Group, or Meta Group, showing the market to be of a certain size. In general, you will not have to worry about presenting this information, because your sales partner will be responsible for this portion of the presentation. However, you are not excused from *knowing* this information, since your position in the market exerts a great deal of influence on your sales strategies. Market data is a great segue for pulling your sales partner back into the conversation when the prospect is trying to steer the discussion away from sales issues.

Technical prospects are sometimes reluctant to deal directly with the sales rep. They may have a tendency to address questions directly to you or to try to steer the conversation to exclude your sales partner. You can use market statistics as a "straight-man" line to give your sales rep an entré back into the conversation. Try something like the following to get your sales rep involved again:

> *"...In fact, this technology is a growing market...* [at this point, you turn to Bob, your sales rep]. *Bob, IDC has recently published some statistics documenting this trend, haven't they?"*

As a sales consultant, you generally enter the picture at the third juncture of the slide presentation. This section is called the product architecture discussion. You will find that the product architecture slides are generally of two basic types—those that *spread the religion* or those that offer *product differentiation.*

If you are selling in what was then, or is now, a new product category, such as relational databases (early 1980s), client/server computing (late 1980s), application servers (late 1990s), or portals (today), you may have to educate your prospect about the particulars of the overall product segment. In sales consultant jargon, this is typically referred to as

Making Effective Technical Sales Presentations — Chapter 9

spreading the religion, and it is often one of the most difficult tasks to perform. This type of approach is typical for the early stages of a market.

Conversely, if you are selling a product in an established marketplace, then the architecture portion of your presentation is typically geared toward *product differentiation*. In the first case, your audience may not be familiar with all of the specific features and advantages of products of your ilk. They need you to explain these basics to them before you can begin positioning the specific advantages of your particular product offering. In the second case, your audience is much more likely to understand the basic product category and is only relying on you to describe the specific advantages of your product.

> If you were selling relational database software back in the early 1980s, your prospects might not have been familiar with the benefits of relational databases versus other, more traditional, data storage technologies. Therefore, the architectural slides within your presentation were more likely dealing with fundamental category issues such as SQL and the relational model. However, if you are working for a relational database vendor in today's marketplace, you will find that the average prospect is familiar with the basic components of a relational database. In this case, your architectural pitch is more likely to be composed of specific features that differentiate your database from the competition's, such as bitmapped indexes or data replication.

Once the sales representative has given the basic company and market presentation, he or she will typically turn the presentation over to you. Since you will probably be doing at least part of the slide presentation, we will look at basic strategies for giving slide presentations.

Making the PowerPoint Presentation

Your corporate marketing department has gone to great lengths to build presentations that reflect the basic product message. However, marketing is not always the same as selling, and you will no doubt find the need to make adjustments to the slide materials. You should try to build your message around the slides where you can, minimizing the number of changes that you make. There is a great deal of benefit to having a consistent product message, and building your own custom presentation may work at cross-purposes to this goal.

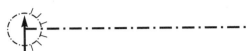

This is not to say that you should sacrifice the effectiveness of your presentation simply to remain consistent with the company's message. Rather, keep the product messaging and positioning in mind when you consider adding or removing slides from your presentation.

In this respect, the advent of PowerPoint has been both good and bad for the business of technical selling. In the old days of the true slide presentation, you were forced to use materials that the marketing department provided to you, and new slides tended to be released on a quarterly basis at best. Furthermore, you couldn't easily add your own slides, since the color scheme—which ties the entire presentation together—would not match the corporate standard.

> Most companies make the logo and color scheme part of the corporate "brand." Collateral materials such as brochures and slides will be rendered using this same color scheme. When you add your own slides that may have a different color scheme, it can distract from the standard branding message. Your prospects will see the different colors (even if they only take notice on a subconscious level) as distracting.

Even worse, when new slide presentations were introduced by the marketing department, they often included a new color scheme. This meant that you had to drop any of your existing slides in order to make use of any of the new presentation materials.

Of course, with electronic slide presentations, you can change the content of the slides much more easily. But you should still try to take a think-twice-and-change-once approach to modifying the basic slide show from your corporate marketing group.

Although slides had their problems, the fact that every member of the sales team had a similar set of materials almost guaranteed that the message was at least somewhat consistent. With the advent of PowerPoint, there has been a tendency to change the content of slide presentations at the drop of a hat. Avoid this common pitfall. The advantage to presentation software like PowerPoint is that you can easily make changes to your presentation as necessary. The trick is to avoid *constantly* tinkering with the presentation.

I have worked with sales consultants who change their slides after every presentation in response to an issue or issues raised during a previous meeting. The result was that they were never completely comfortable with the slides set (because they changed all the time). It is important to have a consistent presentation.

If you find that a topic is not adequately covered with the slide materials that you have, you may need to modify existing slides or add new slides. In any case, do not overload yourself with too many slides.

As a general rule, the average amount of time that you should spend on each slide in a presentation is about three minutes.

Although this may seem like a lot of time per slide, it generally represents an average for all of your slides. Some slides will be very short, and others will take a lot more time, but the average should be about three minutes per slide. You also have to allow time for some interaction with the audience, which is crucial to obtaining the information you need for closing the sale.

Fifteen slides probably means about forty-five minutes. Audiences have a limited capacity for attention, and you will find that the prospect is going to have a hard time paying attention for *longer* than forty-five minutes using any single medium. Therefore, don't load up your slide presentation with too many slides, or you are going to lose your audience. And *everyone* in the audience is much happier to see a slide presentation end a little early.

After you have pulled together your feature/benefit list, you should walk through your slide presentation and tie each major feature/benefit item to an element *specific* to your prospect's situation. Make sure that you walk through the slides with this list in mind *before* the actual presentation. The content on the slides has to be automatically available to you—you cannot keep looking through the slides before trying to make your point. You want to be able to click to the next slide and start speaking without having to look at the slide itself. If you have to look at a slide to figure out the point you were trying to make, it is going to appear as if you do not know what you are talking about. Furthermore, when you finally make the point, it will not have the impact that you want it to have.

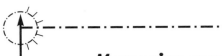

Memorize your slides and tie specific feature/benefit points to the content of the slides and face the audience, not the screen.

Even if you have to glance at the screen from time to time, you must never, never, never make the mistake of speaking while facing the screen. Not only is it difficult for the audience to hear you, but it is quite rude not to face people when you are speaking to them.

> I have always found it helpful to have a printout of the presentation handy, so I can glance at the hard copy without having to turn around to face the screen. You can make notes on the hard copy to remind yourself to focus on certain key points for your prospect.

Normally, the slide presentation is the least interactive of the three "weapons" in your arsenal (slides, chalk talk, and demonstration). You can ask for feedback during the slide presentation, but try not to get too sidetracked. If you find that a certain slide or topic always invokes extensive side dialogue, consider removing the slide and covering the same topic elsewhere in the meeting.

Slides are the best medium for setting up the basic value proposition, but they are more generic than either the chalk talk or the demonstration. The slide presentation should be used to *set the prospect up* for the chalk talk and demonstration.

Let's go back to the SuperServer product we mentioned before. Assume that the top three features of SuperServer are the following capabilities:

- It is very portable
- It is known for fast performance
- It has been praised for its ease of administration

During the slide presentation, you should cover all of these major features (and associated benefits)—repeatedly, if necessary. The demonstration section of your presentation is used to *prove* to the prospect (or at least to start the proof process) that these basic assertions are true. In the slide presentation, you are effectively telling the prospect, "Here's why my product is the right choice for your situation."

For example:

> *"As you can see on this slide, SuperServer is written in Java and it is very portable. You can run SuperServer on Windows NT and more than twenty different flavors of UNIX. I know that here at Federated you have several different brands, and with SuperServer you can leverage your investments in these platforms.*
>
> *"In a few minutes, I am going to demonstrate this capability by running an application here locally on my laptop, and then we'll connect via the Internet to a server at our headquarters that runs UNIX so you can see it for yourself."*

The one suggestion that we make, regardless of the type of product, is to avoid the classic technician's trap: excessive slide builds. Most presentation software allows you to build portions of your slides a piece at a time with each click of your mouse. We like builds, too. The problem is that they just don't work all that well in *real life*. Audiences spend more time wondering when the next bullet point will appear rather than concentrating on the point that you are trying to make. If your presentation style lends itself to using slide builds, then by all means use them, but make them simple and consistent.

Finally, you need to consider whether to hand out copies of the slides in advance of the presentation. You should always make copies of the slides available to your audience, but giving them out before or after your presentation is a matter of personal preference. The benefit to handing them out ahead of time is that the audience can take notes directly on the slides as necessary. The downside is that they will have a tendency to flip through the presentation while you are talking.

The Chalk Talk

Certain types of content do not work well in the classic slide presentation. This is the case with topics that are either very customer-specific or overly complex. An alternative presentation format is to create the presentation on the fly using a whiteboard and dry-erase markers.

Why is the format called the chalk talk? Before the age of computers, most offices had actual chalkboards on which to write. When technicians wanted to make a special point, they would draw out the point on the chalk board. Ergo, the "chalk talk." Today, most offices feature whiteboards, the modern equivalent of the chalkboard. The presentation format is still called the "chalk talk."

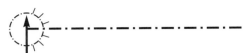

Not every room you work in will have a dry-erase board. Make sure you can reproduce your chalk talk presentation on a paper flip chart, if necessary, and be prepared to bring one to the meeting if none is available.

The chalk talk is the best vehicle for describing highly technical issues or to lay out your product's architecture in a format that allows you to insert specific references to the customer's situation. You start by drawing some simple shapes to represent the various pieces of your product's architecture. Each shape represents part of your solution, and you describe the various pieces as you draw them:

> *"This first box represents your database. Next, we add the SuperServer engine to access the database..."*

or

> *"Let's say your biggest customer places a big order for widgets. We can start by showing the electronic transaction coming into our purchasing application here..."*

or

> *"You already have an existing AS/400 server here. Our XQ-400 disk drive array plugs right into the backplane of the AS/400 like so..."*

Next, you fill in each basic shape with an appropriate label. (Do this while describing what the shape represents in the overall scheme.) In effect, you are building a diagram of your solution as it fits in with the prospect's requirements. A chalk talk can be designed to present any type of technical issue including the following:

- Product architecture
- Business process flow (purchase orders, sales, etc.)
- Hardware layouts
- Network designs
- Product interoperability
- Implementation plans

The specific focus of your technical chalk talk is to describe the major components of your solution in terms that your prospect will understand. For instance, if you are selling an application development tool, the chalk talk might illustrate a workflow of how applications are designed, built, and tested. On the other hand, if you are selling enterprise resource planning software, your talk might visualize how all of the various software modules fit into the prospect's current environment.

The secret of the chalk talk is to carefully build the overall diagram so that it presents your product as the solution to the prospect's problem. The result is a very clever psychological ploy to get your prospect to "see" your product as part of his or her environment. By seeing his or her applications intermixed with your product, your prospect will conceptualize your product as part of their solution.

No matter how off-the-cuff the chalk talk appears to be, it should actually be a carefully crafted presentation that will help your client conceptualize the solution. In general, you will develop a single basic chalk talk that will serve as the framework, and then you will add the prospect's environment to the diagram. Your chalk talk has the twin virtues of emphasizing, through its basic structure, the key features of your product, while also being specifically tailored to your prospect.

The final diagram will almost always have the same basic components. The major difference will come from the labels that you will use for the various shapes.

Take the case of SuperServer for a moment. The chalk talk diagram for SuperServer might look like the one shown in Figure 9.1:

Figure 9.1
SuperServer
initial chalk
talk diagram.

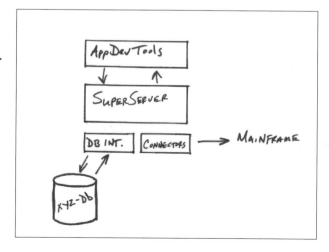

Notice, in the figure, how boxes represent all the possible aspects to the solution, including connections to mainframe systems and third-party application software. Not every client is going to need every piece of the solution, but you have to treat the chalk talk like a story board. The final picture has to contain all the pieces of the puzzle. When you draw the diagram for the client, you simply leave off the pieces that do not apply and label the remaining pieces to reflect the prospect's own situation.

If we use the Federated Department Stores example once again, you will remember that their three main technical requirements were as follows:

- Must be written in Java

- Federated plans on using XYZ-Db as the database for this new project

- Must interface to the JHacker programming tool that the company has standardized on

Therefore, when we modify the chalk talk diagram to account for Federated's specific needs, we might get the picture that is shown in Figure 9.2:

Figure 9.2
Completed chalk talk for Federated.

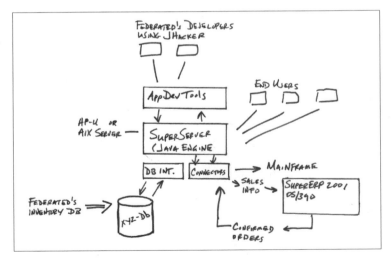

The final rendering of the chalk talk includes the special capabilities of your product, along with the elements that are specific to your prospect's situation. The result is an informal picture of how your product fits into the prospect's environment. In our example case, we've shown how the SuperServer engine will work with Federated's mainframe and XYZ-Db database.

Chalk talks seem informal, so they tend to encourage more interaction with your prospect than a slide presentation can. Audiences tend to look at slide presentations as a one-way medium—you talk and they listen. The chalk talk, by contrast, has a less formal *flow*, so your prospect will be encouraged to ask questions and provide feedback during the pitch.

Since the chalk talk is a different medium than a slide presentation or demo, it can break up the monotony of a meeting and recapture the attention of the audience.

You can even encourage audience participation by staging frequent checkpoints during the chalk talk. Use these as opportunities to ask for feedback:

> *"Here we see SuperServer running in front of your XYZ-Db database, managing the inventory transactions. Everyone with me so far? Susan, does running SuperServer on your HP-UX machine make sense, or do you plan to run SuperServer on the AIX machine?"*

> *"Here I show data from your existing sales order entry system feeding back into the booking module of SuperERP 2001. Can you see how the transaction would come in right here, and how we can then push the content right into the open interface? Does this make sense from a business flow perspective?"*

In order to maximize the impact of your chalk talk, you need to follow some basic rules of thumb. Take note of the following tips:

Don't try to draw beyond your artistic abilities.

This shouldn't be an issue for most chalk talks, since your drawing abilities probably won't need to extend beyond creating simple geometric shapes and possibly an iconic representation of a computer or device. If you really can't draw at all, it is worth the time for you to take some basic art lessons. It can be very painful for an audience to watch a person who can't draw very well chicken-scratch away on a whiteboard. Instead of concentrating on the substance of the chalk talk, your prospects will be involved in the inevitable fascination with a developing artistic disaster.

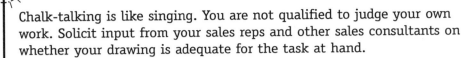

Chalk-talking is like singing. You are not qualified to judge your own work. Solicit input from your sales reps and other sales consultants on whether your drawing is adequate for the task at hand.

Bring your own dry-erase markers.

A master swordsman does not rely on the opponent to bring along an extra sword! Although it's hard to make blanket statements that apply to all prospects, we can tell you that unless you are pitching a deal to Staples (the office supply people), the dry-erase markers that your supplier will have on hand probably pre-date "Welcome Back, Kotter." Bring your own dry-erase markers.

Use several colors, but do not go overboard.

Color is great, because it helps make the diagram more interesting to look at. But you are not Jackson Pollock or Andy Warhol. Use colors where appropriate, and use them consistently. If you decide to draw network connections in red, *always* draw them in red. Don't switch pens like George Steinbrenner switches managers.

Follow the draw'n'talk methodology, and do not get overly elaborate.

You aren't Michelangelo, either. Keep your drawings relatively simple. Draw quickly. Do not spend ten minutes drawing a detailed picture and then start talking. Build the picture a little at a time. Draw a few shapes and then talk about what they represent. Then draw a little more.

You might be tempted just to ditch slides altogether and go with the chalk talk as the main presentation method of choice, but it doesn't work that way. Your audience isn't going to sit still while you draw page after page on the whiteboard. Slides are still the best format for most of your pre-demonstration.

Slides are ideal for more-or-less static data, while the chalk talk is better suited for customized presentations.

Chalk talks work well as a supplement, not as a replacement. The exceptions to this rule include those times when you are given only a few minutes to make your point, and you don't have a chance to use your slides. In such cases, the chalk talk can be the vehicle for making a few key points in lieu of a complete presentation.

Final Thoughts

If you have ever watched a baseball game, you will notice that a pitcher always throws a few pitches for practice before the game begins. You would think that after all the pitches the guy has thrown in his life, he wouldn't need to take a few practice throws to do his job. So why does he do it?

He's warming up, and you should, too. It does not matter how many times you've given your slide pitch or your chalk talk—you should warm up before every game. If you are making a presentation first thing in the morning, get up early and walk through your slides. You don't even need to turn your computer on. Just print a copy of the slides and flip through them with your coffee. While you flip, jot down some of the prospect's requirements on the appropriate pages to make sure that the data is fresh in your mind. When you are finished, get out a blank sheet of paper and quickly sketch out your chalk talk pitch. The whole process shouldn't take you more than ten to fifteen minutes. You will be surprised at how much more effective you will be once you get in the habit of warming up.

Wrapping Up

Through the slide presentation and the chalk talk, you have set the stage. Now, it's time to prove that your product is all that you say it is. The next chapter introduces you to the process of giving powerful product demonstrations. With slides and the whiteboard, you talk the talk. With the demo, it's time to walk the walk.

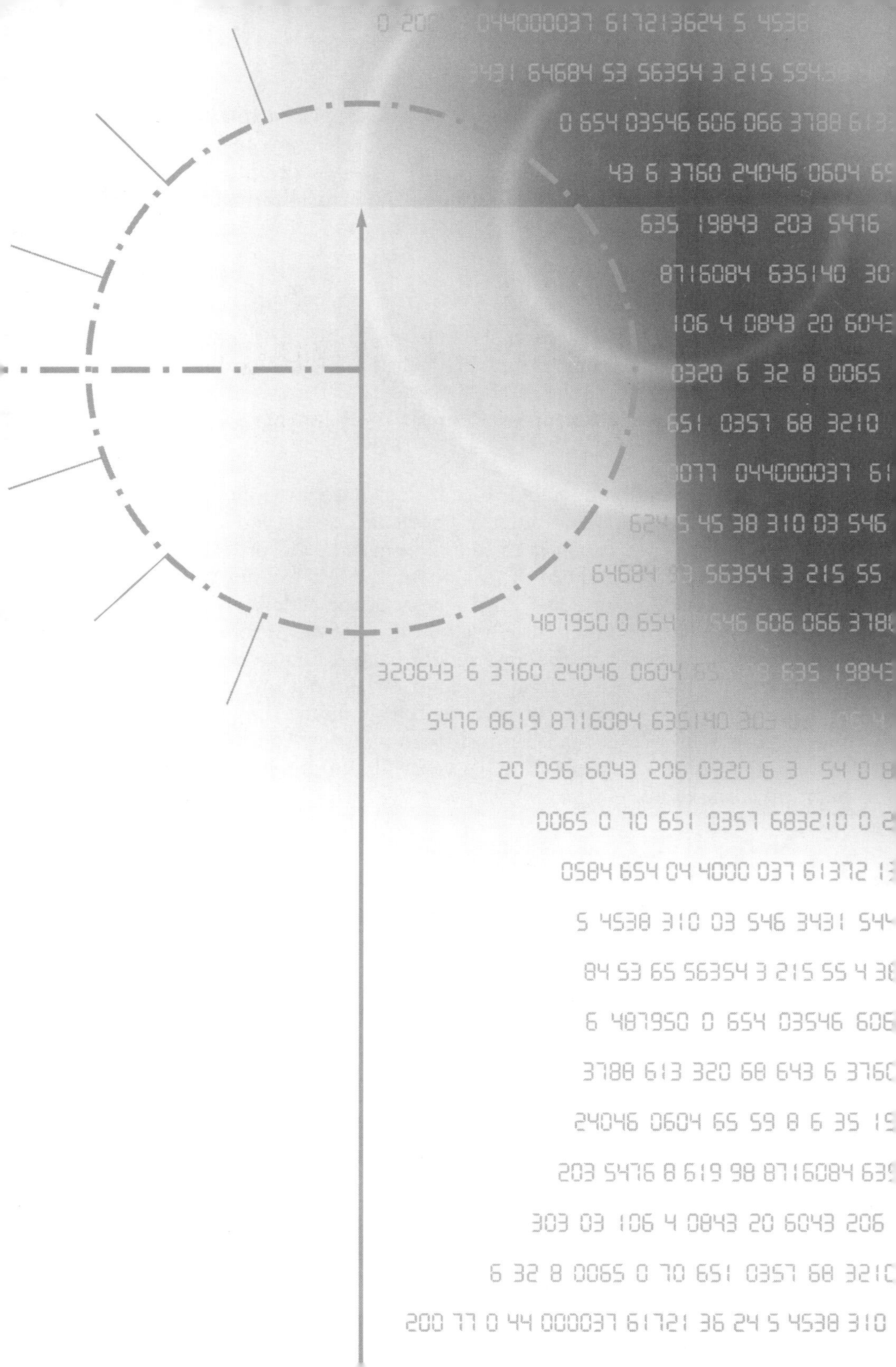

Delivering Effective Product Demonstrations

Throughout this book, we have stressed the importance of the product demonstration in the sales cycle process. In this chapter, we will look at the techniques you will need to master in order to give an effective product demonstration.

Features, with their associated benefits, are the entire point of the demo. However, since every offering has a different set of features and benefits, we will be addressing more of the "how" techniques for creating optimal product demonstrations, rather than the "what" (content) of the demo.

The Importance of the Demo

While you can definitely position your product effectively with a powerful slide presentation and chalk talk, most prospects will need to see a product demonstration in order to truly believe in your product. Slides and chalk talks can help the prospect envision the capabilities of your solution, but they do not serve as a proof step. A slick presentation shows you can talk the talk, but you still need to give a solid demonstration in order to prove that you can back up all that talk by walking the walk.

The age-old adage that "seeing is believing" is certainly true when selling technical products. Very few prospects will actually make a purchasing decision on the strength of your demonstration, but the demo will set the stage for the evaluation phase of the sales process. An effective demonstration can put you in the front-runner's position. While this does not guarantee you a sale, it does make it easier for you and your sales rep to control the remaining phases of the sales cycle. On the other hand, a poor demo can knock you down a few of pegs, even if your product is the best fit for the prospect's needs.

Basic Definitions

The first key to an effective product demonstration is to understand just what constitutes a "demo."

A product demonstration is a live, interactive display of your product in action.

Although it may seem like we're stating the obvious here, the first element of a product demonstration is that it has to be a "live" show. Your prospect needs to see the product as it actually lives and breathes. He or she has to be able to see and touch the product. Most prospects are highly skeptical of being shown a mock-up, and the solution is to have your product live in all its glory.

It's like the difference between watching a television show about tigers or seeing tigers live in a zoo. Sure, in a zoo they aren't in their natural habitat and are certainly not as intimidating when they are behind the bars of the cage. Yet, they *seem* much more real to you because you see them live and in person (so to speak). While the television show about tigers may allow you to see tigers in the wild doing exciting tiger-like things, the presentation doesn't seem all that real. When you demo your product to the prospect, the very same rules apply. Showing a "screen cam" or a mocked-up version of your application just doesn't cut it.

A product demonstration is also interactive. Your prospect needs to feel like he or she has some control over the flow of the demonstration. You cannot simply stick to the script and hold questions until the end of the demonstration. You have to allow your prospect to interact with you *during* the demonstration. Doing so will help you to dispel the impression that the demonstration is scripted in some way. It will also help you to gather information about the prospect's needs that will help you close the deal.

This brings us to the third element of the demo—action. The demo has to involve some action and excitement. There has to be something for the prospect to see. After all, seeing is believing. This is not always an easy task to accomplish, since many technical products do not have much of a visual aspect to them. You might have to get creative in order to add action to your product, but it is an important aspect of your demonstration.

Consider the example of a race car. While it might be interesting to see and touch a Formula One race car, it is much more exciting to see one zip past you at 150 miles per hour. After all, can I really describe what 150 miles per hour is like in any meaningful way? I might be able to make you understand how fast that is, but it will be a lot more effective for you to understand the concept when an actual race car goes whizzing by you. Action is the difference between the two—and action is what makes your demo a proof step rather than just another description of your product.

The purpose of the demonstration still boils down to *FBA*—feature, benefit, and acceptance of the benefit—as described in Chapter 6 on feature benefit selling.

The very nature of the demonstration requires you to make features and benefits seem real by adding live, interactive, and action-oriented displays of your technology. As with most of the other tasks in the sales process, the key to giving an effective demonstration is in large part an exercise in preparation.

What if you can't show a live product? Perhaps your prospect has requested to see beta features, which are not yet accessible to you. Or perhaps you are delivering a customized application that has not been completed. If conditions force you to show a smoke-and-mirrors demo, where you are displaying only a simulation, you should always tell your prospect well in advance of the demo. Explain why the demo is not live and make sure that the circumstances are acceptable to the prospect. You can minimize some of the potential problems by showing parts of your product that *are* live, or by demonstrating a similar, completed application before moving on to the section that is not live.

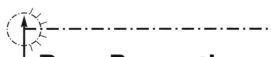

Demo Preparation

As we discussed in Chapter 7, "Mastering The Demo," you must first master your own product before you can hope to give an effective product demonstration. While the demo itself follows a general script and flow, you will need to interact with the prospect during the demonstration. Your prospect will tend to drive the demonstration in different directions; therefore, you will need to be fully prepared to deal with these little excursions as they occur. If you have not mastered your own product, you are not ready to give demos.

Certain demo situations, such as trade shows and seminars, do not require complete mastery of your product. We will examine these specific situations in detail later in this chapter. In the meantime, you should consider mastery of your product to be the foundation upon which a good demonstration is based.

Assuming that you have mastered your product, the next step in the demonstration process is the preparation phase. You should focus on two main areas while preparing for product demonstrations. The first stage is to create your own standard demonstration kit, and the second is to modify this standard kit to take into consideration the specific needs of your prospect.

Most technical products have a standard demonstration kit that is produced by the marketing organization. As we discussed in Chapter 7, this demo kit is usually composed of three parts—the product, a script, and some sample data. The basic idea of a demo is for the prospect to see your product in action. It's sort of like test-driving a new car, except that you do the driving and the prospect comes along for the ride. With high-technology products, things work a little differently. Prospects are rarely able to use your product "right out of the box" without training or instruction. Therefore, it is somewhat difficult for them to take a test drive alone.

— · — · —

> Some companies have been able to create their own "test-drive" kits, which include a version of the product and a booklet that will lead prospects through some tasks. These test drives have gotten more popular with the growth of the Internet. Companies that lack the resources to hire complete sales teams, or those that sell products that do not warrant the expense of a direct sales team, will generally favor the "test-drive" approach.

— · — · —

When you give a demo, you are effectively giving prospects a type of test drive. If they like what they see, they will probably decide to invest in some training and "test drive" the product for themselves. At this point, the sales cycle moves into the evaluation phase (discussed in the next chapter). In any event, your prospects need to see your product in action. You either have to bring the product to the prospects or bring the prospects to the product in order to give a real demonstration. Showing your prospects a videotape or a screen-cam recording does not count as a demonstration.

Choosing the Venue

One of the first things to decide is *where* you are going to conduct the demo. There are basically four ways to get your prospect in front of the product for a demonstration:

- Carry all the equipment with you.
- Load the product into your prospect's environment.
- Take the customer to a demo facility.
- 'Net demo

Although it may sound more complex, the simplest way to bring your product to the customer is to carry it all with you. This technique is often the most common method for demonstrating software, since most products can be made to fit on a laptop running Windows NT or a portable Linux machine. This is not necessarily the best way in which to demo your software, but it is certainly the safest. Since you have control over the entire environment, you can set the demonstration up to be virtually error free.

If your product is portable enough and relatively easy to set up and configure, an alternative strategy is to install it into your prospect's environment. This was a very common practice for software vendors in the minicomputer era, but it has fallen out of vogue. It is an incredibly powerful technique if you can pull it off, since your prospect will get the ultimate opportunity to see your product working in his or her own environment.

On the other hand, demonstrating your product in the prospect's environment is much more resource-intensive than any other demonstration technique. Not only will you have to set up and configure your product in a foreign environment, but you will also have to coordinate this work with resources on your prospect's side. This is not

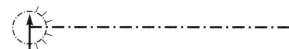

always an easy task. After all, you might be selling to the application development group but need to work with the systems management group in order to get your product installed and configured.

If you have to demonstrate your product in the prospect's environment, you need to consider several factors:

Separate the presentation/chalk talk from the demonstration event.

Although this is not always possible to accomplish from a travel perspective, you should consider making a presentation to the prospect apart from the demonstration. This will give you a chance to huddle with the sales rep to decide if your prospect is worth the effort required to set up and conduct the on-site demo.

This separation also flies in the face of one of the first principles discussed in Chapter 1. Since you have a limited amount of face time with a prospect, why separate the initial presentation from the demo? We have found in our experience that there are so many possible slipups in installing software in the customer environment that you may be more likely to imperil the presentation rather than save time by combining the two.

This is a good rule of thumb for any product that requires substantial effort on your part to demonstrate.

Create a checklist of configuration requirements.

Create a simple checklist of all the elements necessary to get your product installed and configured. Make sure you consider every element, including items like security settings and whether you require privileged access to the system or network. We recommend that you fax or e-mail this list to your technical sponsor and then review the list via conference call in advance. You will want to have your technical contact gather all of the necessary parties on his or her end for this call.

Give yourself plenty of lead time.

No matter how often you have installed and configured your product, you will undoubtedly run into problems at the customer site. Double any time estimates for installing your product—period. Even if a problem is not related to your own product, you will invariably be blamed for delays in starting the demo. Better that you should have a couple of hours to burn than have to delay the start of the demo because you are working through installation problems.

There is a slight downside to this approach. Your prospect may get the idea that your software is difficult to install, based on the excessive amount of time you require to set up. But most prospects will understand the virtue of this "better safe than sorry" approach, and you may be able to use any idle time to get to know some of the people at the prospect organization and to gather information about the account.

While demonstrating your system on the prospect's equipment can be a winning strategy, you may not always be able to do it. Sometimes, your product is not by nature portable, in which case you will have to bring your prospect to the product. Even if the product is portable, it may appear to be less powerful in its portable format.

For example, consider how you would demonstrate a high-end UNIX Server system. Sure, UNIX server vendors make portable workstations that are easy to carry to the customer's site. However, what if the customer is interested in taking advantage of features such as failover or load balancing? You cannot demonstrate these high-end features with a portable demonstration kit. In such cases, it makes sense to escort your customer to a demonstration site where these capabilities can be demonstrated in all of their glory.

If your product is not portable, your company will likely have a number of demonstration facilities configured for demonstration purposes. Such demonstrations can be very effective by virtue of the fact that you can get the prospect out of his or her own environment and into yours. Of course, your own environment can frequently be very comfortable, and if the prospect has to travel to reach it, you can supplement an actual demo with a business lunch or dinner, which will allow you to learn more about your prospect and his or her needs.

Bringing prospects into your demo can work against you if key members of the evaluation team are unable to attend the demonstration. One hybrid of this approach is to demonstrate key capabilities locally and then remote-connect for certain portions of the demo.

If your product is difficult to install, your prospect does not necessarily warrant the expense of a local install, or your prospect does not care to go to an external demo facility, you can opt for a "remote host" demonstration. Products like Traveling Software's LapLink or Symantec's PC-Anywhere will allow you to connect back to your system from a remote location or demo through a Web browser. Under this model, you conduct the demonstration in front of your prospect, but the actual product is running at a remote location. This is the least desirable solution of the three and is completely unworkable for many products. However, in some cases it is the only option.

The decision about which technique to use to demonstrate the actual product will vary by prospect, to a certain degree. The contents of the demo will also vary accordingly.

The Demo Script

Most products come with a standard demo script that highlights the important features of the product. Sometimes, these scripts hit the mark; sometimes, they don't. More often than not, these scripts do not do the complete job for any particular prospect. This is not marketing's fault, because in the real world one size rarely fits all. The *standard* demo script should be the starting point for the demo script that you use with any particular prospect. The standard script will provide you with a logical flow, which you can use as a framework for giving the demonstration. More than likely, your prospect will be interested in the same features that are shown as part of the standard demo script.

> *Make sure that the demonstration script matches the needs of your prospect and the critical features of your product.*

Generally speaking, the marketing campaigns and advertising materials for your product will highlight the major features of your product. Your product has some special capabilities. Prospects become interested by being exposed to these capabilities through marketing efforts.

The simplest examples of this phenomenon are advertisements for movies. Movie ads typically highlight two key features—the movie genre and the stars. Each piece of marketing material for a movie tells you in no uncertain terms what kind of movie you are going to see: comedy, horror, drama, or action. They also tell you which stars you can expect to see in the film. Now, what would happen if you actually went to the movie and the genre didn't match the ads and none of the stars who were advertised were actually in the movie?

Remember, the key features of your product should be represented in the demo script. These features should mark the starting point for your demo. If you have followed the basic game plan for attacking the sales cycle, you should have a technical match-up document with the appropriate features/benefits listed for your prospect. Compare the technical match-up document to the standard demo script; look for mismatches between the two. Consider the following:

You are a sales consultant representing the SuperServer Java Server engine. The marketing campaign for SuperServer focuses on the following elements:

- Connects to many relational database sources

- Integrates with popular Java Development Environments

- Supports Enterprise Java Beans

- Provides sophisticated transaction failover

Your prospect has identified the following technical/application requirements:

- Prospect wants to build an electronic storefront to sell office supplies

- Prospect has data in XYZ-Db and IEM Dbx databases

- Prospect develops programs with the JHacker Java Development Environment

- Programs will be developed with Java servlets that connect to the databases

- Server will run on Linux

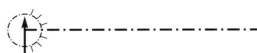

Your product comes with a standard demo script that highlights the following:

- Demo application is a virtual online bookstore
- Demo platform is an NT server
- Demo database is XYZ-Db database
- Demo script shows the completed bookstore application, then walks the prospect through the development of a new servlet and the creation of an EJB object, which is then deployed to the server
- Code is developed using the XYZ-Db JavaWriter development tool

You will notice that there is a basic match between SuperServer and the prospect's technical requirements. The overall marketing campaign focuses on some key elements of the SuperServer product, and your prospect may have been drawn in by marketing's pitch. It is not a perfect match-up, but products rarely *are* in the real world. In particular, you will notice several key intersections between marketing's pitch and the identified needs of the prospect.

Table 10.1
Matching technical requirements.

SuperServer's Advertised Capabilities:	Prospect's qualified needs:
Connects to many relational database sources	Prospect has data in XYZ-Db and IEM Dbx
Integrates with popular Java Development Environments	Prospect develops programs with JHacker Java Development Environment

The preceding pairs of capabilities and technical requirements are *direct hits*. The advertised capabilities of your product match up directly with the specific needs of your prospect. These are not just generic capabilities that are of interest to your prospect, since they match key requirements that you have identified as part of the qualification process.

Exact matches between your capabilities and your prospect's identified requirements should become focal points for your demonstration.

Your prospect has identified SuperServer as a possible solution for his or her needs, based upon the marketing campaign for SuperServer. Through a detailed qualification process, you have identified which specific technical features of SuperServer match with specific technical requirements for your prospect. Ideally, the standard demo script already focuses on some of these same intersection points. As you plan your demo for this prospect, you will need to remember to focus on demonstrating those features that the prospect has identified as being important. During the presentation and chalk talk, you will highlight the features and benefits as they relate to the client. When you get to the demonstration portion of the meeting, it is time for you to *prove* that your product actually meets these requirements.

Prospects must have proof that a product meets their technical requirements before they will buy that product.

The first part of the proof process is the demonstration. If you can show the prospect that your product actually lives up to its advanced billing, you will have already gone a long way toward fulfilling the proof steps. We don't mean to mislead you into thinking that you will not have to provide additional proof steps in the form of customer references, prototypes, or trials. Most prospects will still need to move into the evaluation phase of the sales cycle before purchasing your product. However, if you are able to show the prospect that your product can do the things that your company has said it can do, then you are much better positioned for the advanced stages of the sales cycle.

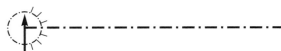

When you compare the intersection between the example prospect's requirements, your capabilities, and the demo script, you will notice that some holes exist:

- Demo database is XYZ-Db only
- Demo runs on Windows NT
- Java development is accomplished using XYZ-Db JavaWriter

You are going to have a hard time making these points of your demo stick, especially when the prospect has identified critical requirements that you cannot show with your demo.

The first element in the list is an example of a *direct hit*. As stated, a direct hit in a demo responds directly to a prospect's requirement. In this case, the prospect has the need to access XYZ-Db data and your demo platform and script uses XYZ-Db as the database. (You might argue that this case is not really a direct hit, since the prospect also wants to access IEM Dbx data, and you are not addressing this at all in the demo.) A direct hit in a demo is a lot like a hand grenade: You don't have to hit dead center to score a direct hit. You can focus, instead, on showing the XYZ-Db-specific capabilities of SuperServer and then talk about how SuperServer supports similar extensions for IEM Dbx. The result is sort of like a mathematical proof. SuperServer claims to support XYZ-Db and IEM Dbx, and you have *shown* how SuperServer supports XYZ-Db. Therefore, the reasoning goes, you *could* show how SuperServer supports similar concepts within IEM Dbx. The situation is not ideal, and you will have to address the IEM Dbx issue during the evaluation phase of the sales cycle, but you will at least have acknowledged the issue during the demo process. The prospect will likely give you a pass on the IEM Dbx issue for now because you have offered a demo proof for at least part of the requirement.

There is a simple way to find out if your plan to handle the IEM Dbx issue is acceptable to your prospect:

Confirm your demonstration plan with the prospect in advance.

You will have a better chance of ensuring that your prospect will accept the XYZ-Db-only demo by reviewing your demonstration plan with him or her before you arrive for the demo. Consider these words:

Sales Consultant: *Joe, SuperServer supports both XYZ-Db and IEM Dbx on all of our platforms. For demonstration purposes, we use XYZ-Db as the demo database, but I will come prepared to talk about our interface for IEM Dbx. Will this meet your needs for the purposes of the demo meeting?*

The prospect will usually not object to this strategy, as long as you are addressing part of the requirement. However, this is not always the case. Consider the second element in the preceding list. While the prospect plans on running SuperServer on a UNIX platform, your standard demo kit runs on the Windows NT platform. Technically speaking, this is probably not a big deal. If you have access to a Linux machine, you could probably give the demonstration without much difficulty. However, the reality is that you do not have a UNIX platform available for demonstration purposes. You will have to address this issue during your confirmation call to the prospect.

If the prospect digs in his or her heels on this issue, you will need to huddle with your sales rep to work through the problem. If the prospect is important and well qualified, you may decide to install the product on the prospect's platform for the purposes of the demo. The sales rep can often negotiate such requirements out of the demo, but you will still face the issue during the evaluation phase.

If every other vendor in the deal is in a similar situation, your sales rep should be able to finesse the issue. However, if your competitors can address an issue more directly, you endanger the sale.

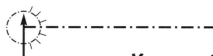

You must be careful not to be the "odd man out."

If every vendor is conducting the UNIX and you are the only one using Windows NT, you may face a very real problem. Even though your product may be the front-runner when all things are considered, if you are the only vendor not showing a critical feature during the demonstration, you may find yourself falling out of contention for the business.

The last item in the list of holes shown above is the most critical of the three from a demo perspective. Moving a demo from Windows NT to UNIX is probably not a major undertaking, especially if your product supports both platforms equally well. Even if you cannot show the server running on UNIX, operating system issues are generally not a big problem. However, using JavaWriter as the development environment for SuperServer when the prospect has standardized on JHacker is a more difficult issue to address. Since you will be using the development environment extensively throughout the demo, and since the client will be unfamiliar with your environment, you are in danger of decreasing the effectiveness of the demo.

While SuperServer takes an "agnostic" view of the development environment, making the use of *any* development environment equally possible, you as a sales consultant have no such luxury. You may have spent many hours learning to use JavaWriter in order to master the SuperServer demonstration. The conversion to JHacker is not necessarily a simple one from a resource perspective. The toughest part of this problem is that you are not actually endorsing one product over another. It just so happens that you need to use one particular third-party product to demonstrate *your* product.

If one of your competitors happens to use the preferred third-party product in his or her environment, you may find yourself in a bit of a pickle. Even though your product is perfectly capable of working with the correct product, you as a sales consultant may not be familiar with that product. There are several steps you can take to minimize the impact of this problem:

Gain agreement with your prospect on compromises in the demo in advance.

We've mentioned this tactic earlier, and it makes sense to consider it here as well. During a conversation before the actual demonstration, you will need to bring this compromise to the attention of your technical contact. This is very different than a showstopper, because your product actually *fulfills* the technical requirement (you just aren't able to show this fact during the demo). Make sure that the prospect understands that for the purposes of the demo, you will be using a similar, but different, companion product.

Do some basic research before you conduct the demo on the alternative technology.

If your company supports the alternative product, you should find white papers or promotional materials that support this fact. Bring them with you to the demo. Make a point, at the appropriate portion of the demo, of walking the prospect through these materials. You may already have other customers who are using the alternative product, so you can work with your sales rep to line them up as references. In some cases, you may not find any company data to support the use of the alternative product with your solution. If worse comes to worst, you will have to contact the company yourself to pull together the materials for the demo. Remember, your prospect is already "sold" on the alternative product, so by singing its praises, to some degree, you should find ready agreement.

While handling such mismatches can be problematic, you likely will encounter even more difficult problems while giving product demonstrations. If you look back at the requirements list, you will notice that two key features of your product are not specifically included in the prospect's requirement list: EJB support and transaction failover. These are examples of two different types of demonstration elements commonly encountered by sales consultants.

In the first case, your product supports a major capability that does not appear in the buyer's criteria list. If this feature is a major differentiator for your product, you will be sorely tempted to focus a large portion of the product demonstration on showing off this feature. However, despite the fact that this is an important feature, your prospect may not care about it in the least. You should certainly attempt to articulate the value of this feature during the slide presentation and chalk talk. But if the prospect does not respond to this pitch, do not focus on it during the demo.

Demonstrating features that do not apply to the prospect is a major tactical error.

The demonstration is part of the proof process. To waste time "proving" features that the prospect is not interested in is a counterproductive use of your sales time. If the prospect specifically tells you that he or she understands the capabilities of a certain feature and that the feature is not of interest to him or her, it is time to move on to other things.

> I have worked with many, many sales consultants who break this rule over and over again. They become fixated on a particular feature and insist on including it in the standard demo, even when prospects specifically state that they are not interested in it. *You have got to remember to concentrate your selling on the elements that the prospect is interested in buying.* This is a very difficult and subtle issue to master.
>
> On the one hand, it is important that you learn how to help your prospects to see value in the special features of your product. Once a prospect attaches value to one of your features, you will have created a significant barrier to entry for your competitors. On the other hand, you can try the prospect's patience if you continue to hit him or her over the head with the need for an unwanted feature.

Sometimes, your product will include features that are of value to the prospect, but the prospect has not grasped them as such. The feature "transaction failover" in the preceding section is an example of one such element. The prospect intends to build an online store for selling office supplies and should be interested in providing support for transaction failover. After all, such a prospect does not want to force customers to have to re-enter data if one of their servers fail. Conceptually, there is no reason that the prospect *wouldn't* want to make use of this feature. However, he or she may not attach any value to the feature either because he or she:

- Does not understand it
- Assumes it is part of every product

Sometimes, a prospect may not understand the value of the feature and how it works. You will want to make sure that you cover this feature during the presentation and chalk talk phase of the meeting. Ask for feedback and make sure that the feature is understood before you take the time to show it during the demo. Alternately, the prospect may not attach any value to the feature if he or she assumed that it is a standard component for every product. In the example case, the prospect might believe that every Java Server product supports automatic failover. If this is not the case, you need to point out this fact during the presentation and then show how it works during the demonstration.

If you look closely at the criteria list for our example sale, you will notice one additional element of concern: the application itself. We are using a "bookstore" as our example, while the prospect is planning on building an "office supply" application. The final element in your demonstration kit is the data. The demo script helps you to tell the story, but it is often the data that helps your prospects to understand how a particular feature works.

Demonstration Data

One of the most commonly overlooked elements in a demo is the data used to demonstrate the product. It doesn't matter what type of product you are selling—from routers to development tools to enterprise resource planning applications. Data is vitally important. Data is made up of two elements: the business framework on which the data is based and the actual data itself. The business framework is the fictional application upon which the demonstration is based. Vendors use a number of common applications in their product demonstrations, such as:

- Winery
- Bookstore
- Employee/Department

- Student information system
- Widget manufacturer

The type of technical product that you are selling does not matter. You will always have some sort of basic "business story" to accompany your demo. Even companies that primarily sell hardware (servers or routers, for example) will have a fictional network or server environment that they use as a means for showing off their product. Of course, applications vendors, database vendors, and development tool vendors are the most prolific designers of fictional applications. If your company is especially blessed with resources, it might build several business frameworks for each of its vertical marketplaces, such as telecom, financials, and manufacturing—but this is less common than having a single framework.

As a sales consultant, you will generally have to translate the capabilities and requirements of the sample business framework to the actual business of your prospect. With our ongoing SuperServer example, you will need to compare the bookstore application with the office supply application that the prospect plans to build. It is up to you to connect the dots for the prospect. Do not assume that prospects will be able to translate your examples to their requirements. You need to build these conceptual bridges yourself. Consider this approach:

> **Sales Consultant:** *In our example case, we have used SuperServer to build a report that shows the various books for sale in our virtual bookstore. Now, Joe, in your case you can use the very same concept to display a page of office-supply products. Although we only allow the user to enter a quantity of one for each book, it would be a simple process to have SuperServer load a page to allow the entry of a quantity value for each item as needed for your office supplies application. Let me show you where we would make the change...*

It is up to you to make the connection between your demo and your prospect's application environment. Even if your demo application offers an exact match for the prospect's line of business, it will never be as comprehensive as a "real" business. Help the prospect to "see" his or her business as it relates to the demo application. No matter which method you choose, you should consider the following:

Do not criticize your company's demo application.

Sales consultants are always tempted to curry favor with the prospect by disparaging the demo application. Don't fall into this trap. If you criticize your own demo application, you will only create an objection in your prospect's mind.

You don't have to apologize for the scope of the demo application. Remember, you are not there to sell widgets or wines from a make-believe winery; you are there to sell your product. Demo applications are supposed to be relatively simple. Their purpose is to show off concepts, and they do not have to represent a completed solution. You need not apologize for the fact that the demo application is simplistic or limited. It is a vehicle for showing off the features of your product—nothing more.

> In the case of applications software, the issue typically involves the depth and amount of data being handled by the demo application. After all, there is no "demo application" per se with enterprise resource planning products. The "demo" is the actual application, using sample data.

Do not get caught up in the non-essential elements of the demo application.

Sales consultants often go too far in another direction by spending inordinate amounts of time describing the details of the fictional application framework. The framework is supposed to be just a means of explaining how your product works. You aren't there to talk about all the ins and outs of how a winery or bookstore or widget factory works.

If one half of the demo is the application framework, the other half is the actual data that is used by the application. This data can take forms such as these:

- Customer data—names, addresses
- Product information—names, codes, prices
- Demographics
- Transactional records

- Scripts and code (application development tools)
- Network diagrams and server charts (network management tools)

The nature of your product will dictate the relative importance of data to the overall demonstration. Consider Figure 10.1:

Figure 10.1
Technology versus applications.

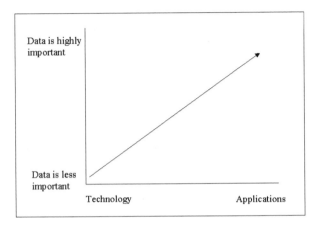

As your product moves along the horizontal scale from a pure-technology product toward a finished application, the need for appropriate data becomes much more important to the demonstration. Products such as language compilers still need data in the form of scripts and programs in order to demonstrate compilation techniques, but the meaning of the sample programs is somewhat irrelevant. To prove the virtues of a compiler, it doesn't really matter what the sample programs represent, just that they represent some type of realistic application. Utility products such as report writers and databases fall somewhere in the middle of the curve, since some data is required to show the product in action. At the far end of the spectrum are the finished applications such as business intelligence tools, enterprise resource planning applications, and customer relationship management programs. These products need data to show off their capabilities, and the more comprehensive their data sets are, the easier it will be to demonstrate these products.

The SuperServer example does not require much in the way of data for the bookstore application in order to show off the capabilities of the server. The data is somewhat incidental to the product. But what if we were selling a *complete* application for running a Web-based office supplies store to the same prospect? It would become more important to have office products and customer data within the application in order to demonstrate the various features of the product.

As a sales consultant for application-style products, you will need to identify your own sets of data that flow completely through the application. It is not enough simply to take whatever data comes with the application. If you are going to show off features of your product that involve data, you must make sure that there are sufficient data to match your demo requirements.

There is nothing worse than running queries in an application demo that do not return any data. I have seen many sales consultants talking around the fact that they cannot show a certain capability due to lack of data. In such cases, phrases like "if we had a customer record with New York as the state" comes across as "this is a bad example," or, even worse, an example of a *lack* of capability in the product. A query that returns no results usually seems like a failed query, especially since many products do not handle a blank result gracefully.

Take the time to load your demo with appropriate data.

Add and modify records in your application until you have enough information to show off all the capabilities of your product. Make sure that you fill in all the fields with interesting data. Don't leave fields blank unless you are trying to make a point about how your application handles missing data. Screens and reports that appear with blank records and fields look terrible, while those that are filled with data make your product appear to be more robust and complete.

Filling in extra data may take quite a bit of effort, but it can really make the difference in a demo. Each time a blank result or set of obviously repeated data appears, you interrupt the flow of the demo. What should be a gentle progression from one miracle of technology to another is interrupted as the audience ponders a lack of information.

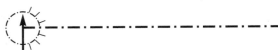

Make sure that your records contain politically correct information for race, gender, and religious references. For example, avoid examples in which you only use male bosses and female subordinates. In our diverse world, it is also important to include names other than "Joe Smith" and "Sally Green" in your data.

Diversifying your data will help more users identify with your product. Diversification will also make forms and reports look more interesting. Seeing page after page of "Joe Smith" data is exceedingly dull.

Proper data can often make applications products easier to sell. Even if your demo application features a different line of business (i.e., online bookstore vs. office supply), you can make use of demographic information appropriate to the prospect. Using address and record information that matches your prospect's vertical market segment can often help the prospect identify with your application. You can draw some of this information out of the prospect during the qualification meeting and pre-demonstration conference call.

Your demo preparation is ultimately composed of three elements: product, demo script, and data. How and where you decide to conduct the demonstration and the focal points of your demo will be heavily influenced by the needs of your prospect. The actual execution of the demo is similar to that of a presentation, but some rules are unique to the process of giving the demonstration itself, as you will see in the next section.

Demo Tips

Many of the basic tips outlined in Chapter 9, on making effective sales presentations, also apply to giving the actual product demo. However, certain aspects of the demo are unique.

You will want to limit the amount of time spent on any one activity. It helps to switch between your demo and a chalk talk every fifteen to twenty minutes, so that you can keep your prospect's attention. Switching between your slide presentation and the demo can sometimes be effective, but this is not as useful when your demo is running on the same system. To the prospect, what you are doing is just more of the same—since he or she is looking at the screen in both cases. With standard software demos, we recommend that you make use of the whiteboard as a way to break things up a little over a long demo.

The whiteboard is an excellent vehicle for explaining features that you are not able to actually demonstrate.

Take the example case of SuperServer in which you are using XYZ-Db as the demo database, but the prospect also has an interest in connecting to IEM Dbx data on a mainframe. You can show SuperServer interacting with XYZ-Db and then use the whiteboard to draw a diagram that connects SuperServer to the IEM Dbx data. This will help reinforce the fact that SuperServer can meet their needs even though you are not able to demonstrate this particular capability for them.

Address questions as they are asked.

As we discussed in Chapter 7, you will need to know what *every* feature is used for on any panel that you show in the demo. Prospects will interrupt with questions as the demo proceeds; make every effort to answer questions as they arise and then prove the answer by explaining the appropriate panels in the product. There will be cases where the question is better answered later on, especially if the answer is based upon a feature you have not yet introduced. If you defer the answer to the question, take the time to note the question on the whiteboard so that you will be sure to answer it later on. By writing the question down, you are less likely to forget to answer it and you will be subtly complimenting the originator of the question. In effect, you are acknowledging the importance of the question.

The exception to this rule is at seminars. You are often on a fixed time budget during seminars, and it is too easy to get off-track. I generally ask seminar audiences to hold their questions until the end of the seminar or to approach me during the break.

Follow through.

You may not be able to answer every question or demonstrate each and every feature that your prospect wants to see. Make sure that you keep a running list of issues as the demonstration proceeds. Be sure to review this list with your prospect at the end of the demo session. Set expectations as to when you will be getting back with these answers, and then stick to your commitment. We recommend that you always respond

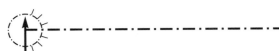

to such questions in writing and that you identify a point of contact for all communications, such as the person who is the leader of the group attending the demonstration.

Consider the complete solution.

Your product will often be used in conjunction with other hardware and software. Familiarize yourself with these ancillary products before you arrive for the demo. From the prospect's perspective, the interface between your product and the prospect's existing technology forms the "complete solution." For example, if you are representing a customer relationship management application, it pays to know at least a little bit about the relational databases on which they run. You do not have to be a database expert, but if you understand the basics, your prospect will be more comfortable knowing that you have a more complete understanding of his or her needs.

Build on a strong foundation of understanding.

On the one hand, many technology products have a rich array of functionality, and buyers want to pick the product with the best range of functionality. On the other hand, one of the most common complaints about technology products is that they are too complex. Many a deal has been lost because of this problem.

The best way to walk this tightrope is to make sure that all the standard explanations you have for your product's features start with an easily explained benefit and only gradually reach a level of more complexity and a greater number of options. If you take this approach, you will rarely find that you have left your prospects with the feeling that your product is too complex.

The impression of product complexity is often a result of confusion in the audience.

It is easy to blame a prospect's confusion on an inherent complexity in the product or presentation, rather than on a lack of understanding on their part. It is, after all, *your* responsibility to make sure the prospect understands the capabilities of your solution.

Use a structured approach for any ad hoc explanations you have to give during a demonstration. Start from a place you are sure the audience understands and then walk, step by step, to the more detailed explanation.

Make sure you are always moving toward an answer. Avoid tossing in too many details along the way. Hold off on the details until you get to the level in the product that you wish to explain. Remember, hardly anyone thinks a product is too complex if they understand what you are saying.

Solicit feedback along the way.

Allow for multiple checkpoints during the demonstration process. You need to make sure that your audience is with you and that you are not talking above or below their level. Since you are already familiar with the tenets of feature/benefit selling, this should be second nature to you during a demo process.

> **Sales Consultant:** *On this panel, you can see how the bookstore product page connects to the database and is loaded by the SuperServer engine. In your case, this page could just as easily be a set of office products, and the data could be coming from both XYZ-Db and IEM Dbx. Joe, is this how you envisioned connecting the server to these databases? Folks, before we move on, does anyone have any additional questions? ...How are we doing with the demo portion? Am I moving too fast, or do you want me to pick up the pace a little? Sue, you okay so far? Bob? Jane?*

Don't expect the audience to grant you their attention; it's up to *you* to ask for feedback and keep them involved in the demo process. Make sure that you involve every member of your audience. You will want to spread the attention around in order to keep everyone involved. Above all, remember to call everyone by name.

Don't waste time trying to fix problems.

If you hit a problem area with your demo, don't spend lots of time trying to fix it. Prospects are more forgiving than you might think, and accidents do happen. You will only draw more attention to a problem if you waste precious demo minutes trying to make something work.

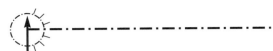

Lawyers supposedly never ask questions to which they do not already know the answer—and *you* should never try to demo a feature if you are not positive that it will work. Trying something "on the fly" almost always leads to problems. It is better to show what you can and then finish up by drawing on the whiteboard than it is to fiddle around with your product in front of the prospect. Your audience will just start feeling bad for you. But prospects generally do not buy based on pity.

> If you encounter a problem, do not make things worse by blaming the product or the operating system or claiming that the "sun was in your eyes." Unless you are sure that the problem will interfere with the rest of your demo, just move on. This does not mean that you never attempt to make it *look* like you are trying something new. I generally have some additional demo features in my repertoire that I pull out when appropriate. I always try to add value and importance to these additions by explaining that "I am trying something new, just for you."

> An effective technique to try when something unplanned *does* happen is simply to say, "You see, this is not a canned demo," and move on. You will frequently get a laugh—so long as you don't have to use this statement more than once.

Always warm up.

It is always a good idea to warm up before a demo. You can walk through the demo in the morning before a sales call at triple speed, just to get yourself into the swing of things. Performing a demo is a lot like being an actor: It helps to go through the lines in your head before you actually give the demo. No matter how many times you have demonstrated the product, each demo will vary slightly depending upon the needs of the prospect. A dry run will help you to reinforce the key ideas in your mind and to work out the kinks that always creep into even the best demonstrations.

Keep irrelevant information out of the demo.

One of the very last things that you want to keep in mind as far as demonstrations go is to *get yourself a reliable, repeatable configuration.* Do not clutter up your laptop computer with personal programs, screen savers, and icons. Keep your desktop clear and well organized, and make sure you have a mechanism for cleaning up the machine between demonstrations.

It is bad practice to show previous demo information or personal data in your demo.

Once you have shown a demo to a prospect, you will want to clean any custom information off your computer (or whatever other hardware you are using for demo purposes). You do not want Prospect B seeing what you demonstrated to Prospect A. When you give a demo that includes a special focus on the items of particular interest to your prospect, you are acting like a partner, not a vendor. If the prospect can see the demo that you gave earlier, you spoil the illusion that you are completely focused on his or her needs.

Personal content such as wallpaper or screen savers that feature your dog are also distracting, and prospects might find them offensive. Keep personal stuff off your demo machine, or at least keep it well hidden.

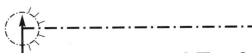

Seminars and Trade Shows

Seminars and trade shows are open to demonstrations that often require special kinds of preparation. Seminars are typically held in a hotel ballroom and are scheduled by the marketing department. Prospects in the early stages of the sales cycle will typically be herded into a seminar, where they can be pitched to in a cost-effective manner. After the seminar, interested parties will move into the prospect phase of the sales cycle, while "tire kickers," who are not really interested in purchasing your offerings, will be funneled into the lead-tracking process.

Seminars require a personal invitation on the part of your company for prospects to get a look at your technology. You owe these people special consideration by virtue of this fact. The main problem is that there are likely to be only a few good "A" prospects in the room, along with many more "B" and "C" prospects. The trick is to be polite to everyone while keeping a sharp eye out for real prospects. Trade shows are similar to seminars but are typically organized around a theme. They also involve multiple vendors (including your competitors).

Most specific industries have their own trade shows that are generally attended by a cast of thousands. From a qualifications perspective, they are worse than seminars. At least with a seminar your company extends a *personal* invitation to prospects; with a trade show, however, you are forced to deal with every Tom, Dick, and Harry who stops by your booth. While you will always have detailed information about your prospect's needs before you give a demo, you will almost never know what your prospect is looking for at a seminar or trade show.

> Trade shows are the one venue where you can add value to yourself as a new sales consultant long before you have mastered your product. The vast majority of prospects who come into your booth will not be qualified, so you can learn a lot by giving repetitive, short demos of your product.

While many of the basic tenets of giving a proper demo still apply, these alternative venues also have their own specific rules:

Stick to the company message.

While you will customize the standard demo script to address the specific needs of the client when you make individual presentations, this rule does not apply for seminars. Stick to the standard company message and keep the demonstration simple and to the point. Your demo should reinforce the major marketing message that is being put forth by your company. If a prospect becomes interested after attending the seminar, you can then take the time to qualify him or her and massage the demo to address specific needs.

Speak slowly and relax.

You can turn to many resources for getting help with public speaking; but this is a subject outside the scope of this chapter. In general, we have found that even the best presenters have a tendency to speak too quickly when presenting at a seminar. You may want to cut some material out of the demo in order to allow yourself time to speak more slowly than usual. Work hard at relaxing before you begin speaking. This will help you to slow down.

> One of the biggest mistakes you can make while presenting demos at an event is to sit down in front of your laptop and "blab away." You will definitely lose the audience this way and will often end up speaking too quickly. Display a panel and then get up from your seat and face the audience. Let your eyes move around the crowd and slowly make your point. When you've said your piece, go back to the workstation and move to the next panel.

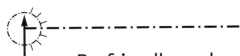

Be friendly and polite, but keep it moving.

Make an effort to "work the crowd" before and after the demo, as well as during the breaks. Don't spend time socializing with the other members of your team (there is plenty of time for this at the bar the night before!). You are there to work the crowd. Introduce yourself, exchange business cards, and be friendly. You will find that if you warm up the crowd before the show starts, they will be much easier to work with. Treat the seminar like your wedding day—make sure that you stop at every table, but do not spend too much time at any *one* table. This is particularly true with trade shows.

When you spend your time at a trade show locked in private conversation with your peers, a prospect feels like a party crasher. If you must have a chat with someone else who is staffing the booth, at least move away from the booth so as not to turn off the prospects coming in.

Keep it short and sweet.

At trade shows, you will want to keep your demo presentation short and to the point. Some vendors have addressed this problem by scheduling mini-demos every hour, while others leave it up to you as a sales consultant to make a short presentation to trade show crowds. Stick to the basic marketing message and concentrate on generating interest in your product. If you come across a prospect who appears to be qualified, get your sales rep into the loop.

Wrapping Up

Product demonstrations are the lifeblood of a sales consultant. When you score with a great product demonstration, you will find it to be one of the most rewarding experiences in your role as a sales consultant. All of the attention and focus is on you. Through you, your product comes alive. If you handle the product demonstration just right by combining your product with a good demo script, with the prospect's needs, and with an effective presentation, you can take the lead in the sales cycle.

The next phase of the selling process is the evaluation phase. If you have gained the lead after the product demonstration stage, you stand a much better chance of winning the evaluation. In the next chapter, we will look at managing the evaluation phase of the sales process in detail.

CHAPTER 11

Managing Product Evaluations

To make purchasing decisions, prospects will generally need to look at your product in more detail than your presentation and demonstration provide. This next phase of the sales cycle, known as product evaluation, is where technical decisions are made. Your company can win the deal despite losing the technical evaluation, but it is much tougher to do so. For the sales consultant, this phase represents the last of the heavy lifting as far as your involvement in the cycle goes. In this chapter, we'll take a look at the different types of product evaluations and how to manage each of them.

The Product Evaluation Phase

In most cases, prospects will come out of the demonstration phase of the sales cycle with several possible vendors in contention for the deal. In this case, the prospect will conduct a further evaluation of each of the finalists.

Occasionally, a prospect will complete a product evaluation for only one vendor, usually because of resource limitations on the part of the prospect team. However, even in these situations, you can lose the deal if you perform poorly in the evaluation phase.

During product evaluation, the prospect looks for *proof points* on which to make a decision among the remaining vendors. Proof points verify all the claims that you made during the earlier stages of the sales cycle. From a technical perspective, the product evaluation phase boils down to proving that you meet the prospect's identified technical requirements.

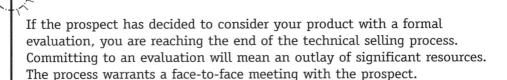

If the prospect has decided to consider your product with a formal evaluation, you are reaching the end of the technical selling process. Committing to an evaluation will mean an outlay of significant resources. The process warrants a face-to-face meeting with the prospect.

The evaluation phase of the sales cycle should always start with a planning meeting.

The sales rep will manage the evaluation meeting itself, but you will be intimately involved in the meeting from an information-gathering perspective. Although evaluation planning sessions are highly technical events, they also involve the commitment of resources. The sales rep has the authority to decide whether to commit these resources. During the planning meeting, it will be up to you to document the four elements of the evaluation, described below.

There is one important rule for you to follow during this meeting:

Do not agree to any of the prospect's demands—let the sales rep or account manager negotiate the terms and conditions of the evaluation.

You do not have the authority as a sales consultant to commit to any specific evaluation steps. The sales rep has to be the one either to agree or disagree to any element of the evaluation. The product evaluation stage signals the start of the negotiation process for your sales rep. He or she will want to use the evaluation process as a means of drawing concessions out of the prospect. Consider the following exchange:

Joe Prospect: *We'd also like to get a copy of your documentation for all of our evaluation team members.*

Sales Consultant: *Sure Joe, no problem.*

This exchange represents a major tactical error on the part of the sales consultant. The sales rep is in charge of the deal; therefore, he or she is responsible for agreeing or disagreeing to any request that the prospect makes. In most cases, the rep will use these exchanges to get the prospect to put some "skin in the game" as is illustrated in the following dialogue:

Joe Prospect: *We'd also like to get a copy of your documentation for all of our evaluation team members.*

Sales Representative: *That's no problem Joe, I'm happy to do it. However, we are selling a lot of product right now and extra documentation sets are at a premium. I am happy to get this for you, but I would really appreciate it if you could get a copy of our contract proposal to your legal team in parallel.*

The prospect still got his documentation—but the sales rep was able to extract a condition. As a sales consultant, making the mistake of agreeing to a demand is very difficult to undo. It is much safer to let the sales rep run the meeting and have him or her control your participation in the discussion. You need to be part of the meeting, since many of the issues that will arise are technical in nature, but you want the sales rep to control its flow.

It is important to determine a game plan with your sales rep before you begin the actual planning meeting. Some reps that I have worked with preferred that I remain quiet during the planning meeting and then debrief with them after the meeting. As long as you can raise issues without creating objections, most sales reps will prefer that you speak up during these meetings.

There are essentially four elements to the evaluation phase that you need to negotiate with your prospect:

- What does the prospect want to prove? *(Technical proof points)*
- How does he or she want to prove it? *(Evaluation process)*
- Who will be involved in the evaluation? *(Team members)*
- Which vendors are participating in the evaluation? *(Competitors)*

We will explore each of these elements in detail. At this point, it is important for you to understand how they all fit together. The starting point for the evaluation process is to understand exactly *what* the prospects want to prove through the evaluation process. They created a set of technical requirements and you matched your product's capabilities to this list during the presentation and demonstration. If they have agreed to proceed to an evaluation, they are looking for proof points that your product actually fulfills these requirements.

Once they have decided what they want to prove, they need to determine the methodology to use. Do they want to install and use the product in their environment, or would they prefer to talk with existing customers? In a word, *how* do they plan on conducting the evaluation?

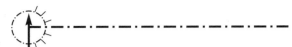

You and your prospect will be committing resources to the process, so you will need to identify what these resources are. You need to know which members of the prospect team will be responsible for which parts of the evaluation.

Finally, you also need to know which other solutions the prospect is planning on evaluating. When do they plan to complete the evaluation process? Although, as we will discuss in Chapter 15, "Working the Competition," you should always be able to find out who your competitors are, you also should expect at this point in the sales cycle to have developed a good enough professional relationship with your prospect to get a straight answer about your competitors.

These four elements are inextricably linked. This is what makes the evaluation process so difficult. Each element is affected by the other elements. A change in one has a domino effect on the others. In the following sections, we'll take a more detailed look at each of these elements.

Technical Proof Points

The technical requirements are the list of features and functions that you created as part of the qualification process. They serve as a type of contract with your prospect. If you successfully prove that your product meets the necessary technical requirements, then you should win the evaluation and secure the deal. During the qualification process, you built up a list of technical requirements and then planned your presentation and demonstration events around these requirements. You also applied the special capabilities of your product to the qualification set. Ideally, during the presentation and demonstration phase, you will have successfully fueled a demand in your prospect for features *specific* to your product.

During the evaluation, your prospect will want to see proof of two types of technical items:

- Critical items
- Your product's unique features that caught their attention during the demonstration process

As part of the qualification process, the prospect identified a list of critical technical requirements. The prospect now believes that your offering matches these requirements in one way or another; this is why you have reached the evaluation phase. Your prospect will now want proof that you actually meet these critical requirements.

Let the prospect build
the revised list of critical items.

You will want to let the prospect build a revised list of critical items for the evaluation. Although you already have a list of items that you created during the qualification process, it is now time to refresh the list. Since the evaluation phase is designed to prove your capabilities in the *prospect*'s mind, your own list is no longer absolutely relevant. If your competitors have shown off some special functionality of their own, this functionality may end up becoming a critical item in the evaluation. When the prospect is asked to build the list of critical items at this stage, you can compare this list with the initial list. Any new items and any items that have been dropped from the critical list are worthy of discussion. Consider the following criteria list:

Critical items identified during the initial qualification:

- Must support UNIX, Windows NT, and Linux
- Must include support for servlets
- Must support Java 2 EE

Revised list:

- Must support Windows NT
- Must include support for servlets
- Must support Java 2 EE

Here, the prospect dropped support for UNIX and Linux off the list of critical items. The question is *why?* It is possible that the needs of the prospect have changed. He or she may have found it difficult to find a sufficient number of vendors with solutions that matched the requirements. However, it is more likely that one of your competitors has successfully convinced the prospect to use his or her company's solution, and that the prospect has dropped the requirement because your competitor does not support it. You need to find out why the items were dropped. The answer will tell you a lot about where you stand in the deal. Consider the following exchange:

Sales Consultant: *Joe, I noticed that your evaluation criteria does not include testing the product on either UNIX or Linux. Are these platforms still important to you in your application?*

Joe: *Actually, we've decided to run the application server on the Windows NT platform. We've felt that Linux is too complicated for us from a support perspective, and UNIX is too expensive as a Java server platform.*

Maybe Joe is being square with you, or maybe one of your competitors has provided Joe with the reasons that he is giving you for no longer needing UNIX and Linux . It works the other way too—you may notice that *new* critical requirements have appeared as a result of the competition's pitch as well. Your job is to notice discrepancies and call them to your sales rep's attention. The sales rep will then decide on how to proceed in light of the change. In some cases, the prospect will include your special features as critical items for the technical evaluation. This is a good sign that you are in the pole position as far as the deal goes. Your competitors will have a hard time matching the revised requirements in such cases.

> More often than not, your prospect
> will be interested in taking a closer look
> at your special features during the evaluation
> process, but he or she will not include
> them on the critical items list.

In most cases, new requirements appear on the criteria list as a result of the selling efforts of you and your competitors. This gives your sales rep some room to negotiate. It makes sense that your prospect wants to take a closer look at your special features. It also makes sense from a sales perspective to attach some value to these features. If none of your unique capabilities shows up on the revised technical criteria list, it's probably a bad omen for you. It is rare for two competing products to have exactly the same set of features. If you have had any success selling to the prospect during the earlier phases of the sales cycle, some unique capabilities of your product should make their way to the critical items list.

— • — • —

A unique feature of an application development tool that I represented was its capability to support multiple operating platforms including Windows and UNIX. Our primary competitor in this market was PowerBuilder, which was limited to supporting Windows-based platforms at the time.

The inclusion of proof steps involving UNIX platforms in the evaluation phase was a strong indicator that our message had gotten through. Conversely, if this requirement had been either dropped from technical criteria, or not considered altogether, we were probably in trouble, which could have called for a re-evaluation of our participation in the sales cycle.

Once you have the list of items the prospect intends to test out, you need to learn how the prospect plans to accomplish the testing process.

Evaluation Process

The requirements list forms the heart and soul of the evaluation phase, but the process still requires more effort. The prospect has a defined set of needs, and you have now offered up your product as a solution. It all looks good thus far, but how do you prove that your product is all you claim it to be? Sometimes, the prospect will have a pre-defined game plan to accomplish the testing process; other times it will be left up to you, as the sales team, to recommend a strategy. There are almost as many ways to complete the proof process as there are products in the market. You will constantly be faced with new evaluation plans. Despite this fact, there are a number of basic evaluation strategies, as listed below:

- Customer references
- Customer site visits
- Trials
- Prototypes
- Benchmarks
- Corporate site visits

Customer References

Customer references are often the simplest and most direct method for providing proof points for the prospect's technical requirements. Almost every deal will involve customer references to one degree or another, but they are more important in the later stages of a product's lifecycle. Prospects like to talk to customer references; doing so requires fewer resources and less work on their end. Customers are also thought to be more forthcoming than you might be.

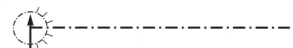

Most good sales teams develop a network of positive customer references within their territory. These customers generally know how the game is played. They are not going to lie on your behalf to the prospects (nor do you want them to). At the same time, they are unlikely to raise new objections or be overly zealous in pointing out the flaws of your product. As a sales consultant, you are generally going to be less involved in the actual reference visit or call, but there are some things that you can do to make the process go more smoothly.

Prepare a briefing document on the customer reference for the sales rep.

The briefing document is a short review of the prospect's technical requirements. It describes what the prospect expects to do with your product. Your sales rep can use this document to brief the reference customer on what to expect from the prospect. This will give your sales rep a chance to qualify the customer as to his or her willingness to offer proof points for the various technical requirements. There will be cases in which a single customer cannot provide testimony for all of the technical requirements. In such cases, you may have to create multiple briefing documents for each customer to whom the prospect will be speaking.

Use your network of fellow sales consultants to locate appropriate customer references.

Your team members in other territories may have some experience with similar prospects and customers in their own regions. It's worth your time to send out e-mails and make a few phone calls to see if any of your compatriots have run into similar evaluation scenarios.

Of course, when you are on the receiving end of one of these types of e-mails, you should also try to help out. You will find that when you need help, you will get a better response from fellow sales consultants who have benefited from your assistance in the past.

Customer references are typically combined with other evaluation process events.

Customer Site Visits

Site visits are much more resource-intensive, since they require your customer to host the prospect over an extended period of time. While a reference call can often be handled in a half hour, a site visit can take a half day or more of your customer's time. There is the added effort for your customer of having to escort the prospect around and interrupt normal business operations. Although a customer site visit can be an incredibly effective selling vehicle if done right, these visits can also be incredibly resource intensive. Furthermore, most of the resources have to come from your customer's organization. Site visits are much more common for products that are too large or complex to evaluate in any other way. Large-scale enterprise resource planning applications such as SAP, XYZ-Db, and PeopleSoft are often evaluated through customer site visits because of the complexity involved in evaluating these products.

Site visits are easier to arrange when the majority of your customer base has evaluated the solution in the very same manner. That's why it is much more common with ERP packages and CRM software—most customers use site visits when they make their decision, too.

While you and your sales rep are responsible for arranging the site visit, some prospects will not want you to attend the actual event. However, keep the following tip in mind:

Letting prospects attend site visits on their own is asking for trouble.

Always be involved in the actual site visit itself. You do not want to rely on interpretations from either the customer or the prospect about how the site visit was conducted. *You* need to be there to make sure that the prospect gets the needed information and to protect the interests of your customer. If you are not present, you risk losing control of this part of the sales process.

> I have attended site visits in which the prospect started bullying my customer or asking for information that was proprietary to the customer's business. Losing a sale is bad enough, but getting one of your customers mad at you in the process of losing the sale is even worse.

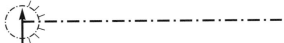

There are several key things to remember when mapping out a site visit.

Brief the customer in advance of the reference visit or call.

You should spend some time with your customer before the visit. You will have the technical requirements document in hand before the site visit, and you should take the time to brief the customer before the meeting. The customer may not be schooled in the art of technical selling and will find it helpful to be instructed about what the prospect needs to see during the site visit. We're not suggesting that you try to put words in the customer's mouth, but rather that you guide the discussion toward those critical items that need to be "proved." Remember to keep the technical requirements document in mind at all times. You do not want to go to the expense of a site visit, only to have the prospect claim that he or she didn't get the data needed to make a decision. Site visits are partly social and partly business—and the business portion is primarily geared toward nailing the proof points.

Site visits require a lot of your time and effort—indirectly.

It is a common misconception that site visits do not require much time and effort for sales consultants. You are likely to acquire extra customer work as "payment" for the site visit. Customers will always be short on technical resources, and there is nothing that they would like better than to get some of your valuable time. This is part of the cost of doing business and it's the right thing to do. The trick is to make sure that your sales rep partner understands these indirect costs. Sure, the site visit itself might only take a day of your time, but the extra work that you need to do for your customer may involve a serious time commitment. Factor this into the equation when you plan your schedule.

Keep a low profile during customer reference visits.

Your main job during the site visit is to assist and observe. Keep your direct participation to a minimum. The sales rep will help to keep the meeting on track; but *your* time is better spent listening to the conversation and taking copious notes for the debriefing after the meeting. Listening to your customer talk about your product is a lot like watching your child star in a school play. Your heart will be in your mouth the whole time. Don't worry about it: Prospects tend to be very forgiving with other customers. They would prefer to hear what they perceive as "the truth" about a product, warts and all, than hearing an overly positive report. If you get nervous about some of the things a customer is saying, hold back. If you think the customer has truly misrepresented your product, deal with it later. You don't want to make things worse by trying to talk over your customer during the meeting.

Trials

Your prospects will often want to try the products themselves. We call this a trial. Trials are inherently the most dangerous of all evaluations because circumstances are not completely under your control. However, a well-conducted trial can seal the deal for you because the prospect gets to see your product work in his or her own environment. Trials can eliminate some of the wariness over the viability of your solution, since the customer gets to see how the product operates in the real world. Trials are more commonly used with application development products, databases, and utilities. They are less commonly used in large-scale enterprise applications.

> With the rise of the Internet, many high-tech companies are adopting the strategy of offering free trial versions of their products that can be downloaded over the Web or shipped out on a CD-ROM. This is not the kind of trial that we are discussing, since it does not really involve sales consulting resources. There is not a lot of technical selling involved in these deals—the company relies on the focus of its marketing message to reach the target prospects.

Sales consultants are normally heavily involved in trials, but you cannot be with the prospect at every moment. Problems will arise and you will have to deal with them on the fly. Conducting a successful trial requires some very special skills and strategies. Here are some tips:

Always have a written trial plan.

Without a written trial plan, you are dead meat—period. The purpose of an evaluation is for the prospect to get proof points for the technical requirements. A written trial plan that reflects these requirements will give the trial a focus. Without a plan, the prospect will undoubtedly spend endless cycles on tangential issues. The trial will linger on and on. Will prospects get sidetracked even with a plan in place? Sure, they will. But if you have a trial plan, you will have a document that you can use to get the trial back on track. Trial plans should have the basic elements shown in Table 11.1:

Table 11.1
Trial plan elements.

Who	*Who,* from both sides of the table, is going to be involved in the trial?
What	*What* are they going to test? This list should match their critical requirements.
Where	*Where* are they going to conduct the trial? On which machines are they going to load the software? You should get critical configuration information about the machine(s) to be used in the trial.
When	*When* are they going to complete the trial? Do they have a timeline for the evaluation?

The trial plan has to be written before you install your product at the prospect's location. The written plan is the ticket to the show—no ticket, no trial.

Install the product yourself for all trials.

First impressions are lasting impressions. Take the time to install the product at your prospect's location. In some cases, the installation itself is part of the trial and the prospect will want to perform this task alone. You should still be there to shepherd the process through. If the prospect has problems with the installation, you will hear about this throughout the trial.

A sales consultant's measure of his or her product often includes a rating of the *OBE*—the out-of-the-box experience. If the product is easy to install and prospects can work with it without training, it is said to have good OBE. Conversely, products that are difficult to install or that have a steep learning curve are said to have a bad OBE. The worse the OBE, the more important it is for you alone to get the product installed and configured for your prospect.

Trials should involve some training.

Trials go much more smoothly if the prospect knows what to do. As a sales consultant, you will have to make a judgment call as to whether the prospect needs to attend formal product training before using your product. Most enterprise-class products are too complicated for the prospect to use without some formal training. You have two choices: Either give a "mini-class" yourself, or get the prospect's evaluation team to attend product training. Formal product training is a double-edged sword, as the prospect will get a firm understanding of your product but will also get exposure to some of the uglier stuff, too.

On the whole, we recommend that prospects go to formal product training if they are going to conduct a trial. Exceptions can be made if the product is incredibly easy to use or does not require much interaction on the part of the prospect. For example, you might be able to install a router for a 30-day trial without formal training. However, I would never let a prospect conduct a trial of an application development tool without formal training of some sort.

If prospects decline formal training on the product, take this as a sign that they will be giving a lot of weight to the "ease-of-use" of the product, whether they say so or not.

Manage the trial yourself.

It will be up to you to keep the prospect on track. The simplest way to accomplish this task is to hold frequent checkpoints with the evaluation team. You do not want to let a week go by before checking in with the prospect to see how the evaluation is going. In most cases, you will be on site for the start of the trial (and for the first few days) to make sure that things get started on the right foot. After that, it is important to

hold frequent, routine checkpoints on the status of the trial. The goal is to keep track of two issues:

- Problems
- Timeline

Problems will inevitably occur during the trial period. The sooner you know about them, the easier it will be to deal with them. Certain problems will bring the trial to a halt until they are resolved. Prospects are usually pretty good about calling you when there are problems, but sometimes telephone technical support is the first line of defense. In such cases, the prospect might not call you to keep you in the loop, so it becomes your responsibility to call and stay on top of any issues. You also want to make sure that they are sticking with the timeline that has been established for the trial. The longer the trial drags on, the harder it becomes to bring it to a close. If you hold frequent checkpoints, you will be able to prevent the trial from getting too far off track.

Schedule a summary event for all trials.

Typically, the prospect will have a subset of the evaluation team working on the trial itself. This sub-team will keep the rest of the organization informed as the trial proceeds, but the larger group will not necessarily be involved in day-to-day operations. Once the trial has been completed, it is very useful to hold a meeting with the entire evaluation team (and any other interested parties) to present the results of the trial and show off the work that was done.

Make the evaluation team members part of the presentation at the summary event.

The sales team will be responsible for arranging and coordinating this presentation, but you should be sure that the hands-on evaluators are part of the presentation, too. From a psychological perspective, it helps prospects to buy into your product, since they feel like they are part of the solution. You do not want to make any of the team members uncomfortable, so don't make anyone a presenter who is reluctant to do so. There will always be one or two players on whom you can rely to help with the presentation. The presentation should begin with introductory slides to explain the process. It should then segue into a demonstration, and finish with a set of closing slides that "sum up" the trial. We recommend that you spend a day with the prospect before the presentation to "clean up" any issues and formalize the presentation itself.

If the product does not lend itself to a summary demo event, you can always "rig up" something. Take some digital pictures of the product in action with the prospect or create graphs that summarize performance results. The demo itself isn't as important as getting the team members involved in the presentation.

When the lights are on, many prospects will rise to the moment. We often find that prospects become much more positive and excited about the product as they make their presentation to the other members of their company. They tend to get swept up in the enthusiasm, and this carries over to the audience. You can help this process along by singing the praises of all of the team members on an individual basis:

> **Sales Consultant:** *Jack did a marvelous job getting the server up and running, as you can see here. Sue was responsible for building all of these data entry screens to fill the database using SuperServer. Sue, maybe you could talk about the process that you followed to build the screens...*

The trick is to get prospects talking about the product. They have all heard *you* talk about it—now, it is time to get them to talk about the benefits in their own words.

One common variation on the trial theme is called an *acceptance,* which can be used when you are the only vendor remaining in the evaluation. An acceptance follows the same plan as a regular trial, but the prospect agrees to buy the system at a negotiated price if the product meets all of the requirements as specified in the trial plan. In the case of an acceptance, winning the trial means winning the deal, so it is doubly important to stay close to the prospect during the acceptance process.

Prototypes

Prototypes are variations on the trial. The main difference is that with a prototype, *you* will drive the hands-on process. In a trial situation, the prospect is in the driver's seat from a control perspective. Sure, you have put a plan for the trial in place, but the prospect implements it and you merely serve as an advisor. In the case of a prototype, the roles are reversed. Prospects decide what they want to see and you, as the sales consultant, provide the hands-on expertise.

Prototypes are most often used when your product has a steep learning curve or requires a complex installation that is not practical for a trial.

Consider the following example:

You are working for ABC Robotics, manufacturers of oversized inventory control robots that pull bins from multi-story parts warehouses.

Let's say that the prospect wants to see these robots in action, and that he or she needs proof that the robots can handle the complex arrangement of bins that is required. It is unlikely that you would install the robots at your prospect's location, since the installation would probably take weeks. In a case like this, it makes sense to bring your prospects to your location to conduct the prototype. You will still create a trial plan in cooperation with your prospect, but you will act as the driver for the evaluation.

Prototypes can also be used to speed up an evaluation, since you can skip the formal training altogether. You will be driving and the prospect will never be left alone with the product, so training is no longer necessary. Prototypes can still stretch over a number of days, and you will still want to conduct a summary presentation.

Benchmarks

Benchmarks have gone out of style to a large degree, but they were once the preferred method of evaluating relational database engines. As Web application servers grow in importance in the marketplace, we are starting to see the benchmark re-emerge.

A benchmark is a special type of trial in which the performance of the product is the key criteria for the evaluation process. Benchmarks are most often used when the prospect is trying to decide among a group of products that all have the same basic set of features. The one element that the prospect can use to differentiate between products in such cases is performance.

Vendors have tried to use benchmarking standards, such as the Transaction Processing Council (TPC) suite for RDBMS engines, as a means of giving the public unbiased benchmarks for a category of product. The idea is to use an agreed-upon suite of tests as a measure of performance in order to minimize the amount of benchmarking in the field.

While product marketing has made great use of these efforts with glitzy advertisements that graph the industry-leading performance of the product, these benchmark suites have not really helped the cause of the sales consultant.

Prospects generally view these standardized benchmarks with a heavy degree of skepticism. In many ways, they are right. The classic TPC benchmark suite (one of several offered by the TPC) shows very high transaction performance numbers, but I would be hard-pressed to tell you how they would translate into performance measures for a real application.

In the early days of the RDBMS marketplace, most users ignored the application development tools that were packaged with the database and built most applications in "C" code. Since all of the database products were SQL-based, they were all somewhat interchangeable. Each product did have some unique features, but performance was the key differentiator in many ways. The application server marketplace (and the OLAP marketplace) are showing similar trends. The tools are very similar in many cases, and it is the performance of the server that makes or breaks the deal.

Know the performance parameters of your product.

Most products have little features or anomalies that make them faster at some things than at others. If your product is likely to be involved in benchmarks, it pays to understand its performance characteristics. Product engineering and other sales consultants are the best sources for this information, because they will have direct experience with how the product performs.

Set expectations for the benchmark up front.

Find out exactly what the prospect is proposing to test and how he or she proposes to measure and compare the results. You will want to get this information up front and then go over it in detail with a performance specialist within your company. Find a sales consultant with experience or get in touch with product engineering directly. The key is to understand how your product is likely to perform before you even start the benchmark. It is much easier to try to convince a prospect to run a test

using different criteria before any benchmark results are in. Once the numbers are in, the prospect will find most of your arguments about the testing methodology to be self-serving.

The major areas of discussion are going to concern those tests that favor a competitor, yet are not indicative of real-world conditions. Benchmark tests should reflect the actual needs of the prospect and not some fictional standard. Tests that favor one of your competitors should be noted up front. If a test is slanted too much in favor of a competitive product, you are probably better off declining to participate in the benchmark.

Bend the rules of the benchmark to your advantage.

Most benchmarks will come with a set of standards that define the "rules" of the benchmark. You should take these rules at face value and try to implement tricks to get the best performance possible out of your product. Remember, a benchmark is a contest with a single result—a number that indicates the overall performance on the benchmark.

If you see an undefined area that might let your product score higher on the benchmark, take advantage of it. Don't even question your prospect as to whether you should be allowed to take advantage of the undefined area, if it will result in a better benchmark for your product. You should, of course, be aware that you are using a special "trick" to boost your performance in the benchmark, just in case your prospect asks or if the competition brings it up.

The bottom line is that no benchmark reflects a real-life situation. Real life is far too messy for adequate comparisons. To properly understand how a product performs over the course of a month or two in a real-life situation, the prospect would have to use all the products under evaluation in actual situations—which would require him or her to commit an enormous amount of resources.

We are not telling you to lie or mislead your prospect. If you do use certain advantages of your product to gain an edge in a benchmark, you should at least let your prospect know after the evaluation has been completed, in the form of a briefing or documentation on performance optimization. But the winner of a benchmark is the vendor with the best score, not the best excuses. Your competitors will probably be trying everything they can to achieve the best score—so you should, too.

One of my first assignments as a sales consultant was to work on a benchmark between different 4GL vendors for their performance on a set of programs supplied by the prospect. We turned in the best benchmark score—primarily because we organized the underlying data in a way that allowed very rapid access, while our competitor did not.

Would a prospect be able to organize the data in a similar manner in the real world? To some extent, yes, but certainly not to the lengths we went to in the benchmark. This benchmark experience taught me a valuable lesson—it's not just two products competing, but the complete vendor packages, which include the product and the expertise of the sales teams.

Prepare for the worst.

If you are not going to win a benchmark, it is important for you to prepare your sales representative for the bad news—in advance. Your rep will have to convince your prospect that your product does not have to win the benchmark; it just has to be fast enough to do the job. You will be unlikely to convince the prospect's team that "fast enough" is good enough without calling on higher-level executives in the prospect's organization. If your sales rep does not already have a good working relationship with these executives, then you might be in trouble.

Of course, your product will need to have some other advantages that alleviate the performance disadvantage. A talented sales rep can sell around performance issues, but you are in a different position. You will be forced to deal with the prospect during the benchmark if your numbers are sub-par. If you are able to set expectations up front and communicate with your sales rep during the benchmarking process, you may be able to win the deal, even if your product is not the fastest.

If your product performs significantly better than those of your competition, then benchmarking can often be a winning strategy. While benchmarking is resource-intensive, it is even more so for your competitors, who will be forced to spend extra cycles trying to squeeze precious improvements out of their systems to compete with you.

This is an especially good strategy when your product is weak in other areas such as feature support, usability, and company size.

Benchmarks are a game. The best strategy is to take a two-pronged approach—either win the game or reduce the importance of the results in the overall purchase decision.

Corporate Site Visits

Corporate site visits require you to escort the prospect to your corporate headquarters. A typical corporate visit will include discussions with your executive management as well as product-related activities, such as seeing beta features of your product. You will be playing host while your prospect listens to your executive management. Corporate site visits are especially resource-intensive because they involve resources outside your sphere of control. Corporate visits are typically used for large enterprise-class sales or site license deals; you will normally conduct them for only a few prospects in any given year. They are more common for enterprise application sales and large computer hardware deals in which trials and prototypes are somewhat difficult to arrange.

Most of the large computer manufacturers, such as IBM, Sun, and Hewlett-Packard, all have corporate site visit teams to pitch large clients. It is not always practical for these vendors to install hardware at an account for a trial. The corporate visit serves as a viable proof step in these cases. All major vendors have large-scale laboratories at headquarters where they have an array of their latest equipment for demonstration purposes.

Corporate visits are the ultimate schmoozing event. The prospect is surrounded by an army of your associates doing their utmost to sell your solution. If your company has an impressive headquarters operation, the visit can be an ideal event for closing your prospect. Although you will be less directly involved in the actual event, you will be heavily involved in the planning stages and behind the scenes.

Get a fixed point-of-contact for corporate visits at headquarters.

Most large corporations have dedicated teams that handle all aspects of the site visit from a logistical perspective. They can handle anything from catering, to hotel reservations, to social events for your prospect. If your company does not have such a team, it will fall to you to manage the logistics. In either case, you need to set up a single point of contact at corporate headquarters for communication. It's important to have a single point of contact on both sides, and it will typically be the sales rep on your end. You can be part of the conversations between the sales rep and the headquarters contact person, but let your sales rep serve as the contact point. Headquarters visits can be used to address technical requirements, but they are also social events. Your sales rep is the captain of the team from your local perspective.

Identify the critical issues and the appropriate headquarters resources.

The purpose of the headquarters visit is to make the prospect feel comfortable with your company and your product so that he or she will make a purchasing decision. While there is typically a standard corporate visit pitch, there will also be some issues unique to the needs of the prospect. You need to use your technical requirements document to identify issues that need to be "proved" to the prospect. Once you have organized this list, you will have to coordinate with your contact back at headquarters to identify resources needed for addressing these issues. Some members of the team will remain consistent across prospects—such as the vice president of sales, the chief financial officer, the company president, and other members of the executive team.

Except with the largest customers, you will be unable to get all of these heavyweights together for every customer visit. Be sure that you emphasize to your prospects that you are bringing the *right* people to the presentation, so they will not feel slighted if a full all-star team does not show up. Even the smallest prospect wants to feel deserving of the attention of the highest levels of a vendor's organization—regardless of whether the proposed purchase calls for this involvement.

However, each prospect will have needs that will require specialized presentations and team members—product managers, technical support managers, or even engineering resources. Your job is to help the sales rep identify and schedule the right resources for the visit.

Create a written briefing document for headquarters personnel involved in the visit.

As with customer site visits, it is vitally important that you create a briefing document for the corporate visit. You need to brief the team at corporate headquarters on the specific needs of the prospect, and you should do this in advance of the event itself. A thorough briefing document can be sent to the team members ahead of your visit. You can use this document to walk them through the prospect's specific needs. Make sure that you include the following information:

- Business background of the prospect
- Biographical sketches of the prospect's team members
- Application description—how does your prospect plan on using your product?
- Technical requirements
- Specific questions that need to be addressed

The corporate presenters will use the data in this document to customize their presentations, and you will need to help them through this process.

The higher you go in your organization, the more necessary a detailed briefing document becomes. Frequently, the executive management in your company will be basically wheeled in to a corporate site visit, so the less time they have to spend preparing for an intelligent conversation with your prospect, the more likely it is that this type of discussion will actually take place.

Brief the corporate team in advance.

You will want to get out to corporate headquarters a day ahead of your prospect's scheduled visit. This will give you a chance to brief the presenters on an individual basis to make sure they understand the prospect's needs.

The briefing document should arrive in advance of your visit, so that the corporate team has time to study the information before you arrive. This will allow you to brief them quickly without having to take up too much of their time. It will also give you a chance to take stock of the various presenters, so you will know how you might need to pitch in.

Many of the team members at headquarters will be experts in their respective fields, but they are not necessarily experts in making technical sales presentations. During the briefing session, you can work out a strategy for staying involved in the presentations as necessary. Some of the corporate presenters may have come from the sales consulting ranks and will be experienced in making technical presentations—if so, just let them work their magic. Other members of the team may be less experienced; you will have to work out a game plan with them for acting as a coach when necessary. Ideally, you will get them to involve you directly. In the worst case, you can use the question-and-answer session at the end of each presentation to draw the data out of the key presenters, as in this example:

> **Sales Consultant:** *Bob [engineering manager], the folks at ABC Corp. are very interested in working with Enterprise Java Beans 1.1 with SuperServer. Could you spend a few minutes talking about how they can use our EJB interface to access their mainframe data?*

You do not want to create a presentation for them, but you want to make sure that your prospect's needs are addressed. Brief the presenters in advance, and monitor the presentations as they are given.

Evaluation Team Members

The evaluation process itself is an important component to the overall sale, but an equally important piece of the puzzle is made up of the team members involved in the evaluation. Regardless of which type of evaluation process prospects elect to use, they will typically deploy a subset of their staff for the evaluation phase. Presentation and demonstration sessions will be filled with staff from the prospect's organization who have an interest in your solution in some manner.

However, many of these people will not be central to the evaluation itself. The size and composition of the "hands-on" team will vary with the type of solution that you are selling. For example, application development tools will always be evaluated by the development team, which itself may or may not be part of the central information technology organization. Companies that have a large application development staff will typically designate a smaller task force to handle the hands-on portion of the sales cycle. Tactical applications such as general ledger or accounts payable will have different sized teams and will be composed of different players. In these cases, the hands-on team will be composed of staff from the accounting or finance departments with one or two representatives from the IT staff. Enterprise applications such as enterprise resource planning and customer relationship management solutions often require multiple hands-on teams with different specialties. The prospect might field several different teams of evaluators (inventory, accounting, purchasing) to focus on each subspecialty of your solution.

The composition of the evaluation team will have a significant impact on your success.

The make-up of the evaluation team will have serious implications for the evaluation—both positive and negative. In general, you want the team to be composed of senior people with authority and experience, and you want the smartest people possible. Senior staff generally have the connections with upper management and the respect of the junior staff members; therefore, their opinions often carry much more weight during the technical evaluation. When you have problems in a trial or prototype (and you will), the senior people can save you from disaster.

> I once worked a trial in which the CD was corrupted and the back-up CD that I was carrying had also gone bad. The prospect team members were skeptical that two CDs could be corrupted and insisted that my product was just unreliable. One of the senior systems managers at the account was part of the evaluation team, and he weighed in with the opinion that media problems were a very common occurrence with all products. His opinion swayed the mood of the group, allowing me to steer the team to spend the day working on the whiteboard while we waited for a new CD to arrive by Federal Express. The whiteboard session turned out to be a great day of interaction with the prospect team, and the new CD was used to install the software the next morning without difficulty.

Your evaluation team members should have four vital characteristics:

- Authority
- Respect
- Intelligence
- Impartiality

Evaluation team members with *authority* can help you to cut through red tape, close down trivial issues, and allow you to keep the focus on the proof steps. Although it is unlikely that you will have a vice president or director actively involved in the hands-on evaluation, a person in this position may act as a sponsor for the evaluation.

You also want your technical lead to have the respect of the other team members. Authority without the respect of the other team members results in a "Dilbert" boss—and this is not good. Authority provides help to get issues closed, but respect is crucial in getting the rest of the evaluation team to tow the line.

Respect itself has several facets, one of which is basic *intelligence*. In many instances, the smartest member of the evaluation team can also be the most obnoxious, which can be detrimental to your evaluation. Team members who lord it over the rest of the evaluation team can hurt you regardless of whether they are "for" your product or against it. Intelligence paired with respect is a much better combination.

The only remaining element is *impartiality* (and it's only important if you are not in the lead spot). If you are not the leading product going into an evaluation, impartiality can be an important component in the evaluation. It is possible to come from behind to win a deal in the evaluation stage, but you need your prospect to be open-minded in order to do so. Certain products will look better during the demonstration and presentation phase, while others are more impressive during hands-on testing. If your product trials better than it demos, you will need your prospect to be open-minded in order to win the deal.

Find the prospect team member with the best combination of authority, respect and intelligence to spearhead the evaluation.

You may not have much choice about the make-up of the evaluation team, but you need to identify the best member of the team to spearhead the evaluation. This person may also serve as your "coach" in the deal, though this is not always the case. Sometimes your biggest fan will be a manager or a contact who is not directly involved in the evaluation. You will still want to work with your coach as part of the deal, but you need to find a team member to focus on for the evaluation stage itself.

It is incredibly difficult to win an evaluation if you do not have a team member to serve as your champion during the evaluation—and you need someone with authority, respect, and intelligence to boot. We are not at all suggesting that you ignore the rest of the evaluation team. Rather, identify a key person with whom you can both work to resolve issues and funnel critical information to.

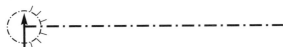

One of the worst, but very common, situations from a team standpoint is what we call the parallel bake-off. In this scenario, your prospect is evaluating multiple vendors at the same time and using different teams for each vendor.

Getting a bad team means tough sledding during a parallel evaluation.

You are unlikely to win the evaluation if you have a sub-par team. The key is to have at least *one* solid team member who can both control his or her own team as well as someone who can carry your message back to the other teams at the end of the evaluation. As a sales consultant, your responsibility is to provide an evaluation of the technical evaluation team for your sales rep. It's not your call to abort the evaluation, but your sales rep may decide to call a meeting with the main contacts in the deal before proceeding with an evaluation with a bad team. There will be cases in which it doesn't matter, especially when the evaluation is a formality and the sales rep has sold the prospect at a higher level. Your responsibility is always to work the evaluation and keep the channels of communication open with your sales rep.

Competition

Competition is such an important topic that we have devoted an entire chapter to it, but it still bears mentioning in the context of the evaluation process. Most prospects will evaluate several vendors in the course of making their decision. From the point of view of your prospect, it is critical to have several possible solutions in the pipeline in order to negotiate the best deal. For this reason alone, your prospect will likely carry several vendors into the evaluation phase of the deal. It's extremely important to know which of your competitors are being evaluated, and why your prospect has included them in the evaluation. This is a good time to reflect on the Bulldozer and BMW assessment that we introduced in Chapter 8, "Qualification and Planning for Presentations and Demonstrations."

Prospects may include a large number of competitors early in the sales cycle. However, by the time of the evaluation phase, they should have narrowed the list of competitors to a more focused group. Typically, product evaluations are limited to the top few vendors in contention for the deal. Although there are exceptions to this rule, it is important to find out from your prospect which of the original proposed solutions are still in the running, and why. Product evaluations take time and resources on both your part and the prospect's part. Evaluations that involve a large number of vendors indicate that the prospect does not have a firm understanding of his or her own needs.

> In my experience, most prospects have identified the product they are most likely to buy at the end of the demonstration phase. While the prospect may put several vendors through their places during the evaluation, they generally know which product they really want at this late stage of the selling process. Despite the fact that I have found myself in second or third place heading into product evaluation, I often have won deals "coming from behind." Frequently, this was the result of a stumble on the part of the frontrunner, rather than my own work, but having to depend on this occurrence certainly reduces your control of the sales process. Starting out in the lead is always better, because the prospect tends to cut you some extra slack, but it's not vital.

The exact number of vendors will vary according to the type of evaluation and the nature of the product that you represent. The usual approach for a prospect is to request a hands-on evaluation, such as a trial or prototype, with two vendors. In such cases, the prospect will usually evaluate the two leading vendors and leave the remaining competitors on the back burner in the event that the leading vendors do not make the grade during the trial or prototype.

If the evaluation criteria significantly favor your competition, you are in trouble.

When the critical technical criteria match your product's capabilities, you are in the winning position for the evaluation phase of the sales cycle. However, if the technical criteria better match the features of your competition, you need to question your participation in the deal. Consider the following scenario:

Prospect's Criteria:

- Support for NT, UNIX and Linux
- Interface with IEM Dbx database
- Support for Java servlets
- Load balancing
- Failover

SuperServer:

- Supports NT and UNIX
- Interfaces to XYZ-Db database
- Supports servlets
- Supports Enterprise Java Beans
- Failover

UltraServer (your competition):

- Supports NT, UNIX and Linux
- Interfaces with IEM Dbx database
- Supports Java servlets
- Load balancing

In our example, your competitor's product features are a much closer match to the prospect's evaluation criteria. As a sales consultant, you will want to question why you are still working this deal. There may be valid reasons: Your price may be significantly lower, or your sales rep may have a contact with upper management within the prospect's organization. But from a purely technical viewpoint, in this example your competitor is in a significantly stronger position. Early on in the selling process, this advantage is not as serious a problem. If you were able to drop the Linux and IEM Dbx requirements from the critical technical criteria during early phases of the sales cycle, the match-up with UltraServer would be relatively even. But by the time the sales cycle moves into the evaluation phase, this same set of criteria spells trouble for SuperServer in the deal.

Ultimately, your sales rep will have to make the call on whether you carry on in the sales cycle or back out before committing resources to an evaluation. Your job is to make sure that the sales rep is armed with all of the data necessary to make an informed decision about whether or not to proceed. The issue is not whether a given set of criteria is important, but whether the prospect considers it to be important. Think back to the beginning of this chapter: Evaluations are all about the prospect finding proof points for critical technical requirements. Your opportunity to adjust the importance of any given technical requirement essentially ends as soon as the evaluation plan is put into place. There are exceptions to this rule, but the odds are not in your favor.

Wrapping Up

Product evaluations are all about creating proof points for the key technical criteria. Conducting a successful evaluation means managing the prospect through a series of proof steps. The key to evaluations is to get a handle on the critical criteria and then create a process that matches while minimizing the amount of resources that you have to expend.

In the next chapter, we will take a look at how to address situations in which the prospect's stated needs do not match the features of your product.

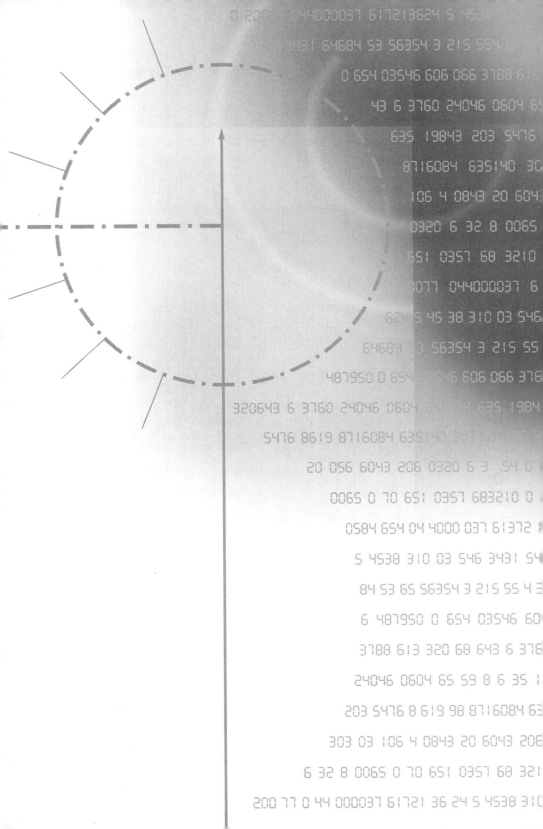

Handling Objections

In every sales situation, you will encounter objections. Every human relationship, from a sales cycle to a friendship to a marriage, inevitably reaches a situation where one participant in the relationship objects to the actions of another person in the relationship.

Objections are inevitable in any significant human interaction.

In this chapter, we will take a close look at how to deal with objections when they come up in a sales situation.

Objections and the Sales Cycle

Your natural inclination may be to think of a sales cycle as a road, with the destination being the successful completion of the sale. With this analogy, it is natural to think of objections as blocks in the path to the sale.

But by thinking of a prospect's objections as simply obstacles to a sale, you will be tempted to take the most direct path through them—by blasting them away. However, this expedient solution will prevent you from using objections to improve your chances in sales situations and maximize the sales revenue available to you.

Since objections are inevitable in a sales cycle, you should use objections to help you to win business. Objections are a form of communication and, as such, can be used to learn more about your prospect's needs, goals, and personalities. In this way, objections can be seen as detours off the main path to a sale. If the detour is small, you can, through working with the prospect, use the objection to expand the road by encompassing

---

its solution into the main route of the sale. If the objection is large and immovable, you may have to find a different prospect to work with, or at least to understand what you will have to do to close the sale.

The rest of this chapter will help you to understand the different types of objections you will encounter and how best to approach each of them.

Types of Objections

Each type of technical product has a different set of objections. Instead of trying to provide a listing of objections that you may encounter, however, we will try to delineate all potential objections into three basic types of objections: philosophical objections, feature objections, and benefit objections. By understanding the differences between these basic types of objections, you will be able to address objections with the most appropriate technique, described later in this chapter, regardless of the substance of the objection.

Philosophical Objections

Philosophical objections come from the inherent mindset of your prospect, rather than from any specific attribute of your product. Philosophical objections are typically based on what a customer thinks is the "right" way to do things. In certain cases, the gap between what the customer believes is right and what you offer is too great for you to deal with and still be able to complete the sales cycle.

Philosophical objections are inevitably pre-existing. The prospect believed in the basis of the objection before you and your product entered the picture. This can be because the prospect has a firm sense of "proper" practices, usually gained either through experience or education.

A philosophical objection often indicates an unobtainable deal.

A philosophical objection can be based on factors other than the exact features of your product. For instance, your prospect may see himself or herself as a technical visionary and, therefore, may give great weight to features that are considered to be the coming thing. Such a prospect may correspondingly object to any other options in your product, simply because these options interfere with his or her pre-established perceptions.

A philosophical objection can also indicate that something is wrong in the sales cycle. Because they are not based on any specific feature of your product, philosophical objections can indicate a hidden agenda on the part of the prospect. Rather than let you in on the agenda, the prospect simply throws up a smoke screen in the form of a philosophical objection. For the same reasons, a philosophical objection is sometimes a marker to a "wired" deal, where the eventual winner of the deal has already been established and the sales cycle is simply a way to justify the decision.

Feature Objections

We have already discussed the importance of connecting the features of a product with the benefits the features deliver. Some objections you may encounter have to do with the lack of certain features in your product, rather than the benefits these features can deliver.

To some extent, feature objections result from years of positioning on the part of vendors. Features are more concrete than the benefits they deliver, so it is more efficient to emphasize a feature you offer, or the lack of it in a competitor, than it is to connect that feature with the benefits it delivers. In an advertisement, the feature is generally writ large, while the supporting benefit connection is in the small type of the ad copy. When potential prospects skim through material, they absorb the feature without connecting the benefit, which leads to the "check-box" approach of product evaluation. The result is a customer who objects because you do not have a particular feature, rather than a customer who objects based on the inability of a product to address his or her needs.

Benefit Objections

Benefit objections are based on the inability of your product to deliver a certain advantage to the user or the delivery of significantly less of that advantage than your competitors can provide.

Benefit objections are closely tied to the real needs of your prospect. Since there are many ways to deliver any particular benefit, benefit objections are also easier to address. When a customer makes an objection based on the inability of your product to address his or her needs, the customer is helping you to understand the situation and is giving you a lot of flexibility in addressing these needs. As you will see below, benefit-based objections are by far the easiest type of objection to deal with.

Scale of Objections

Just as there are different types of objections, objections themselves can have a varying degree of effect on the sales cycle, depending on their scale. For the purposes of this chapter, we place objections into two main categories: *major objections* and *minor objections*.

The difference between major and minor objections is easy to state: A major objection is one that can jeopardize the sales cycle if it is not overcome, while a minor objection is one that, by itself, cannot derail a sale.

Of course, minor objections, as a group or factor, can prevent you from winning a deal. Frequently, the product with the most minor objections will end up losing. Many prospects informally total up the "cost" imposed by minor objections, and this overall perception can cost a deal.

In real life, many objections do not fall into one category or the other, but somewhere in between, as illustrated in Figure 12.1.

Figure 12.1
Major-minor objection categories.

Major   Minor

We are classifying objections by scale as a way to discuss how best to handle the three different types of objections and to understand how objections will have an impact on your sales success.

The Objection Grid

When we combine the type of objections and the scale of objections, we come up with the following objection grid.

Figure 12.2
The objection grid—empty.

	Major	Minor
Philosophical		
Feature		
Benefit		

With this grid, you can classify most objections. Classifying an objection does not solve the problems posed by the objection, but by differentiating between types of objections, you will be able to choose the appropriate technique for handling them. We will revisit this objection grid after we explore the two basic techniques for handling objections. We will also give you concrete examples of different objection categories later in this chapter, once we have introduced information about dealing with objections.

Approaches for Handling Objections

There are two basic approaches for handling objections. You can rebut an objection, or you can educate the prospect to improve his or her understanding of how your product addresses the problem and, in this way, make the objection disappear.

Most of us believe in the product we are selling. We honestly think that our product is as good or better than any other product on the market, and that our product is the best solution for the customer's problems. Because of this, our natural impulse is to handle an objection by rebutting it.

Although rebutting an objection may be our first impulse, it is rarely the best way to handle it. When you try to directly rebut an objection, it may appear you are attacking not only the objection, but also the person making the objection. This type of confrontation tends to close down communication, which is your primary tool for discovering the best approach to your customer and establishing rapport and credibility.

Rebutting an objection closes off communication with the prospect.

Education is a much better technique for handling objections. Education is a two-way process. The first step in an education process is to educate *yourself* about the source of the objection. You can ask your prospect why he or she feels a particular objection is relevant for your product or why a particular objection indicates that your product cannot address his or her problems. Once you have gotten more information on the source and severity of an objection, you can start to sever the connection between an objection and your product. You can educate your prospect about different ways that your product can address the problems that are the source of an objection.

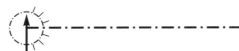

As this mutual educational process is taking place, you are continuing to communicate with your prospect. You can establish rapport through a gentle exploration of your prospect's areas of concern. By helping him or her to understand your product better, you continue to establish your credibility as an expert. And by connecting your product with the solutions to your prospect's problems, you make it much easier for the prospect to select your product.

The Objection Grid Revisited

We can now revisit the objection grid we created above and see the best approach for each different class of objection.

Figure 12.3
The objection grid—filled.

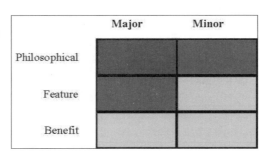

The new version of the grid has three colors that illustrate your three combinations. The white indicates the objections that can be addressed with an educational approach. The black indicates the type of objections that will require rebuttal tactics. The gray areas can be addressed by either education or rebuttal, depending on the exact objection.

Working Down the Grid

You are more likely to be successful in addressing objections with an educational approach than through rebuttal.

> ### The lower an objection is on the grid, the more amenable it is to the educational approach.

One way to deal with objections is to work them down the grid until you can fit them into a category that can be handled more easily.

Your primary weapon in working down the grid is a simple question—"*Why?*" There is a qualitative difference between the different categories of objection. A deep-seated philosophical objection is different from an objection based on the lack of a feature or benefit. However, a philosophical objection could just be an oversimplification or inexact statement of a feature or benefit objection.

When you encounter a philosophical objection, you can try to work down the objection grid by asking your prospect for some of the reasons behind the objection. You could also ask why he or she believes a certain feature is necessary. The answers to these questions may help you to change the type of an objection, which in turn will make it easier to handle.

Of course, this is not a foolproof technique. You may start to explore a feature objection, only to find it has transformed into a philosophical objection. Even this is not entirely bad—at least you have uncovered a formerly invisible obstacle to the sale.

Sometimes, a prospect may react badly to repeated questioning on objections, especially if you are approaching this questioning with the very transparent goal of dismissing the objection. Try at least to make your questions seem like an attempt to understand your prospect's situation more completely, rather than simply using them as a means of countering objections. For example:

> **Sales Consultant:** *Joe, as I understand your application, you plan on implementing the inventory system using Java servlets, which SuperServer definitely supports. Our servlets can cache database connections and they support failover to secondary servers, which seems to meet your requirements. I am a little confused about where you see the need to use Enterprise Java Beans. Could you take me through the development process one more time?*

If you have been frequently interacting with the prospect throughout your contacts, asking them questions about their objections will be just another part of your give-and-take and will not seem so obvious. In this way, the rapport you have established with your prospect will pay off by giving you more flexibility to use the tools at your disposal for handling objections.

An Alternative to Rebuttal

From the grid, we can also see that major philosophical objections are not that amenable to the education technique and, therefore, are the most difficult to handle. Since philosophical objections are generally deeply set in the mind of the objector, even rebutting a particular philosophical objection may not succeed or at least not succeed in the limited time you have for your sales cycle. In these situations, you should

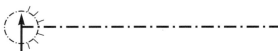

try to reduce the impact of the objection by presenting not just a rebuttal but also a different view of the overall context of the problem your prospect is seeking to address.

Repositioning an objection is an alternative to rebutting it.

You can paint a picture that does not necessarily directly confront the philosophical objection, but that encompasses the objection in the bigger picture. In this way, you can at least hope to diminish the obstacle posed by the objection. Rather than seeming like an enormous boulder blocking your way to a successful sale, the objection can fit into the landscape of the overall environment, revealing a path around the objection.

Although this repositioning may not convert the person making the objection, you may at least be able to reduce the influence of the objection with other people in the decision-making process.

One way to accomplish this repositioning is with an apt comparison or metaphor. Metaphors can be a way of conveying a rich image in just a few words.

A beautiful metaphor can outweigh a thousand words.

We have found that a telling phrase can sometimes turn around an objection or even an entire sales situation. A metaphor can further establish your credibility and the depth of your understanding of a particular problem.

An example of this is applicable when you handle an objection about the learning curve of a product. When people object to the learning curve, they are frequently objecting to its initial few days. They feel that they will not have much to show for their initial effort. However, a sophisticated product that allows a user to accomplish whatever he or she wishes will, of necessity, have more options than a simpler product and therefore will take a little longer to learn to use. Sophistication pays off when the user actually has to accomplish something down the road, but the first steps on the road may look intimidating.

Rather than trying to explain this to a prospect in a sales situation, you could compare the use of a product to a journey to an exotic place. On this type of trip, the traveler is often very anxious about the time it will take to get to the faraway destination, but once he or she arrives, the time and effort it took to reach the spot completely disappear in the beauty and wonder of the destination. If the prospect you are working with loves to travel, this approach can immediately put the learning curve issue in perspective. Your prospect may even associate the use of your product with their love of travel. What starts as a rather difficult philosophical objection evaporates once the prospect is able to map the objection to other situations that have been faced and surmounted. The travel metaphor puts the objection in the context of the larger picture, which is more favorable to your product.

Metaphors are a powerful way to give your prospect another way to look at a given problem, but they can also be dangerous. I have worked with sales consultants who have a real talent for whipping up clear, concise metaphors on the fly. I have also seen sales consultants who use metaphors that are more confusing than the original issue. Have you ever heard Ross Perot's metaphors? You can just hear him saying that he will look under the hood to find a problem with the health care system—then see that quizzical smile that follows, as if he had just said something meaningful. You'll need to practice crafting metaphors before trying them out on prospects.

It can also help if you can graphically minimize an objection with a sketch on a whiteboard or flip chart. The previous example could also use a graphical method by drawing a timeline of the life cycle of product use. As you diagram several years in a line, you can go back to the drawing and indicate the minute portion of the overall use time that will be consumed by training.

Examples of Objection Handling

The best way to understand the different ways of handling objections is to look at a simple case study to illustrate them.

In this section, we will look at examples of each category of objection and provide a brief discussion of the techniques for addressing each category of objection. We will look at a major objection (a complaint that

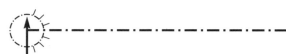

your product is not easy to use) and examine how the same objection can be framed as a philosophical, feature, or benefit objection. We will use the same approach in examining a type of minor objection, which will take the form of a complaint about the difficulty in installing your product.

Handling a Major Objection: Ease of Use

Major objections are objections that can derail a sale. If a product is not easy to use, a prospect may not want to get involved at all. The ease-of-use objection can take any of the three types of objection contexts.

> *Philosophical Objection:* "We cannot invest in a product that is difficult to use."

Your natural response to this type of major philosophical objection might immediately be to begin to rebut it. After all, the prospect seems pretty set in this opinion, so you must smash your way through it by demonstrating that it just isn't true. You can cite studies or customer references.

But this would not be the best approach. With a philosophical objection, you are unlikely to convince proponents that they are just mistaken, since their beliefs likely are grounded outside of your specific sales situation.

You would also be forfeiting the possibility of learning more about the prospect's needs and desires that all objections bring with them. You can discover more by asking why the objector feels this way. Is it because of bad experiences in the past with complex products? His or her experiences may or may not apply to your product. Is he or she actually complaining that the internal staff does not know your product? Or that there do not seem to be many people available with expertise in your product?

Each of these possibilities has an entirely different solution. If you don't delve deeper into the objection, you can find yourself addressing the wrong problem. And if your attempts to find out more about the product are met with resistance, this may tell you that your prospect is less interested in buying your product than you had hoped.

A philosophical objection can disguise a wide range of underlying reasons, so it is best to use very open-ended questions when you explore philosophical objections.

You can often successfully draw out the prospect by agreeing with the basic philosophical objection and then trying to position your solution around this objection. This is illustrated in the following exchange:

> **Sales Consultant:** *Joe, you are absolutely right. I cannot agree more—there is no reason why you should invest in a product that is difficult to use. We have really wrestled with this problem at SuperServer. Our sophisticated customers, like yourself, are very interested in taking advantage of some advanced capabilities such as Java servlets and Enterprise Java Beans. The issue for us has been how to provide support for these inherently complex features without making SuperServer hard to work with. The great thing is that we have insulated new developers from having to deal with these features up front....*

We are not agreeing with the prospect that SuperServer is difficult to use, but we are agreeing with the prospect that he or she should not buy a hard-to-use product. This allows us to start "selling" the prospect without getting into a battle over philosophical issues.

> *Feature Objection:* "Your product does not have wizards that make it easy to use."

You can easily see that a feature objection is much more defined than a philosophical one. At first glance, the feature objection also looks unbeatable. After all, you either have wizards or you don't. But you can still use the same techniques you used with a philosophical objection to discover more about its basis. Does this customer need wizards because he or she has to rapidly create basic applications? If so, templates or pre-existing applications may solve the same problem. Does the customer think that wizards are easier to use? In the short run, this may be true, but in the long run, wizard-generated code may be harder to understand and maintain. Or is the customer only thinking about simple applications that can be addressed by a wizard? In this case, you can point out how a wizard is not as flexible as other methods, and the ease of use may be negated by the difficulty in coding around wizard-driven solutions. For example, you could respond in this way:

> **Sales Consultant:** *Liz, you're right about the wizards. Is your development staff familiar with wizards?*

> **Liz:** *Yes, all of the other tools that we have worked with provide wizards, and my developers were much more productive when they had access to wizards.*

Sales Consultant: *That's a good point. Our engineering staff actually looked at putting wizards into the development interface for SuperServer, but they found that the standard wizard interface limited the flexibility of the programming. Features such as servlets and Enterprise Java Beans have a wide variety of options to them and the wizards themselves became much too complicated. The other thing that we found is that most customers wanted to use a third-party development tool to work with SuperServer, and having our own wizards interfered with that capability. What we have done to address this issue is to provide a comprehensive set of example programs that programmers can use as building blocks. We have found these skeleton programs to be extremely effective in getting programmers up to speed with SuperServer. If you like, I can take you through some of these example programs....*

In our example, the prospect truly has a feature objection: She has used other products that provide support for wizards—and she objects to SuperServer's lack of support for wizards. Our job as sales consultants is to make the issue more generic by tying it to productivity. If we can get the prospect to agree that the real issue is productivity, then we might be able to turn the tables by offering other capabilities that address the underlying issue. We do this by agreeing with the basic premise, that the feature the prospect wants is a desirable one. This will get the prospect talking about the issue in more detail, so that we can be sure where the prospect is coming from. Once we understand the issue, we can sell around it. It does not do us any good to argue that "wizards are bad"; this is just going to cause the prospect to dig his or her heels in. Instead, we attempt to downgrade the feature objection into a benefit objection and then we position around it.

Benefit Objection: "I need to get productive on the product rapidly, since I have a tight deadline."

With a benefit objection, you have not only pinpointed the perceived problem in your product, but you also have a lot of flexibility in delivering a counter to the objection. You could point out the availability of existing solutions that can be adopted, offer consulting help to supplement the current staff, or even suggest training that will get them started fast.

Once you work down to a benefit-based objection, you will have created a partnership with your prospect. Together, you can help to solve the problems. This type of relationship is much more likely to result in a sale.

> **Sales Consultant:** *You are absolutely right. We have a number of features in SuperServer that are architected to address productivity issues. For example, we provide a set of pre-built code modules that your programmers can use as frameworks for their own code. Would you like to take a look at this framework?*

Benefit objections are the easiest to address, since they are not specific to any feature of your product. As always, you want to agree with your prospect's basic objection, but with benefit objections you have much greater liberty in how you address the issue. Because these objections are more generic, in the sense that benefits can be derived from many different sources, it is important for you to get feedback as you go along. This will keep you on the right track. What you want to avoid is simply rambling along describing feature after feature. Instead, point out a feature that addresses the issue and then get feedback. If you haven't put the issue to rest, then you can continue to point out additional features that address the benefit objection as necessary.

Handling a Minor Objection: Installation

As we have said, a minor objection cannot, by itself, derail a sale. A difficult installation indicates a problem, but it is generally not enough to prevent a prospect from buying your product if the prospect's other needs are met.

> *Philosophical Objection:* "A difficult installation process indicates that a product is difficult to customize and maintain."

As with other philosophical objections, this one seems to have its roots outside this sales cycle. In responding to this example, you could try to defeat it by arguing that a difficult installation does not necessarily mean that the product is difficult to customize and maintain.

Or you could try to get more information about the source of this belief, or the problems that the prospect feels really result from a difficult installation. If you work with the prospect, you may end up with a feature or benefit objection, which is easier to handle through an educational approach.

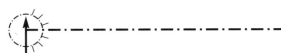

Although this is a relatively minor objection, it is still important to try to knock it down the objection chain as soon as possible. Even minor objections can fester and hurt in later negotiations. If you do not have an answer to the objection, you can sometimes table the issue for the time being by agreeing that there is indeed an issue, as follows:

> **Sales Consultant:** *Sue, that's a great point. I hadn't looked at it that way before. My customers tell me that SuperServer itself is easy to customize, but you are bringing up an interesting perspective. Can we spend a few minutes talking about this at the end of the meeting?*

Although it does not always make sense to table issues, it is a useful strategy for minor philosophical objections. It may turn out that your overall presentation and demonstration will enable you to overcome the issue. You will often make a bigger issue out of it by trying to tackle it right up front. But by agreeing with the prospect and complimenting his or her insight, you have a chance to derail the issue during the course of the meeting.

> *Feature Objection:* "Your product does not have a single installation process."

With this example of a feature objection, you can educate the prospect about ways to circumvent the perceived problem. It might, for instance, be very easy to create a flexible macro that would automatically handle multiple installation processes. The prospect might even be mistaken—there could be a single installation method about which he or she is unaware.

> *Benefit Objection:* "My MIS staff is overworked and cannot spend the time necessary to install this product on each machine."

Once again, an objection based on a perceived lack of benefit can be addressed in a number of ways—from educating the prospect about ways to reduce the burden of multiple installations to offering help in installation. When you help your prospect solve problems, he or she is more likely to become your customer.

Addressing Objections

It is very useful theoretically to understand how to classify objections and how to handle different types. But how should you handle an objection during a live sales presentation?

The most important thing to remember is not to let an objection change the overall flow of a sales presentation. The structure of a presentation is vital. Most people can only absorb a few things from any one presentation, so you should structure your presentations to ensure that your audience will take away the few facts that you want them to remember.

This means introducing those facts early on, spending a significant amount of time on them, and referring to them throughout the presentation. If you let objections dictate the flow of a presentation, they will undercut the focus and reduce the chances that your audience will retain the major points.

Disrupting the flow of a presentation can dramatically reduce its impact.

To avoid disruptions, you should do two things when an objection comes up in a presentation. First, try quickly to understand what type of objection you are dealing with, so that you can ascertain the best technique to handle it.

Second, you should determine how you will address it. Since you may need a little time to make this determination, it can help if you make a habit of repeating an objection when you hear it.

> **Sales Consultant:** *Joe, let me make sure that I have this right. You were hoping to find a product that allowed you to debug Enterprise Java Beans within the server itself. Is this right?*

You have three choices about handling an objection. The first choice is to address it immediately. This approach is appropriate if the objection is fairly minor and you have a quick answer available. You will not disrupt the flow of the presentation or risk becoming diverted into a larger discussion that will take time away from your overall pitch.

Your second option is to reposition the objection. This means that you will restate the objection in such a way that it can be easily addressed or covered later in your presentation. When you reposition an objection, you are restating it in a way that is easier for you to address—such as working it down the objection chain, as discussed above.

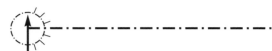

The third option is to "park" the objection. When you park an objection, you write it down, either on a whiteboard or flip chart or in your own notebook. When you do this, you let the prospect know what you have written down by repeating it as you write.

Parking an objection has two big advantages. If there is an objection that you cannot address quickly, parking it does not disrupt the flow of your presentation. It isn't the same as dismissing the objection—the audience can see that you think enough of the objection to actually write it down, so they will rarely resent this technique.

The second advantage of parking an objection is that it lets you prove how responsive you are. At the end of your presentation, walk through the objections that you have parked. If you care to address some of them at this time, you can do so without corrupting the structure of the basic presentation. If you choose not to address the objections right then, you can make a commitment to get back to the prospect with the answers in a short period of time. When you do call the prospect back, your response helps to establish that you feel the prospect is important. It also gives you a chance to see how the prospect feels about you after the sales call. If the prospect seems happy to hear from you, you may be able to get additional information that can help you in your sales effort. If the prospect doesn't take or return you call, it may indicate that something is amiss in the sales cycle.

As we have mentioned in other contexts throughout this book,

Follow-through helps establish rapport and credibility.

The process of parking objections has so many advantages that we will often park one even if we can handle it on the spot. Parking lets us take advantage of the opportunity to contact the prospect again.

One final tip: Try to mix the three techniques of handling objections. If you park all the objections, you will spend quite a bit of time writing everything down, which can take away attention from the presentation. It may also make it seem as though you don't know very much about your own product. If you always address objections, you may seem overly combative. If you always reposition objections, you may seem overly slick.

Wrapping Up

Remember, by offering objections, your prospect is giving you valuable insights into his or her evaluation criteria. Use these objections to understand your prospect's real needs and wants. The purpose of classifying objections is to help you to understand the real purpose behind an objection. All objections have a basis in fact—the fact just might not be stated overtly. By exploring objections, you will help to discover the real source of your prospect's problem. If you don't discover this source, you will waste valuable sales time responding to a problem that doesn't really exist.

By effectively handling objections, you will improve the efficiency of your sales cycle while simultaneously forging stronger links with your customers. You will be establishing your credibility and standing as a trusted partner. At the same time, you will be able to use objections to help you to spot difficult, nonproductive sales situations that can waste your time.

In the next chapter, you will learn how to deal with that dreaded beast: the request for information, or RFI.

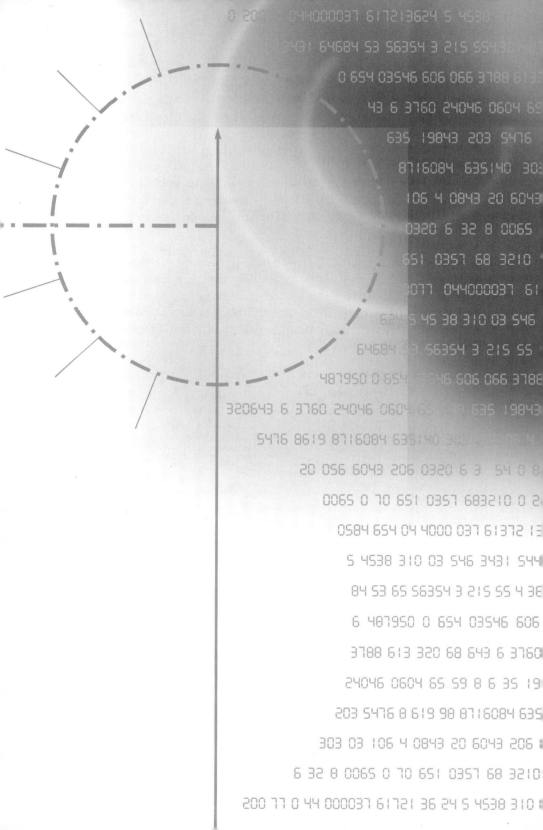

Responding to RFIs

If you are a sales consultant who works with large deals or with a government agency, you will eventually encounter one of the dreaded requests—the request for information (RFI); request for quotation (RFQ); or the request for proposal (RFP). These creatures look like mild-mannered stacks of paper, but they can chew up enormous quantities of your time.

This chapter will help you to understand the prospect's motivation behind unleashing one of these feared beasts. We will teach you how best to deal with one. Just in case you are one of the lucky few who have not yet run across a request, we will start with some definitions.

What is a Request for Information?

A request is a written document that requires a written response from a sales team. Technically, the RFI is a precursor to the beginning of an actual sales cycle. A prospect will request information as a way to approach companies that will be in the competition. In the same way, an RFQ focuses on the cost of a solution, without asking for a lot of extra information. If an RFQ deals only with pricing issues, it is typically not an aspect that will involve you as a sales consultant. An RFP typically combines the purposes of both of the other requests, with a little extra thrown in about pricing terms and conditions.

In practice, a request includes a lot of questions, most not specifically related to price. This means that you will be called in to assist your sales rep in completing a response to a request.

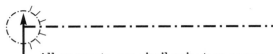

All requests are similar in two ways:

- They require extensive work to complete
- They act as a gateway to the rest of the sales cycle

From this point forward, we will use the term *RFI* to refer to any type of request.

Reasons for an RFI

You may have noticed a tone of mock horror in our use of the term RFI. This is because RFIs have traditionally been one of the sales consultant's least favorite tasks. They generally take a significant amount of time, from several days to several weeks. You spend the time assembling information to create a response to a request, and this time is spent locked up in front of a machine, typing in voluminous answers to questions that you might not fully understand.

A lot of frustration is associated with most RFIs. There's a simple reason for this: By making a written, formal request for information, the prospect prevents you and your sales team from directly interacting with him or her. This barrier, in turn, prevents you from using your formidable sales skills to help gain an edge in the sales cycle. Dealing with an RFI means that most of the other skills and practices we talk about in this book are out of the picture, at least until you have been chosen as a possible vendor through the RFI process.

> ### *The purpose of an RFI is to isolate the decision makers from the vendors.*

Unfortunately, the entire purpose of an RFI is negative—it is usually used to eliminate vendors. This purpose casts a pall over the entire process—you aren't competing to win, but to avoid losing.

Why, oh why, would a customer put you through this type of agony? As with most things in life, there are stated reasons for an RFI and the realities often lie behind those reasons. The reasons will help you to understand the facets behind your prospect's motivation.

You will rarely get a chance to participate in the process that leads up to the distribution of an RFI. But we have found, through years of experience, that there are typically four main reasons why an RFI becomes part of a sales cycle:

- **The RFI is part of a formal process.**
  Some companies, especially large ones, have simply specified that all purchases, or all purchases over a certain amount, require an RFI as part of the formal process of acquisition. Sometimes, the creator of this process has the purchase of objects such as widgets in mind, or other physical items that are not nearly as variable and complex as computer hardware, software, and services.

- **The RFI attempts to establish a neutral standard.**
  When you are dealing with either a vaguely defined solution area (which seems to happen frequently in emerging technology markets, where there is a lack of a common set of features), or when you are dealing with a vaguely defined problem, a prospect might feel overwhelmed trying to match up his or her situation with many different solutions. An RFI is an attempt to put all vendors on neutral, common ground. This approach is also used for situations involving licensing, where different companies can each sport a confusing welter of terms and conditions with their products.

- **The company has a requirement that all significant purchases use an RFI.**
  Some companies feel that the RFI adds a level of safety to the purchase process. Because of this, they will require that an RFI be an automatic segment of any purchase over a certain amount. It is also easier to get vendors to reply to an RFI when there is a larger payoff at the end of the process. However, there is a downside to this approach. If a company issues an RFI to which some potential vendors do not respond, the result may be that the company is forced to purchase a less-than-optimal solution.

Since even a simple request can require a significant resource commitment, smaller companies are less likely to respond to an RFI. If a prospect is looking for a solution in a more cutting-edge arena where many of the best solutions are offered by smaller companies, an RFI may have the unintended side effect of eliminating most of the best solutions.

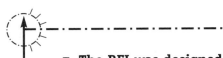

- **The RFI was designed by a consulting company.**
  Many companies hire consultants to help them with their acquisition process. This is especially true when a company is moving into an area of technology in which it does not have a lot of experience and the consultant or consulting firm does. The RFI acts as a kind of bridge—an instrument that can be used to make sure the consultant is finding out the right answers for the eventual user, and for the consultant to make sure the customer is getting the appropriate explanations back. Companies also use consultants to help with the purchase process because their own employees are too busy to devote the appropriate amount of effort to the evaluation and selection of a product or service.

Of course, a company may have embraced more than one of these reasons as justification for an RFI. And, as the next section will illustrate, there is more to the issuance of an RFI than these above-the-board reasons.

RFIs generally appear in the sales process somewhere between lead generation and the initial presentation process. Most prospects will attend a seminar or will request literature before they add you to their list of participating vendors. But this is not a strict rule, especially in the applications marketplace. More and more prospects meet with vendors for a basic presentation before commencing with the RFI process. This can work to your advantage. When you have the chance to pitch your solution in advance of the RFI, you stand a better chance of getting your special features included in the criteria. The downside, of course, is that you will generally have to make a second presentation and demonstration once you make the initial cut imposed by the RFI.

Realities of an RFI

The reasons listed above are publicly stated reasons, the sort of things that a prospect will tell you. However, as with many things in life, there is often a gap between a publicly stated reason and the underlying reality. The underlying reality may not present quite as clean and pretty a picture. Some of the realities behind the use of an RFI include the following:

- Design by committee
- Maintaining control of the sales cycle
- Establishing control for consultant
- Justifying a decision already made
- A rite of passage

Design by Committee

One of the most common reasons to issue an RFI is motivated by the fact that the purchase under consideration will be used by many different people, groups, or departments at the prospect's organization. The RFI produces a single focal point for a decision that is meant to satisfy all of these different entities. Each entity contributes some questions to the RFI.

Decisions made by committee have a wide range of reasons and priorities for purchases.

As you have seen in other chapters, one of the keys in making a sale is to match the features of your product to the most important requirements of your prospect. With this type of RFI, not only do you have different priorities for different capabilities, but you also have different sources for the RFI, all with their own separate sets of priorities. In addition, different contributors to the RFI may have different political standings in the organization, so the top priority for one contributor may not even make the top-ten list of the powerful decision makers.

The person who is your nominal contact may actually not even be aware of the impact or repercussions of some of the questions on the RFI. I once called my contact for an RFI to ask for some clarification on a question, and he said, "Gee, I don't even know what that question means." It was tempting to dismiss the question's importance, but I had no way of knowing if my contact had more standing in the final decision than the author of the question.

When an RFI is used as a "united front" for a wildly diffuse set of requirements, you will find it difficult to gain any sort of control of the sales cycle, at least until the RFI process is completed. In such situations, you should try your best to find some way to communicate with representatives of the various groups involved in the RFI. By speaking with each group, you will not only be able to get clarification on any of the questions, but you can also ask each of them their impression of the process. By using these different views to explore the real influences on the committee, you can often get a good handle on the reality of the decision-making process, which can be of great help to you in winning the business.

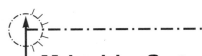

Maintaining Control of the Sales Cycle

Sometimes, an RFI has as its aim imposing a measure of order on the sales cycle. Since the prospect controls the RFI, he or she will control the sales cycle.

Although this is sound reasoning, it is also a sign of a problem with the customer. If a prospect knows what he or she wants and can evaluate responses, the prospect *is* in control of at least the outcome of the sales cycle. If a prospect does not possess the ability to accomplish both of these tasks, you are all in some trouble.

A prospect who suffers from this situation may refuse to communicate with you, since he or she may be afraid of losing control by engaging with you.

**If a prospect refuses to communicate
with you during the RFI process,
this factor could be a sign that something
is amiss in the prospect's organization.**

If you can't communicate with the issuer of an RFI, you can still participate in the process, but you will be flying blind. With any luck, all the other pilots competing for the business will be operating under the same handicap.

Make Work for Consultant

As we mentioned earlier, some RFIs are the result of the intervention of a consultant. Although most consultants are honest in dealing with customers, consultants do charge by the hour, and creating, coordinating, and evaluating RFIs can generate a lot of hours.

If the RFI is strictly a "make work" proposition for a consultant, you should understand that you are trying to sell yourself to the consultant as well as to the prospect. Perhaps you can point out that this sale could mark the beginning of a long and fruitful relationship between the consultant and your company. For more discussion on interacting with consultants, please see Chapter 16, "Eight Challenging Prospects".

Establish Control for Consultant

Account control is all-important, especially for larger consultancies. Some consultants use the RFI as a buffer between the vendor and the eventual user. This can help the consultant to establish his or her own importance to the customer and your prospect.

This can be a frustrating situation, since a consultant in this situation will probably try to block you from direct access to the prospect. Handle these types of situations with sensitivity. Try to work with the consultant in a nonthreatening way. Become a member of the team. Remember, the prospect is paying the consultant for his or her time, so the consultant's value is already established. You will usually lose a showdown with a paid consultant, so it is best to avoid a conflict.

Justify a Decision Already Made

One of the least productive, and most feared, situations is the *wired* RFI. A wired RFI is one that is simply made to justify a choice that has already been decided upon. If you are anyone but the chosen vendor, you are simply wasting your time responding to a wired RFI. There is nothing you can do to change the outcome of the process.

Wired RFIs do occur, but not as frequently as many sales consultants believe. But don't let your reluctance to create a response lead you to believe that *every* RFI is wired. Remember, your prospect, like everyone else, has received information from a variety of sources, including from your competition. If an RFI includes a few questions that sound like they come directly from your competitor's marketing material, it is not enough to reject the RFI. Typically, an RFI contains a few questions like this that could apply to any vendor in the running.

A few "leading" questions in an RFI do not necessarily mean that the RFI is wired.

But if you see that a significant percentage of the RFI is slanted toward features or services that are available only from one competitor, you might consider declining the request to participate. We discuss this topic in more detail in the section on accepting the challenge of an RFI later in this chapter.

A Rite of Passage

This type of RFI is almost a freefloating entity in the sales cycle. In this case, the answers to the RFI matter less than the ability to complete it. An RFI may be the prospect's way of saying that if you do not have the resources to be able to complete an RFI, they do not want to do business with you.

In this scenario, a response to an RFI is your ticket to the dance—no ticket, no sales cycle.

Each of these reasons is a possible motivation behind the use of an RFI. However, sometimes an RFI is added to the sales cycle for a combination of all of the reasons above. It can help to understand why an RFI is being issued. If, for instance, a consultant is using an RFI as a way to make work or to establish control in the account, the consultant may be the actual decision maker. In such cases, you should concentrate your efforts on him or her.

If an RFI is merely a cover for a decision that has already been made, your sales team might be best advised to walk away from the work involved in responding to the RFI. Once an RFI becomes a part of a sales cycle, it can rarely be circumvented. Your only chance to win a deal with an RFI without responding is to hope that other vendors who do respond will all fail—which violates first principles by giving virtually total control of your participation in a sales opportunity to your competitors.

Kickoff Meetings

Since, as we stated above, the purpose of a request is to put some space between the prospect and the vendors, you will rarely have an opportunity to know much about an RFI until it is released into your hands. If your sales representative is working closely with a particular prospect, he or she will often know in advance when an RFI is due to come out. Some RFIs are actually advertised in the classified sections of relevant newspapers and magazines.

Many RFIs begin with a formal kickoff meeting. This meeting is where the actual RFI is distributed and where your sales team will have an opportunity to ask questions of the prospect team or its representative.

Some RFIs will be distributed in advance of a formal kickoff meeting, but the kickoff meeting will still serve the same purpose. The only real difference is that you and the other vendors will come to the meeting with better prepared questions about the RFI.

This meeting will ideally not be the only opportunity for you to ask questions about the RFI. It is essential that you attend the kickoff meeting, for a number of reasons:

First of all, you will get a chance to see who else is receiving the RFI (and even though some RFI processes allow for sending out the written RFI or its electronic equivalent, it is still useful to see who shows up at the meeting). Seeing who your competition is gives you a better idea of how to evaluate your chances.

Second, you always want to hear the questions that other vendors are asking. Listen carefully to the answers given by the prospect. In a very formal RFI situation, the prospects will promise to post any answers to publicly raised questions so that everyone can share the information. Even if a prospect successfully follows through on this promise, you can't get the same visual cues from a written document that you can from seeing a live person answer. For example, did the person answer the question quickly and confidently, or did he or she have to think about the answer? Little tips can help you to understand the process that a prospect went through in creating the RFI.

It is also extremely useful to see if the subsequent written answers to the questions raised by vendors are different from those given at the meeting. This not-uncommon occurrence can clue you into the fact that there is some other source running at least part of the RFI process.

If there is any chance that you will even consider answering an RFI, you should attend the kickoff meeting. After the meeting, you will face the most difficult question in the entire RFI process: Should you even participate?

Accepting the Challenge of an RFI

An RFI presents a challenge to your sales team. It is a challenge you can choose to accept or decline. There are repercussions with either response.

If you choose to create a response for an RFI, you should do so only if you are willing to complete it. We will discuss what you have to do to complete an RFI in the next section, but you should have already estimated the time it will take to respond, and plan that time into the schedules of everyone who will be involved with the response. If you tell the issuer of an RFI that you will respond to it and then don't follow up, you likely will have ruined your credibility with that individual or organization. You will have made only one significant commitment and failed to deliver. Even if your failure is due to changing circumstances, such as the pressure of more important tasks coming up, it will still look as though you do not value your commitments. This is a bad image to present. The loss of credibility can affect you long into the future—it can hurt your chances of ever working with the issuing company again.

Do not agree to participate in an RFI process unless you plan to complete a response to it.

You also have the option of declining to participate in an RFI. There is absolutely nothing wrong with declining an RFI. You may look at the questions on the RFI, balancing the amount of work required for completion against your likelihood of winning the deal, and conclude that answering it would not be a valuable use of your time.

— · — · —

In gathering a list of companies to participate in an RFI that I was issuing, I once was impressed with the sales ability and products that came from one smaller company. We had several discussions about their products over the phone. I sent them a copy of the RFI, and the sales rep called me several days later to tell me he would not be participating.

He explained that they did not have the resources to adequately complete a response. I encouraged him to attempt it as much as I could without revealing his favored position, but he was unable to commit to the process. I left the interaction even more impressed with the professionalism of the company and subsequently recommended their technology to other clients.

This story also illustrates one of the dangers of the RFI process for the customer. Even if his company had the best solution, the interaction between the RFI process and his company's resources eliminated them from consideration— and eliminated a potentially good solution for the prospect's problem without allowing for any consideration of the solution.

— · — · —

For an overwhelming majority of the time, declining to submit a response to an RFI will eliminate you from consideration in a deal. However, there are times when, for one reason or another, an RFI does not turn up an adequate candidate for purchase. In these cases, you may be called back, even if you did not participate in the RFI process. You should make sure that all your interactions with the people handling the RFI are professional and that you try to do a little bit of selling in these interactions, since you want to leave a good impression. Even if you aren't called back into the process, it always helps to leave a prospect with a favorable view of your company, for there may be other opportunities, either with this company or, if the individuals you are dealing with change jobs, with other companies.

You should work with your sales team to determine if you should take on an RFI. Although a sales rep will probably not be as directly involved with the creation of the response as you will be, he or she should still recognize the advisability of taking on an RFI.

If you really don't have enough time to create a professional response to an RFI, just convey this information to your rep. They should see this as the danger sign that it is, because no one benefits from a sloppy or hasty response.

Before you decide to reject an RFI, you should always evaluate it in terms of how well your main competitors would do in responding to it. Remember, the RFI process, like the sales process, is a comparative venture: The winner does not necessarily have *the* answer, just the best available answer. Even if you do not know which of your competitors will be responding to the RFI, you can still go through a hypothetical competition in your mind to determine if you have a decent chance to make it through the RFI gate.

How to Answer

Once your sales team has decided to respond to an RFI, there is only one way to move forward:

Once your sales team accepts the challenge of an RFI, you must pursue it aggressively.

You should try to make your response as good as possible. No one on the prospect's team cares about your issues with the RFI. They don't know about your time constraints or your disagreements with your sales rep over the feasibility of responding to the RFI. The entire purpose of the RFI process is to get a response, and you will be judged heavily on the quality of that response. Submitting an incomplete or unprofessional response will accomplish only one thing: The prospect will think less of you and your company.

Although an RFI is designed to elicit direct responses, you should always try to include as much of the selling techniques, such as feature-benefit selling, as you can in your response. This doesn't mean that you should simply insert your marketing materials in response to questions. The prospect evaluating your response will just get frustrated if he or she has to wade through irrelevant "marketspeak" in your response. That frustration typically results in a lower opinion of you and your company.

It always helps if your company has some type of boilerplate for RFIs, or answers to the typical questions on a response. You can save some typing time by taking the basic facts from pre-existing materials. But don't simply create your response by cutting and pasting the most relevant information. You have to customize your response to the specific situation of your prospect—as much as you can determine that situation from the RFI and other interactions. Don't just cut and paste together the complete response.

It really puts a prospect off to see a cut-and-paste response to an RFI.

If your company does not have some type of boilerplate for responding to an RFI, you should make it your business to create one, even if it is for your own personal use. Part of the job of responding to an RFI is pure grunt work, so any manner in which you can capitalize on your own earlier work or the work of others will leave you more time to polish the rest of the response.

Even creating a repository of RFI responses on a corporate server can significantly help in the creation of future responses. This collection can help other sales consultants to pick and choose the optimal response from previously completed RFIs. A more productive solution would be to create some type of response generator, but this type of aid typically requires some additional programming work.

Keep in mind that your response is a fairly formal document and should be presented with the care that a formal document deserves. Take a little extra time to format the questions and answers attractively. Go out and buy a plastic cover for your response or have it bound at a local copy shop. Create a cover page with your company's logo or some other attractive graphic.

And please—always spell check and proofread the response more than once before you send it out. Your sole interest at the end of creating a response may be to get it out the door, but your prospect will be spending many hours looking at your work. Making sure that your response to an RFI is attractive and correct may not get you to the list of participating vendors, but handing in sloppy work will reflect badly on your company and could very well end up contributing to your elimination.

Winning the RFI

There is one goal in your participation in an RFI. That is to advance to the next step in the sales process, whether that is a purchase order or further work with the prospect toward that end. You should understand several techniques if you want to increase your chances of making it past the RFI gate.

Getting to Yes

We've gone through a lot of material about an RFI, but we haven't actually discussed how you should answer the questions that make up the RFI. The reason for this is quite simple. There is only one best answer for any question in an RFI—"Yes."

Remember, a complete sales cycle usually includes a lot more give-and-take than a formal RFI process. As you have read throughout this book, there are many ways to shape and reposition a question so that you can give a good answer. Unfortunately, the elimination of that interaction makes this type of modification impossible, so you should feel free to shape your answers to the RFI to place your company in the best possible light.

Let's say the RFI asks for a capability that you can do only in an awkward, workaround way. You should feel free to answer that you have that capability. Depending on your impression of the prospect, you may or may not want to include some explanation in your answer.

For instance, perhaps your SuperServer product can do a particular type of operation only with extensive coding (so extensive that no one ever does it) or can do it only through the use of a third-party tool. You have several possible responses to this type of question:

- "No, SuperServer does not have that capability."
- "Yes, SuperServer can provide that capability, but only with extensive coding or an additional purchase."

  Or
- "Yes, SuperServer gives you two ways to implement that functionality—through customization in your code or with third-party assistance."

Which sounds better? Did any of them mislead the prospect? If this capability is really important to the prospect, he or she should ask you more about it later in the sales cycle. If this capability is not important to the customer, you have been able to answer "yes" and can give your weakness a positive spin.

> Of course, you should never lie to the prospect. But keep in mind the reality of the situation. The issuer of the RFI, in many cases, simply goes down the answers in your response and sees if you have said "yes" to each answer. If you have, you get credit. If you don't, you don't get credit.

Forcing an Opening

An RFI always starts out as a formal process. But you may still be able to carry on part of your normal sales cycle activities in addition to answering the RFI. You may have one or more contacts at the prospect to whom you can direct questions. You should try to use any opening you can to interact with the prospect.

Call your contact for the RFI before a kickoff meeting or the actual issuance of the RFI. Suggest giving a live demo of your product. Ideally, you should set up these meetings *before* the RFI is issued, since you can use the information you gather to help determine if you should participate in the process, as well as potentially be able to modify the questions that end up on the RFI.

Don't be surprised if you are rebuffed in this attempt, since, let's face it, you are trying to circumvent one of the key goals of the RFI process. But try to make every contact with the prospect or with his or her representative pleasant and attempt to have every contact lead to another contact.

Be polite and professional, but keep gently trying. You should also not be surprised if some RFI prospects refuse to return your phone calls or do not respond to your requests. One of the purposes of the RFI is to set up a buffer between you, the vendor, and the prospect. As we noted above, this type of action is often a sign of insecurity on the part of the prospect, but that doesn't mean this situation does not occasionally happen.

The exceptions to this rule are RFIs and RFQs that are issued by government bureaus or the military. These prospects often have extensive "rules of engagement" that they are forced to follow in order to comply with legal requirements.

Making the Cut

The goal of the RFI process, from your point of view, is to make the cut by being one of the top respondents. Most RFIs do not simply award a contract to the "winning" response, but rather use the RFI process as a device to narrow the field of competitors down to a more manageable number.

You should, if at all possible, try to determine where you are leading in the RFI competition and where you are trailing. Of course, you will not be able to see the responses being prepared by your competition, but if you have established a good relationship with your prospect, you may be able to find out what areas of the RFI other vendors are asking about. Your competitors' questions can be signposts to difficulties they are having with any particular questions on the RFI.

You should find an opportunity to change or rebut your answers as part of the RFI process. The prospect might get a preliminary copy of your response, skim through it, and give you feedback before you submit a final, formal response.

Why would the prospect allow this? Isn't he or she trying to avoid interacting with you? Well, yes, but the prospect should also be trying to get the best solution for the problem the RFI is designed to address. If the prospect can read through your response and give you feedback, you will be able to shape your answers better in the final, formal document. You will be getting more information, but so will the prospect.

Sometimes, you can find a coach at the prospect's organization to help you through this process. The feedback you get does not have to be through the standard RFI channels, but it will still be helpful.

The bottom line for an RFI is simple— making the cut is virtually always the only way to eventually win the deal.

At the end of the day, it comes up the same. To paraphrase a famous talk show host—"RFIs—you love 'em, you hate 'em, you can't live without 'em."

Wrapping Up

For better or worse, RFIs are a part of the overall sales landscape. This chapter has given you some insight into the ups and downs of the RFI process and has offered some tips for dealing with them.

The next chapter will move onto a slightly different type of sale: Add-on sales to existing customers.

CHAPTER 14

Working the Installed Base and Alternative Sales Channels

The focus of your sales team is typically on new prospects, since it is they who are the primary vehicle for making quota. While this fact certainly makes sense from a simplistic and pragmatic point of view, it is important to recognize that there are several additional paths for getting to prospects. Business partners and existing customers represent an excellent channel for reaching new prospects and extending your reach beyond what you alone can handle. In this chapter, we'll take a look at the various alternative channels and learn how to work these channels to reach new sales opportunities.

Working the Customer Base

Common sense will tell you that among your best sources for information are the existing customers in your territory. For one thing, they made the decision to purchase your product at some point in the past. Whether they are currently satisfied with your product and company is another issue altogether—and we'll deal with that issue shortly.

Secondly, as we pointed out earlier in this book, existing customers have firsthand knowledge about the positives and negatives of your product. This data can be invaluable to you as you strive to master your own product. Customers have real-world experience with the things that work and the things that don't work. As a sales consultant, you do not often have the time or resources to try everything yourself. Customers provide you with the opportunity to experience your own product vicariously.

You can leverage this opportunity while you build rapport with your customers, creating a win-win situation for both sides.

Customers are the ultimate laboratory for your product. If several of your customers are having a problem with some facet of your product, it means that there *is* a problem. You probably understand the underlying basis of your product better than your customers, and you definitely have access to more resources to help you understand. But if you are able to use a feature properly and your customers are not, flag this situation as an issue. Do not label the users as less than capable customers; your future customers will probably encounter similar problems.

For the purposes of this discussion, it is important to separate pure-play customers from prospect-customers. Prospect-customers have bought in the past but are once again actively involved in sales cycles. Often, customers will make a small "prototype" purchase of your product, which they will then utilize with the expectation of making a large buy in the future. Such customers should be treated like prospects, since they are still in the midst of an active (albeit extended) sales cycle. Pure-play customers, on the other hand, have already made their major purchases of your product. This does not necessarily mean that they won't buy more product (or additional products) in the future. Rather, pure-play customers are not actively involved in current sales cycles. From the sales rep's perspective, this means that they are not on the current forecast list.

Outside of providing additional revenues, most vendors want one thing from customers—references. One of the keys to many sales cycles and evaluations is the ability to leverage customer references. The specific *relative* importance of customer references will vary according to your product's position in the Technology Life Cycle, as discussed in Chapter 3.

References are always valuable in helping to close a deal, even during the emerging stages of a marketplace. Your sales reps will always have a ready appetite for good, positive customer references.

As you learned in the chapter on managing evaluations, references come in two basic forms—telephone references and site visits. Telephone references are those customers who are willing to take phone calls from other prospects to confirm that your product does all that your company claims that it does. Site visits are much more extensive references, since the customer must be willing to burn at least a half-day of their time hosting the prospect on site. A good site visit can absolutely nail a deal, but it represents a huge investment of time for the customer.

If your sales rep is desperate for good, positive references from customers, what can the rep provide in return? Unfortunately, the answer is "not much." Sure, we're being a little facetious here, but the point is still essentially true. The sales rep can provide discounts on products, but most of these things are negotiated during the closing process. There are occasionally exceptions to this rule, as when a customer burns through allocated licenses prematurely or when he or she needs to use a back-up server for a short time. In general, however, the sales rep provides the most value *during* the sales process, not *after* it.

You are the most valuable contact to the customer.

Once the customer has the product, you become his or her most valuable resource. The support department, engineering, and consulting all provide tremendous value to the customer, but you can be an additional conduit to these organizations. As a sales consultant, you can act as the guide in negotiating through the maze of corporate headquarters organizations. While the personnel in all of these groups are trained professionals, they will not be as familiar with the customer as you are. This is especially true if you are the sales consultant who sold the customer in the first place. In particular, you provide three basic values to the customer:

- Technical knowledge
- Access to resources
- Advocacy

You are a "fountain of technical knowledge" to the customer. You have technical knowledge and information about your product, and this is incredibly valuable to your customer. In fact, you are at your most valuable in this regard when the customer first buys the product. At an early point in the experiences of the customer, you are bound to know more about the product than the customer does. As the customer works with the product over time, he or she will probably surpass you in the category of "hands-on" knowledge. However, you will always have access to certain information, such as data about upcoming versions of the system, that your customer will not necessarily be able to acquire on his or her own.

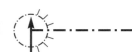

As an employee of the company, you will also have access to resources within the company that an outsider will not have. In particular, this access is to such scarce resources as engineering staff and technical support staff. Customers are typically precluded from calling into the engineering organization directly—at least without an introduction from you. You can act as the go-between to get information out of engineering that is beyond the customer's reach. Should the customer need extra assistance in the event of a serious problem, or if he or she needs an important enhancement, you can also serve in the capacity of an advocate. As an advocate, you can work with engineering to help get an important enhancement into the product plan on behalf of the client.

Be extra careful in this regard. Just because one customer wants a particular feature does not mean that engineering believes that it automatically justifies spending development resources to implement. The reluctance to add custom features grows as a product moves into the later stages of the Technology Life Cycle, when even small changes can affect the product in use at hundreds of customer sites.

Certain enhancements will fall under the category of "customization," a process better handled by the consulting team.

If a customer insists on a feature or capability that has been rejected (at least for the time being) by engineering, you can always bring in consulting to help shape the existing product or to supplement it in some way.

Choosing Your Customers

Now that we've established that you are a valuable resource for your customer, how do you properly work with each customer, and how do you choose which customers to work with? You have an incredibly busy schedule as it is, so you will have a delicate balancing act to manage. One of your goals is to work with the customer to get something back, and that something is primarily a reference. However, always remember that the customer has already given you at least one important item— revenue!

As a sales consultant, you have a fundamental responsibility to support all your customers.

A good working relationship is a two-way street: You get something and they get something. A good customer will want to provide you with the help you need, but you still have to support your customers even if they do not return the favor. Although you should treat all customers with the professional courtesy they deserve, the "gray area" is the degree to which you have to support customers who are "not supporting you back."

Deciding which customers to work with more closely is a matter of judgment. There are three factors to consider when you make your choices:

- Chemistry
- Importance and influence
- Responsiveness

Your selection of customers will partly be a matter of chemistry. You will get along better with certain customers, just as you have both "acquaintances" and "friends" in your personal life. Some customers will turn out to be friends, and others will remain only acquaintances. As you work with a particular customer over a period of time, you will get a feel for the relationship. Your personality will click with some customers more than with others. Make sure that you factor this into the mix, but remember it's not the only factor.

From a sales perspective, it is much better to have references in your pocket who are important, well known, and influential. For example:

> Who is a more powerful reference: Joe Smith of ACME Pet Food or Bill Gates of Microsoft?

If you can build up a reference base of customers who are well known and influential, they will have a greater impact on your sales cycles. However, deciding who is well known and who is important is not as straightforward as you might think. For instance, consider our example. If you are selling any PC-based product, then having Bill Gates as a reference is obviously the best choice for "well known" and "influential." But what if you are selling a piece of software targeted at the pet foods industry? Maybe Joe Smith *is* the better reference. In fact, sometimes an unknown turns out to be extremely well connected in your particular sales patch. Joe Smith might be the head of the local chapter of an

---

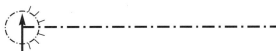

industry group in your territory, so he would have more influence on your immediate attainment of quota than Bill Gates.

How do you decide whom to focus on? Work with your sales rep to prioritize your customers. The sales rep can work with you to identify them. The rep has the territory plan and knows the forecast and pipeline. Work together as a team to decide who the important customers are.

As you begin to work with the customers, start factoring in one final element—*responsiveness*. Which customers call you back right away when you need a reference? Which customers are open about discussing the positives and negatives of your product? A less influential, but responsive, customer is often a better reference than a highly influential and important customer who is hard to reach.

> Certain companies have an official policy against serving as references. You will want to make sure that the customer can serve as a reference before investing too much time with him or her. This may sound cold and callous to you, but it is one of the harsh realities of the world. You owe it to your customers to provide help and assistance, but the difference between good service and great service is a matter of reciprocity.

Selecting the right customers to serve as reference candidates requires a careful balancing of all three elements. In most cases, you will end up with several key reference accounts that are weighted one way or another. Some will have more influence and some will be more responsive. In any case, it is vitally important that you have a good relationship with the customer on a personal level.

Building Up the Relationship

The simplest path to building up a reciprocal relationship with your customer is to make the first move. Don't wait for your customer to call you with a problem; contact the customer proactively on a periodic basis. If you are working a brand-new territory, it is possible that you will not have any customers to work with initially. We call this a "green field." It is always easier to start with a green field, but you will not always have the luxury to start with a green field.

Divide the existing customers among the team.

All the customers in a given territory should be assigned to a member of the sales team. You should generally handle the accounts that you worked as part of a sales cycle, but you will also end up supporting other customer accounts as well. There will be turnover among your fellow consultants as time goes on, so your company will have to make sure these orphaned accounts are transitioned to another sales consultant. Work with the rest of your sales consulting group to divide these customers among yourselves. Some accounts are larger and will require more work than others, so this process of division should not be made simply on a numbers basis. Some companies do not have an official policy for building and maintaining references, and some sales reps are going to be reluctant to have you call into "their" customers. References are an incredibly valuable resource, however, and it will be worthwhile for you to work out a program for managing references among the sales team in the absence of a formal policy.

Dividing all of the customers among the various sales consultants is good practice, regardless of whether these accounts become references or not. As you begin to work with your accounts, they will naturally begin to fall into their proper place for your time and attention. Even if you have targeted a particular account as a key reference account, you will have to build up the relationship over a period of time. Identify a main point of contact within the account, and be sure the contact is well positioned in the organization.

The first step in the process of managing your customer is to agree on a single point of contact for both sides. If you funnel communication from the customer through a single point of contact, you will be better able to manage the workload. Should you find yourself in the situation where a single customer has a number of serious problems, the contact person on your side can help to prioritize the issues.

Work with your sales rep to match a contact person in the customer's organization with an appropriate contact person within your own organization. Your sales rep may identify a customer contact on the business side to work with, and it makes sense for you to have a *separate* technical contact in such cases. You might get calls from other people in the account from time to time, and you will need to make sure that you loop back to your main contact to let him or her know about these calls when they occur.

It is very important to be organized when you call on your customers. Make a schedule of whom to call and try to telephone each customer on a

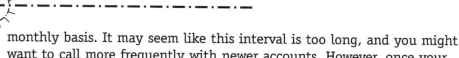

monthly basis. It may seem like this interval is too long, and you might want to call more frequently with newer accounts. However, once your installed base gets sufficiently large, you will find that even calling once a month can be a burden for your contact.

Now comes the tough part. Remember the basic criteria for identifying your best reference customers—*chemistry, importance,* and *reciprocity.* As you gain experience with your customers, you can start prioritizing them from "first" to "last," based on how well they stack up on the criteria. You can monitor your other customers without calling them directly by using your company's hot line support system.

Over the course of my career, I have often been surprised by which customers turned out to be excellent partners and references. In many cases, some of my least favorite clients turned out to be great references after we had gotten a chance to work together. That's why it is important to service all of your accounts, even the ones that you have not targeted as references.

Pull the technical support logs for your target customers on a weekly basis. The technical support system should have all the data that you need to check up on your customers indirectly. Customers who have lots of calls into the support system or have serious bugs that are pending resolution are candidates for a telephone call. Serious problems may even warrant an on-site visit from you. You can also look for customers who are conspicuous by their absence. If a particular customer never appears in the support logs, he or she may warrant a call as well.

Never call on a customer without checking the support logs first.

You should always check the technical support logs before you call on your customer. This will help you to avoid nasty surprises.

Right:

Sales Consultant: *"Hi, Joe. Sorry to bother you, but I noticed from my daily technical report that you've run into a problem. I've been talking with technical support about this problem that you are having with the latest version of SuperServer. Technical support tells me they are working on a patch, which should be ready by next week. Is that going to work for you?"*

Wrong:

Sales Consultant: *"Hey Joe, How is it going?"*

Joe: *"We've got a major problem with SuperServer, that's how it's going."*

The Boy Scout motto, "Be prepared," is a good thing to keep in mind. By gathering data *before* you make the call, you can make sure you are adding real value. Your customers will appreciate the fact that you are on top of the situation. There are still going to be some surprises, and you will not always be able to help directly. However, the more preparation, the fewer nasty surprises.

Checking with technical support before you call on your customers is just one of a number of tactical steps you can take to keep abreast of your customers. Press stories, magazines, and the Internet are all great sources of information about your customers.

The Golden Rules for Working with Existing Customers

There are two golden rules that apply to working with your customers. In fact, they apply to working with prospects also, but they are especially important in maintaining a good and lasting relationship with your customer base.

> *Always set expectations.*
> *Always return phone calls, e-mails*
> *and pages promptly.*

It is very easy to become overwhelmed with work and start to fall behind on your commitments. You can avoid this by being absolutely fanatical about setting proper expectations. Promise only what you can deliver, and be up front with your customer about what you can and cannot do. Consider the following:

- You cannot solve the world's problems. Some things are out of your hands.

- You have a schedule just like anyone else, and you can't do everything right away.

- It is permissible *not* to know the answer off the top of your head.

- You do not have to agree with everything that your customer tells you.

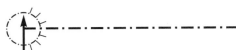

These are not excuses—they are reality. You can keep tempers from flaring and disappointments from occurring by properly setting expectations. Tell the customer what you are going to do in response to his or her request, and say when you are going to do it. If it takes longer than you expect, call the customer and let him or her know that it is taking longer than expected.

In all cases, *promptly return all phone calls, e-mails, and pages from your customers*. You do not have to call back with an answer or a solution, but you have to at least acknowledge the request as soon as possible.

One common mistake that sales consultants have a tendency to make is to let their voice-mail message get outdated. Try to change your voice message on at least a weekly basis.

It will help to set the customer's expectations for a response from you by listing your weekly schedule on your voice mail greeting, and don't give anyone your pager number unless you are prepared to answer the page immediately when your customer uses it.

Consider the following:

Your customer leaves you a message regarding a problem, but you are already booked solid when the message comes in. The right thing to do is to acknowledge the issue and let the customer know exactly what to expect from you, as follows:

> **Sales Consultant:** *Joe, I got your message, and I am sorry to hear that you are having a problem with SuperServer. I have a seminar presentation this morning, but I will look into this for you this afternoon. Could you give me the case number that technical support provided you? I will call them about this case directly after the seminar and find out where we stand. I'll leave a message for you regardless of the outcome to let you know what the plan is for resolving this issue. Joe, I am sorry about this, and I thank you for your continued support and patience.*

In the preceding example, the sales consultant acknowledges the message, even just to say that he is aware of the problem but cannot respond to it right away. Proper expectations are set, including the fact that the sales consultant will let the customer know what is happening, whether the problem is solved or not.

There is another good practice depicted in this example. Although the sales consultant is quick to offer assistance, he also ensures that the customer is making use of the proper support channels by asking for the technical support case number. Customers will run into many problems—some questions, some bugs, some training issues and some situations that require custom coding. Most companies have three distinct types of resources for helping the customer:

- Technical support
- Training
- Consulting

Technical support is available for answering basic questions and to track bugs. The first line of defense for the customer must be the technical support organization. By asking for the technical support case number, you are also making sure the customer is following accepted protocol. Make sure the customer utilizes technical support. You can reinforce this process by verifying the customer has a case number.

Customers who have a high volume of calls are candidates for additional training. The technical support group will bless you eternally for staying on top of customers who are having continuous problems—and this blessing will usually be returned in the form of enhanced cooperation when you have a good customer with a serious problem.

Some types of problems will require custom coding, on-site configuration and tuning, or the addition of new features to the system. In order to solve these problems, you will need to build some consensus among both engineering and technical support. If you have a track record for managing your customers well, it will be a lot easier to get consensus on tough issues with these other teams.

If you think the customer needs additional training or consulting help, get the sales rep involved.

The sales rep is your partner. He or she is trained to manage customers and sell solutions. If you think that a particular customer is having serious problems, get the sales rep involved in the account. The sales team may need to sit down face to face with the customer to put together a more detailed plan to get the customer back on track.

Proactive Customer Management

Up to this point, we have focused mainly on problem resolution, since this is one of your major tasks as a sales consultant. However, this is not the only value that you can bring to the customer. Sales consultants have access to lots of good information, such as innovative uses of the product, the details of forthcoming releases, and access to beta software. As technology companies continue to move to the Web, it is increasingly common that most of the critical information that your customers will need can be found on a Web site's support section. It is very popular to stuff the support site with frequently-asked-questions and how-to documents. Still, your customers want to hear your voice and see your smiling face from time to time. Personal phone calls and visits show that you have a commitment to the customer.

With all of the other important work that you have to do, it can become difficult to reach most of your customers on a personal basis. Important customers, especially those whom you have targeted as likely references, require personal attention. The question is—How do you find time to reach the other customers in your territory?

The answer is the ever-popular user group. User groups are periodic meetings that are organized by a group of customers in a localized territory. Most high-tech companies have a national user group that typically meets once a year in a pleasant locale. The national event takes place in more of a party atmosphere, giving you less of a chance to bond with your local customers. This is not to say that we think that national user group meetings are a waste of time. They are important for your company but less valuable to you in terms of managing your local customers. They offer too many distractions for the customers and for you.

Local and regional user group meetings are a much better venue for working with your customers. First of all, local groups are typically composed of your own customers, as opposed to the national meeting, which is attended by the national body of users. Local user groups do not typically require extensive (or expensive) travel, so most users find it easier to attend local meetings.

User groups are an ideal place for you to meet with all of your local customers. You may not have the bandwidth to call on all of them individually, but you can get to most of them through the user group. Most groups have a formal charter, with rules about allowing vendors to attend group meetings. As a sales consultant, you are typically an exception to such rules, since your technical ability makes you a welcome participant, regardless of your affiliation with the vendor.

Users are sensitive about being "sold to" during user group meetings, and they sometimes exclude sales reps to guard against turning these meetings into sales events.

The key element to making local user groups successful is content, and this is the main value you can bring to user group meetings. You can draw content from many sources, including the following:

- Technical support
- Engineering
- Partners

Local user groups are usually more successful if the users themselves take responsibility for content, but it is your job to help them in this effort. Leverage your contacts within the company to get other members of your corporate team to make presentations to your local user groups. We know that it is expensive to fly people from headquarters out to the local offices, but in this age of the Internet, you can leverage other technologies to accomplish this same feat more economically. You can broadcast content using a browser and have your company resources call in via a conference call or video hookup.

Technical support people are often a wealth of knowledge, and it helps to get them involved directly with customers. Very few users call technical support to express their gratitude on a daily basis: They call technical support because they are having problems. User groups are a perfect venue for technical support staff to address the users proactively. Take note of the following example:

> **Sales Consultant:** *It seems like every customer is having issues with backing up the SuperServer master database. Technical support has been looking at this issue in detail. I have Ken Jackson from our technical support department on the line today, and he's excited to talk with you about some popular techniques for addressing this issue.*

This kills two birds with one stone. Technical support people get to "show their stuff," and they might even be able to knock down the call volume by educating a large group of users at one time. Product engineering offers similar opportunities, especially about the internals of your products.

Be aware that your company, or individual tech support reps, may be leery of letting a group of customers know the identity of a particularly good support rep, since this may lead to direct calls from members of the user group.

Engineering staff are best leveraged for *detailed* technical issues, as opposed to product strategy. Sales consultants are most helpful resources for introducing new features and new releases to the users. This is part of your job.

Many sales consultants make the error of handling all of the "company presentations" to user groups themselves. Don't make this mistake. Your customers will feel better about your company and technology if they see that the company is more than just "you."

User Group Etiquette

There are several important things to remember when working with user groups:

Greet all of the customers personally.

Take the time to shake hands and say "Hello" to everyone in the group, not just the people that you happen to like. Be sincere about it.

Don't take over the meeting.

Feel free to participate, but don't take over the meeting. You are there as a resource, not to run the show. You may have to "run" the first few meetings of a new chapter of a user group to get things off the ground, but it is important to get the users to take control. If you don't, the user group will become more of a burden to you than an asset.

Bring along some "gimmes."

One of the guilty pleasures of being a technologist is getting T-shirts, mugs, mousepads, hats, pens and bags—basically anything with the company logo on it. If your company does not provide such things, work with your regional manager to buy them. Many companies make "gimmes" in smaller quantities for a reasonable price. Bring enough for everyone in the user group, and keep one or two "higher-end" items for the user speakers or meeting-hosts. Customers love these things, and they keep the company name and logo in circulation.

Involve partners in the user group.

Your company undoubtedly has business partnerships with other companies. Partners can be a fountain of knowledge as well as valuable assets for local user groups. Remember to invite your sales consultant counterparts within partner organizations to your local user group events. Partners are an important component of your overall installed base. We will discuss this in detail in this next section.

Partners

There are several different types of customers with whom you will work as part of the installed base. For the most part, sales consultants are involved with direct-sales, end-user customer companies, but these are not the only types of customers. We use the term "end-user" to refer to companies that buy your technology or application for internal use, as opposed to customers who use your technology as part of another application. There are four other classes of customers that you may have to deal with over the course of your career:

- Value-added resellers (VARs)
- Application service providers (ASPs)
- Original equipment manufacturers (OEMs)
- Systems integrators

All of these organizations can be customers, but the way in which you interact with each of them can be quite different as compared to the way you deal with traditional end-user customers. Value-added resellers (VARs) are those companies that use your product as a component of their own product. In essence, your technology is a part of their larger product offering. VARs are very commonly associated with software companies, particularly those software companies that manufacture tools and utilities.

Most database manufacturers (relational, object, etc.) have a large installed base of VARs. In fact, any company that makes and sells an application on top of any database product is by definition a VAR. Companies such as XYZ-Db, Sybase, and Informix have many VARs among their installed base of customers.

VARs are a special kind of end user of your product. Their engineering department uses your product as a component of their solution. Whether the use of your product is visible to users or to the sales teams of the

VAR depends very much upon the nature of your solution. Consider the following two examples:

- ACME Sales applications uses UberJava's Java editor and compiler to build the ACME-Sales-Trakker application.
- ACME Sales applications stores its data in an XYZ-Db database and ships a copy of XYZ-Db with each release of ACME-Sales-Trakker.

ACME is a VAR for both products in the preceding examples. However, in the first case, ACME's developers use UberJava to build their application, but they do not really distribute UberJava to their users. A local sales consultant from UberJava will support the headquarters operation of ACME, but local sales consultants are unlikely to have much interaction with ACME.

ACME also uses XYZ-Db as the database for its Sales-Trakker product, and ships a copy of XYZ-Db with its sales application. In this case, the sales consultants for ACME will be bumping into XYZ-Db issues directly. ACME customers will need to run XYZ-Db in order to use the ACME solution. As a sales consultant for XYZ-Db, you will end up working directly with the local sales consultants for ACME in addition to local ACME customers (who end up as XYZ-Db customers by virtue of the fact that they bought ACME's product). A local VAR can give you tremendous penetration into a territory. The VAR is like having an extra sales team helping you out.

Because VARs have a closer relationship with you, they should also be treated as high-priority customers. A sales consultant who calls on you from a VAR may have a problem that is affecting *multiple* customers, so you would be well advised to make an extra effort to support the VARs in your community. VAR accounts offer tremendous sales potential for the sales team as well. Many times, a VAR will embed a "run-time" copy of your product within its system. This gives you the chance to "upsell" the end-customer a full version of your software for other projects. In effect, the VAR gets your system in the door and you can leverage this into new business.

As a sales consultant for a 4GL software vendor, I had the chance to work with one of the company's largest VARs, who had built a comprehensive asset-management application. I learned a few things about my own product from their engineering team, and we were successfully selling their clients full development licenses for other applications. In fact, I liked their system so much I ultimately went to work for them!

Application service providers (ASPs) are the newest type of partner that you will encounter as a sales consultant. ASPs are similar to your VAR partners in many ways. They, too, license your software for distribution to the end customer, but they differ in the manner in which they deploy the software. While VARs install your product as part of their own offering, ASPs install and manage your software on their own equipment on behalf of the customer. In the Internet age it has become quite common for customers to outsource the management of critical Internet-based systems to these ASPs. ASPs will normally specialize in a finite number of software and hardware products.

Sales consultants from your VAR partners will tend to have the closest relationship with you out of any of the partner types. Original equipment manufacturers (OEMs) will come in a close second, only because of the wide nature of the OEM marketplace. OEMs also have a formal business relationship with your company but do not necessarily work with your product directly. The term *original equipment manufacturer* is a legacy from the early days of the minicomputer, when the primary OEM vendors were the computer hardware companies. OEM relationships are also defined at the highest levels of each company, but the degree to which they penetrate to the local territories varies widely.

This is not to say that OEM relationships are not important, as they can be very valuable. However, deciding how aggressively to work any particular OEM channel will require some judgment on your part.

OEM relationships are inherently more difficult to manage at the local level if your product is just one of many for the OEM partner. This does not excuse you from working with the OEMs, but it does make it more difficult in some cases for you to get their attention. VARs tend to be more intimately involved in your product than most OEMs.

In any case, you will have to keep your eyes open and adjust to the changing tides of the market. As the marketplace changes, your relationship with your VARs and OEMs will change. If you have a good working relationship with your local VARs and OEMs on a personal level, you can often "ride through" the inevitable changes that occur at the corporate level.

The largest partnering category may very well dwarf the influence of VARs and OEMs combined. Systems integrators, consultants, contractors, and professional trainers have a growing influence over the marketplace. These firms tend to work most closely with your product on a daily basis. Indeed, they are often building a business by providing services around

your product, making them extra important to your success. These companies come in forms such as these:

- National firms
- Regional firms
- Vertical specialists
- Independent contractors

National firms such as EDS, Arthur Andersen, and KPMG are typically full-service systems integrators. They have the ability to handle everything from design to implementation, and your company will most likely have a formal business relationship with them. As with the VARs or OEMs, you can develop a personal relationship on a local level with the technical staffs. These firms are less likely to have sales consultants, so you will find yourself more often than not working with project managers or consultants. If your product is important enough, they will develop a "practice" around it. Most of the national firms are focused on large, multimillion-dollar projects.

As of this writing, the key markets for the national firms are customer relationship management (CRM), and e-commerce. Although they have a much broader focus than these two markets alone, many of their high-profile partners are vendors who sell into these two spaces. After all, why spend your time building a small Intranet application when you can generate mega-bucks implementing Ariba or Siebel for many clients, leveraging your expertise?

Often, the smaller, regional firms and local consulting companies will be a better source of partnering opportunities. These firms do not necessarily target projects of the size and scope of the larger companies, and you will find that they have a tendency to be "stickier" as a result. Smaller firms may also require more of your help and resources. Some of these firms specialize in vertical market niches, where their industry expertise can offset the superior resources of the larger firms.

This is reality. Focus on partners who are willing to work with you, and maintain professional standards with those who are in someone else's camp. That's the best that you can do.

The easiest and, in other ways, the most difficult partners to work with are independent contractors. They are the easiest because they tend to be the most closely allied with your product. After all, one person can master only so many products at any given time. Yet because of their dependency upon your product, they can be the most resource-intensive partners to deal with. You have to go back to the root goal of working with customers and partners in order to understand how to deal with individual contractors. You work with customers to get references and to generate more business. Working with a single consultant too closely is not going to maximize either of those goals.

— · — · —

> The exception, of course, is when the individual contractor is a person of extreme influence and stature within your marketplace. I have worked with numerous high-profile contractors in my career when it has been smart to do so. Size doesn't matter; influence does.

— · — · —

Etiquette for Working with Partners

Regardless of the type of partner you are dealing with, there are some basic ground rules to follow:

Introduce yourself to the local sales consultants for all your partners.

Watch for new partnership announcements from your corporate marketing department, and be sure to introduce yourself to the local sales team for every partner.

Invite partners to all of your user-group events.

Partners are customers, too. Remember to invite your partners to all of the local user events, both as participants and as guest speakers. End-user customers will be interested in what your partners are doing with your products. Partner-products can often improve end-user satisfaction.

Start small and work your way up.

Working with a partner on a local level can be rewarding, but you should not expect too much at first. It's easy to over-promise at the start of a new partnership and have the whole thing fizzle out. Start slow, commit to a few events, and then be sure to follow through.

Wrapping Up

Landing a new customer is an expensive proposition. As a sales consultant, you should always be looking for innovative ways to shorten the technical sales cycle. Working with your existing customers to build references can help you with this process, while it also works to keep your existing customers satisfied and happy. Sales consultants are the most important contacts that a customer can have. Sales consultants provide the conduit back to the technical support and engineering organizations. You have access to resources that the customer needs to be successful, and you are more likely to be plugged in to new trends that are developing in the marketplace.

Your partners are special types of customers who can greatly expand the reach of your sales efforts.

In this chapter, we have focused on your friends and allies. In the next chapter, we are going to take a look at the other side of the coin: the competition.

Working the Competition

Throughout this book, we have been repeatedly discussing your interactions with others: your sales rep, your prospects and customers, and the other people in your company. This chapter will also discuss a particular type of interaction, one that is indirect, less than friendly, but still an inevitable component of any sales situation. This chapter covers how you can address the competition for your customer's business.

Why Care About the Competition?

You may be wondering why you should even think about the competition. After all, your goal is to sell your own product, not to deal with other companies and their products.

You *do* have a point if this is your thinking. In fact, we have intentionally placed this chapter on competition near the end of the book to emphasize that you should concentrate on your own products, rather than try to simply defeat the competition.

The reason for giving the competition a secondary place in your sales cycle considerations is simple:

You cannot win a deal by simply defeating the competition.

Although we will be focusing now on the competition, you should never forget your primary goal of selling your own product or service. Nonetheless, knowing about the competition and how to use their strengths and weaknesses to your advantage can help you win your business. Knowing about the competition and, even more importantly, how to use competitive information, can make you into a more valuable sales consultant.

There are two main reasons for concerning yourself with your competition. First, there is *always* competition in a sales situation. Usually, your competition is other products from other companies. If you work for a large company that creates many different products, you may even find yourself competing with other sales teams from your own company's ranks.

But sometimes your competition is not even another product. Your competition, in a broad sense, is any condition that can prevent you from winning your business. Your competition could be some of the staff at your prospect's company who don't want your product for a wide variety of reasons, ranging from a noble sense of dedication to having a different course of action to personal politics. Your competition could even be a more indirect condition, such as a budgetary restraint. Regardless of its shape, you should be able to use the suggestions in this chapter to defuse the threat from the competition.

But what if there really isn't any competition? This situation *could* occur, but the chances are that your sales representative would not even call you in on this type of deal. It is much more likely that there *is* competition, but that you and your sales representative didn't discover this until too late, when your deal had disappeared.

If you don't see competition in a sales situation, you just haven't found it yet.

You would much rather be aware of your competition so that you can deal effectively with them than to be blindsided by an unseen competitor. If an unknown source of competition lurks in the background of a prospect, you can suddenly find yourself losing control of the sales cycle.

The second reason to understand the competition is a corollary of the first. Although you cannot win a deal simply by defeating the competition, you can *lose* to the competition, so the competition will always stand in the way of the successful completion of your sales cycle. Even more importantly, losing a sale can lead to the loss of a customer, an ally, and a source of continuing revenue. If a customer does not purchase your product then, he or she has consciously decided to pursue a different course of action. If the customer chooses to purchase one of your competitors' products, it makes it easier for him or her later to purchase additional products from that competitor. If the customer decides not to purchase any product, you have failed to be convincing about the value of your solution and you may potentially have lost some of the prospect's respect.

Up to this point, we have been identifying any factors that could cause you to lose a business opportunity as your *competition*. It helps, from a conceptual viewpoint, to see this large picture, but from a practical standpoint, internal factors that affect a target customer—such as budget issues or internal politics—are more a part of your sales rep's primary tasks of qualifying and losing. As with all other parts of the sales operation, you should work with your sales rep to seek out and address these types of problems.

The rest of this chapter will focus on the competition you will face from other vendors.

Positioning Against the Competition

The key to working against your competition is to find a way to differentiate your product from theirs. In advertising, this has been called the *unique selling proposition*—exploring what your product can uniquely deliver that your competitors cannot.

In a competitive situation, you must help your prospect to understand what distinguishes your product from your competitors. Your unique selling proposition comes from a juxtaposition of your product's strengths and your competition's weaknesses.

You should start from your product's *sweet spot*—the part of your product that delivers the most powerful benefits.

Then, continually return to the benefits of your product, even when discussing the competition, since your ultimate goal is to sell your product. The "best" features of your product tend to remain relatively constant, but the benefits tied to these features will vary according to the needs of your prospect.

You can also turn your competitors' weaknesses into your strengths. If your competitor cannot provide a particular benefit, you should make this benefit a part of your overall positioning. You can combine these relative strengths in your product with your own sweet spots to win a deal over a particular competitor. For example, note the following:

Consider two products:

- UberServer—Does not provide load balancing
- SuperServer—Offers load balancing

Under normal sales conditions, you may not stress the importance of load balancing with SuperServer. It may not be one of your sweet-spot features. However, if you are competing against UberServer, it makes sense to discuss load balancing as part of the sales cycle, since you know that it will cause problems for the folks at UberServer. Your job is to create a need in the mind of your prospect for load balancing, rather than trying to draw the prospect's attention to the fact that UberServer lacks support for load balancing.

You can only use a competitor's weak points as one of your strengths if your product can deliver some type of countering benefit. If you simply attack a competitor's weakness without offering a corresponding benefit from your product, you risk losing your credibility in two ways. First, people generally don't like negative selling, so you risk losing some of your carefully built-up rapport with the prospect. Second, you can never tell what your competitors are planning for the future. If you attack a weakness in your competitor's product that has been remedied, or that will be shortly, you will have wasted a valuable part of your selling time.

Your competitor always knows more about his or her product than you do.

By coupling a competitor's weakness with one of your strong points, you establish your own strength, even if your competitor can address his or her product's own weakness.

You should be able to adopt your basic positioning for any particular sales situation based on your competitors' position in that situation. Most products have only a limited set of competitors. In fact, competing against inappropriate competitors is a sign of a sales situation gone awry, as shown in the Bulldozer-BMW comparison in Chapter 8, "Qualification and Planning for Presentations and Demos."

If your prospect is looking at products that do not address the same needs as your product, he or she may very well be confused. You will be in for a tough sale if your prospect doesn't recognize his or her own needs, since your goal is to demonstrate how your product answers these requirements. Your most difficult competitive task will be to attempt to educate the prospect about a misconception of a competitor's capabilities. Normally, you should focus on the capabilities of your product and the prospect's needs. However, occasionally you may need to address your

---

competitor's solution directly. This is especially the case when your prospect is misinformed about the competition's capabilities. Although we dealt in detail with this problem in the chapter on objection handling, the subject bears mentioning here as well. If you need to dispute one of your competitor's claims, you need to keep in mind the fact that your competition knows more about the product than you do. Be careful how you react in these situations:

Wrong:

Sales Consultant: *Joe, you are wrong. UberServer does not have a native database driver for IEM Dby. They are lying to you.*

Right:

Sales Consultant: *Joe, I am sure you are right. It was my understanding that UberServer was using a third-party driver to access IEM Dby. This may have changed in the new release. In any event, let me show you how SuperServer works with IEM Dby...*

In the first conversation, the sales consultant errs in telling the prospect that he is wrong. By backing the prospect into a corner, you have forced him to fight. It does not matter whether you are right or wrong about UberServer—all you've done now is angered your prospect. In the second conversation, the sales consultant sells the issue subtly by complimenting the prospect and then offering an alternate opinion. The consultant does not state opinion as fact, but raises the issue in the mind of the prospect and then moves on.

Discovering the Competition

As we have discussed earlier in this book with the Bulldozer-BMW analogy,

Inappropriate competitors are a sign of a confused prospect.

How do you find out who your competitors are in a sale? Believe it or not, the best policy is simply to ask your prospect.

This may seem counter-intuitive in some sense. After all, you are in a battle to win a sale, and you can't expect your prospect to aid you in your quest to defeat the competition. But when you focus on a sales cycle as a battle between you and your competition, you are forgetting the real aim of the cycle—to give your prospect what he or she wants and needs. Your prospect is not some bystander in your own private war with your competitors—he or she is the focus of your efforts. You may win and your competition may lose, or vice versa, but the only way you will achieve lasting sales success is if your prospect wins by getting the product that best suits his or her needs.

It is in the best interest of your prospect to tell you about your competition. Your prospect wants to find the best product, and by informing you, he or she is helping you to illuminate the differences between your product and those of your competitors. There is nothing wrong with asking your prospect about the features of the competition that are most appreciated, or about the features that the prospect feels the other products lack. If the prospect knows what is required, he or she can get the best understanding of the differences between competing products by letting you, and your opposition, know about their respective products.

In some situations, your prospect will not tell you who your competitors are. There could be several reasons for this. One is that you are not engaged in a truly open and fair contest to win the business. The prospect has already decided which product to purchase, and does not want any information delivered that would contradict this choice. Another reason is that your prospect is afraid that you will unduly sway him or her from a particular product if you know who the competition is. This type of prospect typically is not well informed, and therefore does not want to get confused. Although some sales representatives think this type of prospect can be easily educated, this prospect can, in fact, be the most difficult to win over. As the prospect hears from one vendor, he or she accepts that vendor's premises. When the next vendor enters the scene, the prospect adopts a different set of priorities. Since your prospect is not grounded in his or her needs, it is difficult to address issues in any lasting way. We will talk more about problem prospects in the next chapter.

You may not be in the most favorable sales situation if you cannot learn who your competitors are from your prospect.

300

If you can't discover your competition, there is something wrong with the sales situation.

There are times when your prospect asks you to identify some of your significant competitors. This is a potentially dangerous situation that must be handled with care. But don't be afraid to respond to this request. Resist the temptation to say that you don't have any competition. Remember: All products have a set of competitors. Your prospect will eventually find other competitors through advertising or research. By denying the existence of competitors, you may be delaying the discovery of your competitors for a brief time, but you may also be jeopardizing your own credibility.

If you are asked to name your competitors, take advantage of the request to better understand your prospect's needs. It is good technique to tell your prospect that your competitors depend on the prospect's requirements. This type of comment will help you draw out information from the prospect that will assist you to understand how they will choose their eventual product selection.

Let the prospect's needs drive your competitive positioning.

A prospect may be looking to you for validation of potential choices. Don't be afraid to mention some of your competitors, especially your well-known and established ones. A prospect who is even remotely well informed will already know about these choices, so you have endangered neither your sale by bringing in new competition nor your credibility by displaying naiveté about the overall marketplace.

Be aware, however, that some prospects want you to do their market research for them. They expect you to offer up the most likely competitors on a plate, informing them of the competition's strengths versus yours. There is no need to indulge this type of request. You shouldn't be rude when denying the request, but you can demur on the basis of being an expert in your product and not on your competition's.

The goal of making a sale to your customer is to match the prospect's needs with your strengths, not to provide validation for the prospect to choose a different product. As an example, say your prospect asks you for a description of your competitors. You could reply by saying,

> **Sales Consultant:** *"Well, we have some competitors, but the appropriate one in this situation depends on your needs. Could we discuss those in a bit more detail?"*

Usually, this discussion will continue for a while until the prospect backs off from the request. But if he or she still asks, you will at least be armed with some key information about your prospect. You can then suggest a competitor who you know will not be able to address the prospect's needs effectively!

And if this still doesn't work, just say "Microsoft," or "IBM," or "XYZ-Db," or one of the other giants, since they compete with everyone!

In general, you want to avoid disparaging the competition in any way during your exchange with the prospect. The key is to avoid either knocking the competition or validating them in some way other than through some simple platitudes. Consider the following examples:

Wrong:

Sales Consultant: *UberServer? Are you kidding me? That product is a dog with fleas.*

Sales Consultant: *UberServer. Yeah, we run into them all the time.*

Right:

Sales Consultant: *You are looking at UberServer as well? They make a fine product and they have some talented people. Now, one of the ways in which SuperServer can help you is...*

There is no value in disparaging the competition, since you end up insulting the prospect by implying that he or she is considering an inferior solution. You are better off complimenting the competitor as a fine product, and then refocusing the conversation back to your solution. You also do not want to validate the competitor by giving it an important status. Aren't they the competition? Sure. But don't validate them in the deal by mentioning that you compete against them all the time.

How to Use Competitive Information

Competitive information can help you understand the needs and goals of your prospect. If you know your competition's strong points and weaknesses, you can determine the most important qualities of a product for your prospect. For instance, if your prospect is not looking at the leading product in your market segment, you may gather that it is not crucial to your prospect to go with the leader. With this information in hand, you may not have to spend time overcoming the fact that your product may not be the leader in its market.

With some further interaction, you may even be able to find out more about your prospect. You may learn, for instance, that your prospect is predisposed toward a company with a smaller market share, because they think that smaller vendors have a technological edge.

When it comes to introducing competitive information into your sales presentation, you should follow four basic guidelines. By following these guidelines, you will be able to use competitive information most effectively.

Stay centered on your products.

It can be very tempting for you to focus on knocking the competition rather than selling your prospect on the virtues of your product. This is a bad idea for a very simple reason.

You have a single primary objective in your sales cycle: to get the prospect to purchase your product. Competitive information can be used to stop your prospect from buying the competitor's product, but by itself, competitive information does nothing to sell your product. In all sales cycles, you have a finite amount of time to interact with your customer, and you should try to use as much of it as possible to push your product, rather than to knock the competition.

For this reason, you should never lead off a discussion with competitive information. Your prospect may walk away from your meeting with a single thought—and you want it to be about your product, not your competition.

You can maximize the use of competitive positioning and knockoffs by always staying centered on your product's strengths and capabilities. You can always use your competition's weakness as one of your product's strengths. This way, you can keep the focus on your product and still get some digs in at the competition. It is not necessary to identify your competitor's weaknesses by name when you focus on your strengths.

Wrong:

Sales Consultant: *SuperServer has load balancing and UberServer does not.*

Right:

Sales Consultant: *One of the most powerful features of SuperServer is its ability to load balance user connections across multiple servers. You can use this feature to ensure that the response times for your users remain constant during times of heavy use.*

Make sure all competitive information is 100 percent accurate.

Whenever you use competitive information, you are treading into a mine field. You are in grave danger of losing your most valuable asset: your credibility.

Remember, your colleagues with the competition have the same goal as you—to sell their product. And, as we mentioned earlier in this book, to some extent your prospect will buy from the team he or she feels more comfortable with. If you make a misstatement about your competition, you will have to assume that what you say will get back to the competition. They will have caught you in a lie, a lie told for malicious reasons. Your credibility will take a direct, and often fatal, hit, jeopardizing your entire effort. With stakes this high, you should always be as accurate as possible about the competition.

Never lie about the competition!

How can you use any competitive information? After all, you know much more about your product than you know about your competitor's products. Your competitors also have knowledge of forthcoming enhancements and improvements in their own products that will not be immediately available to you.

The most important technique to use is to always caveat your competitive information. It never hurts to use phrases like "I understand" or "I've heard from others" when talking about the competition. These phrases both protect your credibility, in case you are wrong, and invite a response from your prospect if your statements about the competition are incorrect. This will give you a graceful way out of anything you may say about your competition that turns out to be less than accurate.

Of course, you should always protect yourself when you use competitive information. Check out the date of the information. The older the information, the better the chance that your competition either will have fixed the problem or at least have come up with a countering stance or demonstration.

The dangers posed by incorrect competitive information give you all the more reason for staying centered on your own product! It's not worth jeopardizing your credibility for what may be a dubious competitive advantage. You can always avoid painting yourself into a corner by couching your remarks in the context of the market as a whole:

Wrong:

Sales Consultant: *UberServer doesn't support load balancing.*

Right:

Sales Consultant: *Customers tell me that the load balancing feature of SuperServer is unique in the application server marketplace.*

Go for the clean shot.

Just because a piece of competitive information is accurate and timely does not necessarily make it appropriate to use. You always have to remember that in using competitive information, you are not firing at an unarmed opponent. If your prospect is seeking to find the best product for his or her needs, he or she is likely to tell your competitors what you have said about them.

Because of this, you should treat some types of competitive information carefully. There are some competitive knocks, true of virtually every product and company that has ever been in existence: They have some dissatisfied customers, their product has some bugs, and they are occasionally late on delivery dates. Along with these generic types of knockoffs, there may be problems with your competitors' products that are also problems for your *own* products. If you use these types of points as key competitive knockoffs, you may very well find yourself in a spitting contest with your competitors, where you spend more time pointing fingers and defending your product and less time establishing your product as the eventual winner of the sales process.

This isn't to say that you can't use some of this information in the context of weaving a competitive story. If a product has a long reputation as unstable, you can use the information as part of a larger picture of your competition. In such cases, you can say that they have to devote attention to fixing their problems before moving on, or that these problems are the result of a flawed underlying architecture— coupled with a clear and brief explanation of the flaw. This is what we refer to as a *clean shot*—a competitive volley that cannot be easily defused by the competition.

For example, if you say the competitive product is "buggy," all your competition has to do is to produce customer references who are happy with the product or to guide the prospect through a session with the product that does not result in any bugs. Your competition has not only refuted your assertion, but has turned the focus of attention onto their product at the same time.

On the other hand, if you point out that many of the bugs are coming from the way the competitor's product is architected, a simple demonstration or reference call may not be enough to dispel this notion. Your competitor may have to spend his valuable sales time explaining and demonstrating underlying architecture. At the least, you have been able to set the agenda of the sales cycle, giving you more flexibility in your sales cycle and a greater chance to make the sale.

As with your own product positioning, the best way to use competitive information is to make a competitive case. Many individual points combine to create an overwhelming impression of the weaknesses of your competitors' offerings.

Keep it professional.

Even when you follow all of these guidelines, it is very tempting to go after your competition full strength. This approach is especially alluring, since you probably compete against the same product day after day and can build up a bit of animosity over time.

You must resist this temptation and go easy on your competitor. The main reason is quite simple: Someone at your prospect's company chose that competitor. By rabidly attacking a competitor, you are attacking the judgment of the person who initially chose them. Sometimes, your contact will seem to have a predisposition against your competitor. Your prospect may just be acting sly, but more frequently he or she appears this way because someone else at the company selected the competitor.

You must assume your competitors have advocates within your prospect's organization.

Since you must assume that your competitors have advocates within your prospect's organization, you also have to assume that everything you say or imply about a competitor will make its way back to them. Your competitor will have the opportunity to rebut what you have said, sometimes without giving you the chance to counter their rebuttal.

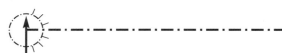

You might say to yourself, "Oh no, this prospect and I trust each other—they won't go to the competition with my slams." And you might be right. But even if you are, you are depending on the good will of your prospect and all of their co-workers. You will have given up some of your control of the sales cycle.

The strategy of having an advocate for a particular product act as the contact for that product's sales team is quite common, since many organizations have to divide up the work of evaluating multiple vendors. Those who favor your solution will be more likely to volunteer to investigate your product. The person you are talking to may genuinely dislike your competition and be willing to believe anything you say about them, but when the sale is being consummated, your contact may very well have a counterpart in the decision-making process who feels just as negatively about you.

You also have to remember that making a sale marks just the *beginning* of a long-term relationship with your customer. It helps get this relationship off to a positive start if you are being perceived as a fair and positive person rather than a piranha who is constantly attacking enemies.

The last reason for going easy on the competition is a simple, logical one. Remember, your object is to find your customers, not destroy the competition's. If you establish credibility and properly link your product's strengths with the needs of your customer, you have gone a long way toward turning your prospect into your customer. When your credibility is established, a simple implication on your part will be as powerful as a direct frontal attack without the backing of your credibility. If you have to go at your competition with hammer and tongs, there is a good chance that something is missing in the relationship with your prospect.

The sales cycle is a gentle dance with your prospect. Match your actions to those of your potential customer. If you have to ride roughshod over the competition, you are probably just increasing the distance between yourself and your prospect and diminishing the possibility of turning that prospect into a customer.

It is imperative to use competitive information with discretion. There are no silver bullets in competitive situations that will always work, and there are rarely times when competitive information alone can win a sale for you. The four guidelines above will help you to use competitive information in an appropriate way.

But how do you work competitive knockoffs into your sales cycle?

Working in Competitive Knockoffs

You don't want to force the mention of the competition into your part of the sales cycle, because this action may not serve to be the most effective use of your sales time. There are several ways to make sure that your competitors' weaknesses are made known to your prospect without distracting from your control of the sales cycle.

As mentioned above, the most effective way to handle competitive information is to use the competitors' weaknesses in your overall positioning. This method helps you avoid the pitfalls that come from a more direct use of competitive information. You are giving your prospect a framework in which to understand your product, and simultaneously orienting them away from your competitors. Since one of your main goals is to get your prospect to accept your positioning, you also do not waste time dealing directly with your competitors' positioning.

Finally, by using positioning, you can implicitly knock your competitors without making direct statements about them. This makes it much harder for your competitor to respond.

You can create a slight variation to this approach by discussing your competitors in a general market overview. This can be a part of your standard presentation. You can fortify your credibility by displaying an understanding of the overall market. This approach makes it appear that you are very familiar with the products on the market, and you can recommend your solution impartially for its obvious superiority.

Of course, you can always mention the competition when you talk of specific points about your product. If you bring up a point as part of your presentation, you can mention how your competitors deal with the situation. This method can be effective, but because it is more specific, your competition has a better chance to refute you, thereby jeopardizing your credibility.

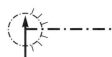

One of our favorite techniques for passing on competitive knockoffs is the *casual aside*. You can always just happen to mention a competitive knockoff in passing. Typically, the casual nature of this type of comment ensures that your prospect will not go back to your competition with your remark. You establish a competitor's problem in your prospect's mind without having to elaborate on specifics.

For example, during a break in the meeting over coffee you might casually make this sort of remark to your key technical contact:

Sales Consultant: *It's interesting that you mention the need for load balancing. It was my impression that UberServer doesn't support load balancing—have they addressed this issue?*

Of course, the casual aside works much better once you have established a good rapport with your prospect. When you are thinking in sync, your prospect will be able to absorb the impact of a negative aside. If, for some reason, your prospect picks up on a comment and asks for details, you can deliver more information, but at least in this situation you are acting in response to your prospect's questioning, so you will not seem to be unduly trashing your competitors.

As a final caution, you should beware the prospect who asks you for dirt about the competition. As we mentioned earlier, this type of prospect may be asking you to do market research for them. The prospect may also be asking for direct competitive points to turn over to your competitors for rebuttal. By having the negatives and the subsequent responses, the prospect can make a very neat case for your competitor and still make it seem like you have been given a fair chance to win the business.

Sometimes, a prospect will ask you to attack your competition as a test of your professionalism. If you attack the competition like a hungry dog going after a piece of steak, you will not seem like the sort of person to trust in a long-term relationship between a customer and a vendor.

One common mistake to guard against is "assuming the competitive objection." You may find yourself running into the same issue with the same competitors over and over again. If you see a particular issue often enough, you may find yourself automatically assuming that every prospect is concerned about it. It's important to let the deal develop naturally. Don't dive into a long response before the prospect even raises an issue. At best, you have appeared somewhat defensive. At worst, you have introduced a powerful competitive issue into a sales cycle that works *against* you.

Where Can You Find Competitive Information?

There are four basic sources for information about your competitors:

- **Public sources**—You can freely gather information about your competitors in the same way that a prospect does. You can request marketing information from a competitor; you can attend a competitor's booth at trade shows; you can read your competitors' ads in trade journals; or you can visit your competitors' Web sites. The disadvantage of gathering information from these public sources is that you will only discover good things about your competitors' products. The advantage of gathering information through public sources is that you will see the same image of your competitor as your prospect will see.

  You can also do more research from public sources, including finding articles in trade journals. These sources may reveal problems with your competitors' products. Anything you can use from a published article is especially useful, since it is as valid as a third-party source.

  You can also visit Web sites that discuss your competitors' products, as well as participate in newsgroups and mailing lists concerning your competition. These sources may yield some weaknesses in the products. However, you generally have to spend time with these sources, since you have to sift through a lot of material to find and confirm negative information.

- **Internal competitive information**—If you work for a larger company, or if your product has a limited number of competitors, you may be able to get competitive information from your colleagues in sales and marketing. Many companies have people whose full- or part-time job involves dissecting the competition.

These people will gather information from public sources as well as do in-depth research on the competitive products. Large companies may even reach out to the competitors' user community through surveys and questionnaires.

It's great to have access to this type of competitive analysis. Competitive analysis not only describes the competitive products, but also illuminates weaknesses in the products and maps out competitive positioning for you. However, because this type of competitive analysis has to be directed to the general needs of the entire company, you may find that you will not be able to use all of the information. In addition, your prospects may be reluctant to take this type of information to heart, since it can be seen as too favorable to your product.

If you do not have a formal competitive group within your organization, you can set up an informal group for sharing competitive information and techniques. By creating a simple online resource, such as a mailing list or a bulletin board, you can not only share the information gathered or possessed by your co-workers, but also create a long-term repository of this information.

- **Your prospects and customers**—Earlier in this chapter, you learned that you should be able to find out who your competitors are from your prospects. Once you have established a good rapport with your prospects, you can speak frankly with them about the competition. Although a prospect may not give you in-depth information about the competition's weaknesses, you should be able to at least find out the strengths of your competition. It doesn't matter if your prospect's viewpoint differs from the established position of the competition. In the end, the competitor you must beat is the competitor as your prospect sees it.

You can also use your established customers as a source for competitive information. Every time you win a deal, you have probably beaten your competition. It makes sense to contact your customers after making a sale, to get their opinions on your competitors' products. Once a customer has chosen your product, he or she will be able to illuminate why you were chosen over your competition. You can use this information for future sales cycles.

By knowing who you beat in a deal, you can also find the most appropriate customer reference to use against similar competition in other deals. Your customer will be able to relate to your prospect's situation and be an appropriate guide.

- **Your co-workers**—Your co-workers are one of the best sources of competitive information. First of all, they will be selling against the same competitors, so they will have hands-on experience about all phases of the competitive battle. This is especially important since competitive information has to be as timely as possible. Even if you have worked against a particular product many times in the past, your co-workers may have seen a new wrinkle in their positioning, or be aware of promised new features or solutions that you have not seen before. By pooling information with your co-workers, you will acquire the omnipotence of many sets of eyes and ears.

In the high turnover world of technical sales, there is also the chance that some of your co-workers may have worked for the competition. These former employees are an invaluable source of information, since they will not only be able to fill you in on the strong and weak points of their old products, but may also be able to enlighten you as to the ways your competitors are positioning themselves against your product.

Wrapping Up

To complete a technical sale successfully, it helps to be aware of the competition. But competitive information must be used with great discretion, since it can, when used incorrectly, damage or ruin your credibility, and actually cause you to lose a sale. As they used to say in a well-known television show, "Be careful out there."

At this point, you should be feeling pretty comfortable about handling your end of the sales process. But the person on the other side of the table—your prospect, the object of your professional attention—can sometimes undercut your best efforts. In the next chapter, you will learn about certain types of prospects who can cause problems in a sales cycle, and the best ways to deal with them.

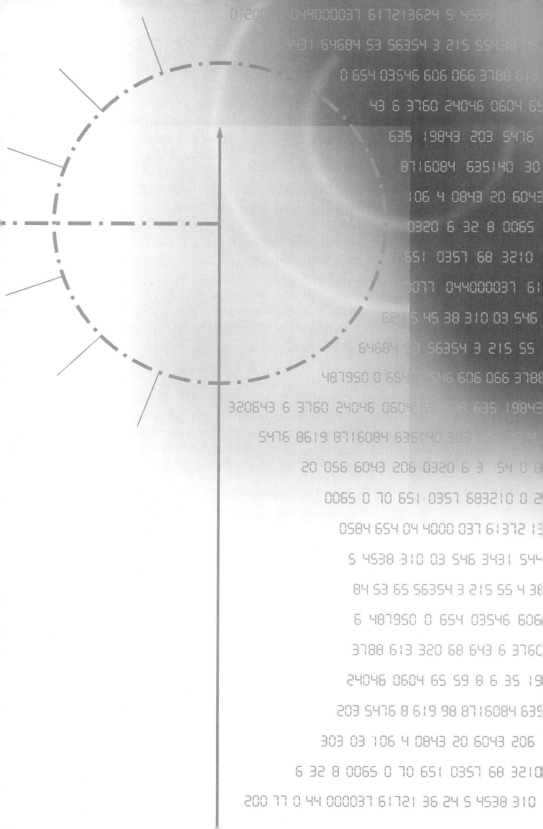

CHAPTER 16

Eight Challenging Prospects

Up to this point, we have tried to focus mostly on positive and practical subjects. In this chapter, we will take a detour into a topic that is primarily negative—dealing with the worst types of sales prospects you will encounter.

Each of these types of prospects should send up a red flag, telling you that there may be difficulties ahead in your sales cycle. For each of these problem prospects, we include suggestions on how best to deal with them.

Uneducated Prospects

The perfect prospect understands not only the technical issues that revolve around your product but can also quickly connect your solutions to technical benefits your product offers. However, at times, your prospects may simply be ignorant about the arena in which your product operates.

With an uneducated prospect, you will find that an increasing amount of your valuable sales time is taken up explaining not only your products, but possibly also some of the basics of your technology and your industry. Your prospect may even be ignorant about computers in general.

If a prospect is uneducated, he or she will typically favor the vendor with the most "mindshare," or public awareness. For instance, everyone knows about Microsoft's phenomenal success. Someone who is not that savvy about the details of technology may tend to give Microsoft products far more credit, based on mindshare, than any of its specific products warrant. If you work for Microsoft, or some other dominant player, uneducated prospects may be oriented toward your solution. Unfortunately for most of you reading this book, Microsoft is a bit of an anomaly as far as public mindshare goes; since it is by far the most widely known and recognized

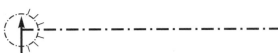

software company, you will normally find that an uneducated prospect is indeed a problem.

> Mindshare can work both ways, of course, as Microsoft's troubles with the Department of Justice have illustrated.

Although an uneducated prospect, in and of itself, is not necessarily bad, the person's lack of awareness can be coupled with an attitude that turns him or her into a virtually impregnable fortress—such an individual may be both uncomprehending and inflexible.

How to Handle the Uneducated Prospect

The uneducated prospect (at least in its benign form) is the least deadly of the types described in this chapter. You can help solve his or her problem by simply providing some education! If you can help the prospect to understand a topic, issue, or problem, you will be establishing your credibility as well as building rapport.

When a prospect starts to show signs of a lack of education, check out his or her understanding more frequently than you might normally do.

> "Checking for understanding" is an instructional process during which you specifically ask a person or audience if they understand a particular point or ask them questions designed both to test their knowledge and to reinforce key points. Although checking for understanding can feel forced, at least at first, it is an invaluable tool for verifying the success of teaching. For example, you could check for understanding about a certain facet of the SuperServer product in the following way:
>
> **Sales Consultant:** *SuperServer runs as a separate Java process on your UNIX server. I don't want to bore you with excessive details about how this works unless you are interested in these details. Should I take a minute to go through how Java servers are architected?*

Although you may find yourself using up a lot of time with this confirmation process, it is far better to spend some time checking on your prospect's understanding than to give an entire explanation that sails right over the prospect's head.

As you work with your product set more and more, you can gather up a set of standard, quick, and clear educational "lessons." One of the best ways to accomplish this is through the use of metaphors. As initially explained in Chapter 12, "Objection Handling," a well-turned comparison will not only connect with your prospects but will illuminate a topic more quickly and deeply than a mere explanation can possibly do.

In a sense, the uneducated prospect is a fertile field waiting to be tilled. If you can educate your prospect about a larger technology issues, you can establish the framework for him or her to select your product or service. When you lay out the ground rules, of course, you will do so in a way that favors your solution.

In a second sense, an uneducated but arrogant prospect is another type of field—a *minefield*. You will have to find a way for this type of individual to absorb some education while he or she avoids "losing face" by admitting ignorance.

One way to handle these problem prospects is to ask, in a conversational way, about a repercussion that resulted from a particular feature. Phrase your discussion in an open way and then lead the prospect to a deeper understanding.

One excellent method for accomplishing this is to use the device of the "other" prospect. You can allude to a customer who had a similar problem but who was not as intelligent or aware:

> **Sales Consultant:** *"I'm sure you are right on this. I once had another customer who was saying the same thing, but he hadn't thought this through, so this problem ended up sneaking up on him."*

You can then all have a good laugh at that "other prospect's" confused ways.

I used to use this tactic frequently, and it was absolutely amazing how often that other prospect was almost *just like the person I was talking with*—except not nearly so perceptive or bright. What a coincidence!

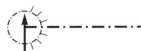

Tire Kickers

Although you may enjoy the actual process of a sales cycle, the cycle is very goal oriented: Its aim is to get the sale! A tire kicker is a prospect who is shopping, but isn't buying. A tire kicker can use up as many resources as a legitimate sales prospect, but with a tire kicker, you will never be able to complete the sales cycle successfully.

Since tire kickers have no intention of buying, they also do not have a specific problem they are trying to solve.

A prospect who demands an excessive breadth of functionality may be a tire kicker.

Of course, the process of qualification, which has been discussed throughout this book, should eliminate tire kicker prospects early in the sales cycle—usually before you get involved with the prospect at all. If you are working with a prospect who has no intention of culminating the evaluation with a purchase, he or she has reached this late stage frequently due to an incomplete or unresolved qualification process.

In other situations, a prospect may seem qualified to your sales rep but may look like a tire kicker to you. For instance, some companies have an extremely long purchasing cycle. Their normal mode of operation involves tire kicking for a year or two and then making a significant purchase. At some point, this prospect will become a real opportunity, but in the early phases they come across as a tire kicker.

> I was once involved in a lengthy sales cycle with one of the Big Three auto companies. Early on in the process, the sales rep asked if the company had money allocated this fiscal year for the project. They honestly answered "No," so the sales rep moved on to greener pastures.
>
> Eighteen months later, the company did make a multimillion-dollar purchase—from a company that had shown more patience with their evaluation process. But the sales rep I had worked with was long gone.

In some situations, there is a disconnection between the people your sales rep talks to and the people you are dealing with. The rep may have discussed the buying process with a senior manager, who assured him or her that a purchase could and would be made this year. You, on the other hand, are talking to the people who will be implementing the product or using your services, and they have informed you that they will not have the time to use your offering for more than a year. In this situation, your sales team should either try to reach a consensus from the prospect team or, with eyes wide open, move forward with the sales cycle anyway.

> You should always defer to your sales rep in these situations, but you should also make sure that you arm your rep with the data points that you have gathered from the technical decision makers.

How to Handle the Tire-Kicking Prospect

The leading creator of tire kickers is a lack of budget. As we have said before, as a sales consultant you should stay away from direct involvement in financial matters. But if you suspect that a prospect is not going to eventually make a purchase, you could ask for proof of intent in other ways.

For instance, you could ask the prospect to show you the milestones in his or her implementation schedule. If the dates and descriptions of the milestones become increasingly hazy as they move forward in time, or if they don't even exist, you might have a reason for concern.

Another factor that creates tire kickers is the infamous "standards committee." As the name implies, this committee is a group of people whose expressed goal is to create standards, which are then used in an actual sales process. With a standards committee, you will have to determine if the investment of time with this committee will create a suitably favorable result—standards for a deal you can win.

Having a tire kicker as a prospect doesn't necessarily mean there is no reason to continue the sale, but you and your rep may want to re-evaluate your resource commitments.

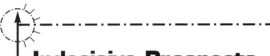

Indecisive Prospects

Indecisive prospects can drive a sales consultant mad. A perfect sales cycle should feel like a funnel: The closer you get to the end of the cycle, the more you hone in on the perfect prospect—product fit. An indecisive prospect cannot commit to a decision, which in turn means he or she cannot move on down the "funnel" of the sales process. An indecisive prospect can throw your sales cycle off the rails.

Many times, an indecisive prospect is simply no more than a prospect who truly does not know what he or she wants. These prospects often will become less and less indecisive as you work with them through the sales process. As with some of the other difficult types described in this chapter, this type of initial indecision is temporary; it usually fades away over the course of your interactions with the prospect.

But for some prospects, the indecision does not go away. Their indecision may come from a variety of sources. They may feel that they are powerless in their role, that any decision they make may be overruled by their senior management. The inability to make a decision is sometimes a part of the corporate culture, especially in the high tech field, where companies are often led by very hands-on executives.

And some people are just indecisive by nature. For many, indecision is a cover for insecurity, which paralyzes them from taking any bold action.

Indecisive prospects also tend to favor the market leaders, since that is the path of least resistance. If you are not a market leader, you will probably find this frustrating.

> You will find more indecisive prospects in the later stages of technology life cycles, since they have fewer decisions to make between the limited vendor choices in these later segments.

If you are a market leader, you may find this delightful. But even if you work for one of the leading vendors, you should not mistake indecision, which can include a lack of negatives for all products, for a favorable attitude toward your offering.

Don't mistake indecisiveness for any type of decision.

This common mistake is one of those glass-is-half-full approaches. You may be thinking, at least the prospect hasn't chosen your competitor. In fact, you should treat the absence of a decision as a reluctance to choose *your* product.

How to Handle the Indecisive Prospect

As frustrating as it may be, the best way to handle an indecisive prospect is to help him or her to take little baby steps. For instance, if such an individual cannot commit to authorizing a full-blown evaluation, perhaps you could get them to attend one of your seminars. Although an indecisive prospect may find the thought of actually making a choice overwhelming, he or she will be less intimidated by a smaller, incremental step.

But always make sure that each interaction is moving the indecisive prospect closer to choosing your solution. Don't let an indecisive prospect "tread water" by revisiting the same topic over and over again.

Indecisive prospects will almost inevitably lengthen the timeframe of the sales cycle, so you should plan on this extended timeframe when you allocate resources for the deal. In many cases, indecisive prospects are those prospects who have been misqualified in the sales funnel. Most sales reps will tell you that prospects need a "compelling event" in order to make a decision to evaluate and then purchase a product. When the pain of remaining where they are becomes bigger than the pain of moving to a new solution, the indecisive prospects will break out of their lethargy.

When you run into an indecisive prospect, this scenario can be a killer—after all, this person may become a real prospect in the future, so you don't want to ruin your chances by ignoring them. The best way to handle an indecisive prospect is to work with the sales rep to either escalate the need to move the prospect toward a decision or downgrade the prospect to a less qualified status in the sales funnel.

Secretive Prospects

In any sales interaction, we firmly believe it is in the best interest of everyone to communicate honestly and openly. When you have a prospect who will not share information with you, your sales cycle and any possibility of a successful conclusion become much more difficult and in doubt.

A secretive prospect may be reluctant to tell you anything at all or may be secretive about just a few topics, such as who your competitors are. They typically don't realize that sharing information with a professional sales team will only help the sales team assist *them* to make the best choice for their purchase.

Frequently, a secretive prospect is trying to protect something. The prospect may not be the master of the destiny of the sale, but he or she doesn't want to let you know this. The prospect may not even be sure of what he or she wants and can be afraid of being overly swayed by the silver tongues of your sales team.

Regardless of the cause, a secretive prospect is difficult to sell to. Throughout the sales cycle, you are looking for feedback—it is the oxygen that feeds the fire of the sales cycle. Without an adequate supply of information, you may find your sales effort directionless and adrift. It is easy to lose control of the selling process.

How to Handle the Secretive Prospect

As we intimated above, the cause of a prospect's secrecy may be fear. The prospect may be afraid of revealing too much to you and prejudicing the evaluation. The prospect may be afraid of his or her own lack of control, in the sales process or in life in general.

The best way to overcome fear is for you to present yourself as a trustworthy and soothing presence. Of course, building trust and rapport is an integral part of building a professional relationship. However, for a secretive prospect, you might want to go the extra mile to make yourself seem less threatening.

Sometimes a prospect may become secretive in response to your manner, rather than due to the substance of your interaction. For instance, some people withdraw from direct questions. It isn't that they don't want to give you information, it is just that they have an instinctual response that causes them to pull back from any type of direct inquiry.

Imagine the direct question, "When will you complete the project?" Imagine that the prospect is filled with anxiety about the entire project. This type of question may cause the prospect to have a withdrawal response.

If you were to phrase the question a different way, such as, "Do you think you will be completing this project by the Christmas (or any other holiday at a suitable distance) break?" you will be asking as much about the prospect's holiday plans, which should be nonthreatening, as you are about the completion of the project.

If your prospect is simply refusing to reveal some information that you think you need, don't keep hammering away. This technique will only stiffen the prospect's resistance. Pull back and perhaps use peripheral questions to get a sense of an answer.

As a last resort, you can simply start hypothesizing about the information. Watch the prospect's body language for clues as to the correct information. Make sure you do this in a lighthearted way.

> If you ask a prospect the scheduling question noted above and he or she refuses to answer while his or her body noticeably stiffens, you might take this as a negative answer. If the same question doesn't result in a direct answer, but the person's posture slackens, you might take this as a confirmation that the project will be completed by Christmas.

If you sense an extreme resistance to revealing any particular piece of information, you may just want to give up on obtaining it. If you are put between the rock of needing a particular piece of the puzzle from your prospect and the hard place of not getting it, you may eventually decide, with your sales rep, that the deal is not worth pursuing. If you come to this impasse, it can never hurt to discuss the situation with your prospect, as a last resort. If the potential customer really wants you in the deal, he or she may relent when seeing your reluctance to continue without better communication.

You're-In-This-Just-to-Make-It-Competitive Prospect

We discussed the subject of "wired" deals in Chapter 13, "Responding to RFIs." A wired deal is one in which the outcome is preordained. The winner has been selected before the contest even begins. Since you are trying to find your customer, and the prospect already belongs to someone else, a wired deal is a gigantic waste of your time and resources.

How do you recognize when you are in a wired deal? In requests, you sometimes spot sentences, paragraphs, and questions that seem to come from one of your competitors' own marketing literature. However, just because some of the language seems to lean toward your competitors, don't immediately jump to the conclusion that you have no chance in a sales situation.

Remember, your prospect has become educated on technology *somewhere*. If he or she learned from a seminar, the seminar was probably sponsored by some company, possibly your competitor, with the corresponding slant to the presentation favoring that company. If your prospect learned from a colleague or teacher, that individual may also have favored a particular company. Even if your prospect learned on his or her own, working with products directly, he or she could have had a significant amount of experience working with a competitor's product but still be open about this purchase.

You will most commonly find a particular slant to a prospect when a field is dominated by a particular company. For instance, a prospect may ask you about supporting Microsoft's COM architecture, because of the dominant presence of Microsoft in the market. In reality, this prospect may actually be asking about component architectures in general and not necessarily be favoring any particular company. They may not realize that the COM architecture is one of several options available for component architecture.

Just as you should not immediately assume that a prospect favors your competition because of the language that he or she uses, you should not necessarily assume that the prospect is in your camp because he or she uses your flavor of terminology.

Make sure that customers walk the walk as well as talk the talk.

You have a deal only when the customer purchases your products or services—not when they agree with you on terms and definitions.

How to Handle the You're-In-This-Just-to-Make-It-Competitive Prospect

As the previous discussion made obvious, your first step in working with a prospect in a wired situation is to make sure that the deal really *is* wired. It can be rather bad form to flat-out ask if the prospect has already made up his or her mind. If he or she has asked you into a deal, you are needed for something. If the prospect were free to simply choose his or her desired vendor, why would you even be there? If you find out the deal is wired and walk away, the prospect can look as if he or she has not done due diligence and will have his or her decision questioned, which is not what the proponent of a wired deal wants. All this makes it much less likely that a prospect will tell you if the deal is wired and more likely that he or she will resent you for asking.

If you indeed decide that the winner has already been chosen, your next step is to make sure the prospect is speaking for the company and not just expressing personal prejudices. Your contact may have already decided the outcome of an evaluation process, but his or her company may not have. This is also a ticklish situation, since your contact will typically have something to gain by the selection of your competitor, so he or she will not take kindly to your trying to go around them for information. If you have a personal relationship—or just a better working relationship—with someone else at the company, you can check to see if any suspicions you have are justified. Although you may not be able to change the situation or its outcome, you can at least make an informed decision about the resources you will devote to this sales cycle.

If your prospect seems to be heavily leaning toward one of your competitors, and winning the bulk of the deal looks improbable, explore the "edges" of the deal. If you cannot sell your main product or service, perhaps you have an auxiliary offering that you can focus on. With this approach, you can recoup some of your investment with the prospect and still leave the door open for other deals in the future.

— · — · —

> You might also want to leave behind a little "gift" for your competitors who remain, such as suggesting to the ex-prospect an additional step for the competitors to go through in the sales cycle. The extra step, such as a "bake-off" or benchmark, will suck up your competitor's valuable time, and, if you suggest it on your way out the door, you will have the added credibility of impartiality, since you will no longer be involved in the deal. And the more time your competitor has to spend on this deal, the less time he or she has for other deals you both may be competing in.

— · — · —

Whatever you do, if you decide to leave a deal, part as friends. The winning vendor may have problems later, so you want to be able to be invited back for possible further consideration. Your particular prospect may move to another company that is more open to your solution, so handling this situation in a professional manner will serve you in good stead down the road.

Consultants as Prospects

You will sometimes encounter situations in which you are not directly dealing with the organization that will use your product or services. You are instead talking to a consultant who works for the eventual customer— either as a technology consultant or a management consultant.

Although there is not necessarily anything wrong with working with this type of prospect, even the most well-intentioned consultant is always at least a step removed from the direct needs and desires of the customer. The level of indirection introduced by the consultant always affects the free flow of information between you and the real prospect. At best, the consultant will simply rephrase or reposition the prospect's wishes. At worst, the consultant will make a purchase decision that is best for his or her own well-being rather than that of the customer.

And, in almost all cases, the consultant will be out of the picture at some later point in time, leaving you to deal directly with the customer. So any miscommunication will eventually cloud your relationship with the real customer, since the consultant will be out of the loop and no longer directly responsible for any statements or promises conveyed to the customer from you.

This potential for calamity is enough to scare any sales team.

How to Handle the Consultant as Prospect

The first thing you should realize is that the prime directive of a consultant is to maintain account control. A consultant with account control can realize a steady source of revenue, while a consultant who loses control of an account can see his or her world turned upside down by the simple act of not renewing a contract. If you try to get to the prospect in some way in which the consultant is not involved, the consultant likely will see it as a threat and react accordingly.

There are certainly times when a consultant may not be treating your sales team fairly, but if you try to get the prospect to trust you instead of the consultant, remember this simple fact:

A consultant is paid for his or her advice, while you give much of yours away for free.

Like it or not, this difference makes the prospect more likely to value the consultant's advice. And, in virtually all circumstances, the consultant is spending a lot more time with the prospect than you are, so he or she has a much greater ability to make a case.

Rather than wait for a problem to arise, it makes good sense to ensure that a member of the prospect's organization is an integral part of the sales cycle. If you ask for this up front, you can claim that getting the prospect involved is a good practice to guarantee better communication among all three of you: your sales team, the consulting company, and the prospect. If you try to bring in a representative of the prospect's company only when things have gone awry between you and the consultant, the request will seem suspicious and it may be too late to save any possible deal.

You should also realize that you are now making two sales—one to the prospect and one to the consultant. There may be ways to entice the consultant into favoring your product, such as helping the consultant out by getting him or her involved with some of your other customers. If you go this route, be sure that the consultant understands that you will help with these contacts only *after the consultant is fully up to speed with your products*. Bringing a competent consulting firm to others in your installed base is a way of performing a service. Trading consulting leads for help in a sales cycle to a less than competent consulting firm does a disservice to the prospect and to your customers.

A consultant who looks for leads in return for helping in a sale is a consultant who lacks integrity.

You can point out to the consultant that there is a demand for skilled professionals who understand your product offerings. In other words, the consultant will be qualified for more work once he or she knows your products. You might offer to find a way for a consultant to get free or discounted training on your products in the event of a successful sale.

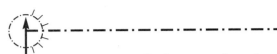

This approach will also appeal to the consultant's need for account control. He or she will be able to rack up more hours with your common customer once having received training on your products.

Finally, you should make sure that your sales rep is directly involved with the consultant and his or her team. Consultants have a tendency to try to get as much from a vendor as possible, and your sales rep can both help to handle these types of requests and also get an up-close-and-personal look at this particular sales opportunity.

Dysfunctional Prospects

Dysfunctional is the politically correct word for a variety of behaviors. We used to refer to dysfunctional people simply as jerks, although we now recognize that their unpleasant behavior may stem from contradictions in their lives.

Your prospect may habitually lie to you or may constantly schedule meetings and then cancel them at the last minute—or not cancel them at all, leaving you waiting for hours in the lobby after you traveled overnight to get to the site.

Dysfunctional prospects typically have one small common trait: Their problems cause them to be difficult for *everyone*, not just for you and your sales team. This may be small comfort when you are suffering from interaction with them, but it is an important data point nonetheless, so that you can understand that their poor behavior is not a reflection on how you are doing in the opportunity.

> ## Dysfunctional prospects do not have a problem with you or your company. They just have a problem.

Keep in mind that the dysfunctional prospect, like some of the other problem types described above, might be caught in a temporarily dysfunctional state. Perhaps your prospect is under a lot of pressure at work or is affected by situations in his or her personal life that cause him or her to react in an inappropriate way.

I once had an editor who was all over the map—waiting until the last minute and then demanding rapid changes and decisions, never providing enough information to move forward, not responding to messages and phone calls. I heard from colleagues that he was going through a particularly difficult personal situation, so I immediately cut him some slack.

Unfortunately, the problems in dealing with him and his company continued long after the personal situation had been resolved. The dysfunction was a part of his corporate culture as well as his own personality. Nonetheless, giving the editor some space did not make the situation any worse, and helped to keep me calmer.

How to Handle the Dysfunctional Prospect

To paraphrase the philosopher Joe Tex, you gotta treat 'em right. Although dysfunctional people rarely realize it, their behavior is sometimes a form of a challenge. If you react to their inappropriate behavior with your own inappropriate behavior, you rapidly end up in a sales-killing death spiral of mutual disdain.

The best advice about handling a dysfunctional prospect is to try, as best you can, to avoid getting infuriated over their behavior. There are two very good reasons to keep a cool head. First of all, you can rarely make the best decisions when you are angry. When you have been jerked around by a prospect, your overwhelming desire is to walk away from the opportunity, regardless of the potential rewards. This feeling can color your decision-making processes.

The second reason is even better: It's no fun being angry. It just makes your life uncomfortable, and anger has an unpleasant habit of interfering with your relationships with those around you. In other words, life is too short to be upset about something as trivial, in the grand scheme of things, as a jerk of a prospect.

There is one more slightly vindictive reason to avoid getting angry over the effects of a dysfunctional prospect. Sometimes, the entire purpose of the person's actions is to make you mad, so that you will terminate the interaction. By not giving in to anger, you are not letting the dysfunctional person get away with these tricks.

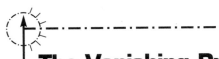

The Vanishing Prospect

One of the most frustrating types of prospects is the amazing vanishing prospect. At some point in the sale, the prospect seems to disappear from the face of the earth. Calls and messages are not returned, meetings cannot be scheduled, and communication grinds to a halt. In most cases, the prospect suddenly vanishes and is now totally out of touch.

The vanishing prospect leaves you hanging uncomfortably in mid-air. Is the prospect unreachable because you have been kicked out of the deal? Although this may be the case, there can be other reasons. Frequently, a particular contact vanishes because something has happened at the company to change his or her position or responsibilities. If your prospect is uncertain of his or her own position at a company, he or she may not be ready to work with an outsider. The prospect may just be stalling you because he or she is waiting to get his or her own feet on the ground.

How to Handle the Vanishing Prospect

Most organizations have layers of intermediaries to protect their employees from unwanted incursions of the outside world. Such layers include administrative assistants and voice mail. If your prospect really wants to avoid you, he or she can make it happen, especially if the person has a fairly responsible position in the company.

You can try to reach the prospect by being gentle but insistent. Don't make yourself a pest by continually calling. Instead, try to make yourself as available as possible by offering to meet or speak at the prospect's convenience.

You should also never, never take out your frustrations on the messenger—the person who is keeping you from contacting your prospect.

An administrative assistant may not be able to get you in touch with a vanishing prospect, but the assistant can definitely prevent you from contacting this person.

In most cases, prospects who are unresponsive to you are also unresponsive to others, so their assistants may very well be used to fielding calls from frustrated sales teams. If you are cheerful and polite, you may get the gatekeeper to warm up to you enough to at least tell you where you stand. If you are being avoided because you have been eliminated from consideration, at least you may find out so that you can stop wasting your time and your hopes chasing an unobtainable goal.

My sales representative and I once encountered a classic vanishing prospect. We had been working with this guy closely for around three months, and all of a sudden he stopped returning phones calls. We couldn't find a time to schedule a meeting with him, either. We decided that we would have to enlist the help of one of the most powerful agents known to man—nicotine.

Our prospect was a fairly heavy smoker in a nonsmoking building. We knew that if we hung around the lobby for an hour or so, we would see him heading for the door for one of his cigarette breaks. My sales rep tried for a week to schedule a meeting with him, which, of course, was turned down. We drove to his office, ninety minutes away, where we called his secretary from the lobby of the building again to see if he was free. Once again, we were told his entire day was booked. We then began to wait, and after about ten minutes, our man came striding toward the door.

We walked up to him and he immediately burst out laughing, saying, "Well, I guess I have to see you now." We went up to his office and he explained that he had been trying to work through some budget issues to make the purchase possible. He gave us a chance to win the business. In fact, he told us that if we could give him a hefty discount, he would write a check on the spot!

In the end, the discount was too steep and management did not approve it. But at least we had resolved the uncertainty that had been hanging over the sales cycle. We were now able to move on to more fruitful leads.

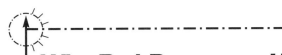

Why Bad Prospects Happen

This chapter, so far, has been about a lot of doom and gloom. The fairly long list of problem prospects we enumerate may leave you feeling a little discouraged, especially since the attributes described above can pertain to pretty much everyone to some extent. After all, how many of us have not had our moments of indecision or been occasionally difficult to get in touch with?

Even if you are pessimistic by nature or through circumstances, you should hesitate before you assign any of your prospects to one of the difficult categories in this chapter. Frequently, a small dose of the remedies proposed in this chapter will be enough to bring a less than ideal prospect into line.

But there are situations where you end up with a prospect who fits squarely into one of these categories. This situation may cause you to think, "Why?" (or at least, "Why me?"), since none of these prospects is appropriately equipped to make the best buying decision. These prospects are problematic not just because they are difficult to sell to but because it is difficult to establish the sort of partnership that results in a good long-term relationship between a customer and a vendor.

You should step back and try to understand the goals of your prospect's organization. Keep in mind that the primary job of this company is *not* buying software—even though your primary goal is to sell them some. The people assigned to the evaluation team may very well not be the most senior or most knowledgeable folks in the company, since they are all busy with what the company sees as more productive tasks. You may get someone who is new to the group or who is not really technically equipped to grasp the subtleties of your solution. You may even get a particularly prickly individual as a prospect simply because no one else in the company wants to deal with them.

If you get an opportunity to speak with others at the company, pay attention to how they refer to your difficult prospect. Although there is usually nothing you can do to get a problem person off the evaluation team, you can at least reassure yourself with a "sanity check." You will realize that the problems you are having with your prospect are not your fault, and, correspondingly, that these problems do not necessarily indicate that you are having problems in the sales cycle.

There is a case, though, where difficult prospects can indicate a problem in a sales cycle. Sometimes, when an organization is looking at several different solutions, they will assign different teams to evaluate different products. If you end up with a team of problem children and your competitors get senior, well-behaved employees, you should smell a rat.

The quality of your individual contacts can indicate a company's opinion of your company.

Of course, it's hard to determine the quality of the people evaluating your competitors' products. The best way to go about gathering this type of intelligence is through oblique references. Pay close attention to how colleagues refer to other people at their company, and see if you can gently probe to find out how these colleagues are perceived.

One way to go about getting some of this information is to ask your prospect for an organizational chart, either a formal diagram or a chalkboard version. As your prospect adds co-workers and superiors to the picture, you can gently probe to see who is above the prospect and who are his or her peers. You will also find out what role the others will play in the evaluation. It is pretty easy for your prospect to let you know that an individual is working on another part of the evaluation, and from there you can find out a little bit more about roles.

There is one more critical piece of information you can gather from an exploration of different evaluation teams. You may very well run across a situation where there are proponents and coaches for both you and your competitors in your prospect's organization. Frequently, these two different groups have been battling for a while, and the evaluation is essentially a political showdown. In these situations, it can be very useful to find out the political lay of the land, since the ultimate victor in this type of battle will be a political victor. By evaluating the respective political power of your supporters, you can get a feeling for the potential outcome of the sales process.

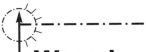

Wrapping Up

In most cases, getting stuck with a prospect who falls into one of the eight unfortunate categories listed here does not necessarily mean that the sales cycle has come to an end. There are ways to work around some of these types of prospects and ways to help these problem prospects overcome the issues that are blocking your path.

But forewarned is forearmed, so if you spot one of these types in a sales situation, you should always discuss the issue with your sales team immediately to make sure that the additional effort you will have to put into the deal will still be spent appropriately.

In this chapter, we have looked at the problems common in your prospects. In the next chapter, we will look within ourselves to see the most common problems in sales consultants.

CHAPTER 17

The Seven Deadly Sins of Sales Consultants

As a sales consultant, you are, of course, an outstanding individual—full of virtue, fire, and music. But you are not flawless. None of us are.

We have found seven common problems that seem to affect a large number of sales consultants. There is a simple reason for this commonality—many of these problems stem from the very strengths that make you a good sales consultant. It's the difference between adding a pinch of salt or a cup of salt to a recipe: The first amount delivers a delicious dish, while the second amount can ruin a meal. By avoiding the deadly sins examined in this chapter, you can ensure that your role as a sales consultant is properly seasoned.

— · — · —

> The chapter title is a bit of an overstatement, in that many of the problems we will discuss are far from the moral failings that a sin denotes. But all of these failings will decrease your effectiveness as a sales consultant and cause disruption or damage in the sales cycle. This makes them sins in the context of your job.

— · — · —

As you read about each of these deadly sins, look within yourself and your daily activities to see if any apply to you or your colleagues.

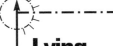

Lying

We have stated this cardinal rule before, but we will state it again because of its importance:

Never lie to a customer or prospect.

Get the picture? As stated earlier, your most valuable asset in dealing with a prospect or customer is your credibility. The foundation of your credibility is the ability of customers and prospects to trust that what you say is accurate. If you are caught lying, this foundation is destroyed.

Of course, portraying things in the best light is marketing, or spin. However, there is a very clear line between presenting an uncomfortable fact in a diminishing way and lying.

Let's say your product can allow an update to just a single customer record at a time. Compare the remarks of the Spinmeister and the Liar in the following dialogue:

> **Customer:** *Can you update multiple customer records at the same time?*
>
> **Spinmeister:** *There are ways that you can create batch jobs to update multiple customer records, but we have found it more effective to update a single record at a time, since this is such an important process.*
>
> **Liar:** *Sure.*

The most damaging thing about lying is that there is no percentage in it. The potential damage is so harmful to your credibility that virtually no short-term advantage can make up for the overall risk involved. A single lie can severely damage a sales cycle in a way that no amount of truth-telling can repair.

> Unlike with baseball, prospects and customers do not consider your "batting average" about being truthful. As Wilson Pickett once sang, "99 percent just won't do."

You may be trying to justify lying in two ways. First of all, you may be worried about losing a deal if you tell the truth about a particular topic. Frankly, this is not your decision to make. You are not the person directly responsible for making a sale—the sales rep is. You are the one who is directly involved with presenting a good image of your company. Lying oversteps the first restriction that dictates that the sales rep makes the call, and it destroys the second responsibility of being a credible advocate for your company.

The second excuse is the thought that, "If they don't catch me, it isn't a lie." Although this is not factually correct (it is still a lie, even if no one is in the forest to hear it told), it leads to its own damage. If the prospect discovers your lie, you are in trouble. Your ability to continue effectively is dependent on the customer not discovering your lie. You are ceding control of the sales cycle to the customer's actions and therefore, losing a handle on the entire process. As the first principles described in Chapter 1 state, you should...

Never willingly give up control of the sales process.

Be extra careful in guarding against several common extensions of lying. The first is the *lie of omission,* in which you let the prospect assume that something is true even though you know that it is not. We're not asking you to make a point of highlighting all of the flaws in your product, but you need to speak up if the prospect is clearly making a buy decision on an assumption that is just wrong. Alternatively, you might call this the lie of *Don't ask, don't tell.* Consider this example:

> *You demonstrate SuperServer to the prospect running on Windows NT. Throughout the sales cycle, the prospect talks about using the AS/400 as a server platform but never asks whether or not you support the AS/400 as a platform. Your marketing literature may even include diagrams that use the AS/400 as a "database server." However, SuperServer itself does not run on the AS/400.*

In this situation, you clearly need to find out whether or not the prospect plans to run the server on the AS/400. Then you need to deal with the issue. Letting the prospect assume that the server will run in the environment is lying.

I once worked with a sales consultant who was running a performance test for a prospect. Our server was architected differently than the competitor's server, and although the elapsed-time numbers were the same between the two products, it appeared that our server used far fewer system resources. It turns out that the prospect was looking at the wrong system process in getting the resource numbers for our server. The sales consultant knew this, but let the prospect go with the incorrect numbers. Eventually, the prospect got wise to the problem, and we were unceremoniously kicked out of the deal.

Equally insidious is the *lie of exaggeration,* in which you widely overstate your product's capabilities. We see this most often when it comes time to address the learning curve for your product. It is *so* tempting to position your product as being much easier to use than it really is. Unlike with the "Borg" in *Star Trek*, resistance is not futile, so resist the temptation! Take note of the following example:

Prospect: *How long will it take my developers to become productive with SuperServer?*

Wrong:
Sales Consultant: *Joe, once your developers complete training, they will be ready to go.*

Right:
Sales Consultant: *Joe, application servers are new technology and there is going to be a learning curve for your team. Most of your staff has extensive client/server experience and that will be a big help, because Web applications are also event-driven. Normally, it takes customers in similar situations three to four weeks after the training period to become productive with the system. SuperServer's training program is very thorough and we believe that our ramp-up period is better than the industry average. However, any competitor who tells you that you can learn their product and be productive in a week's time is understating the complicated nature of this technology.*

Chances are good that your prospect will already have an idea about things like the product learning curve. Exaggerated answers are not going to fool anyone and will hurt your credibility. The better way to deal with the answer, as shown above, actually can enhance your credibility.

In the above example, you also assign the problem to the general product category, rather than to your specific product, to help head off a potential threat to the sales cycle caused by your competitor's exaggerated claims. If you have developed some credibility with your prospect, this approach may help to swing the deal your way.

Whether you lie outright, lie by omission, or lie through exaggeration, the result is the same. You will ultimately pay the price.

So don't lie, OK?

Arrogance

As a sales consultant, you are a fountain of knowledge. When you reach the highest levels of your profession, you will become a true guru about your products and offerings. Indeed, the more expert you are, the more you can contribute to a sales effort.

But notice that the key word in the previous sentence is *can*. Just having knowledge is not enough to make you valuable in a sales cycle. Even if you possess all the requisite communication skills to convey your knowledge, you can still undercut your value with one of the most common sales consultant sins—the sin of arrogance.

Arrogance can cause you problems with your customers, prospects, and co-workers. If your outside audience finds you to be an arrogant person, they will essentially turn off their listening powers. Your manner will interfere with the message you are trying to convey. With your colleagues at work, continued exposure to what they feel is an arrogant attitude will cause them to shut you off, which can make work a far less hospitable place to be.

Arrogance is common because it is simply an extension of one of the chief virtues of a sales consultant. You want to be a credible source, and part of the process of establishing credibility is to display your in-depth knowledge of your products, services, and the technology market in general.

There's a thin line between arrogance and confidence. An arrogant person dispenses knowledge in appropriate amounts, with a side order of diminishment. When information is delivered in an arrogant manner, the audience is made to feel less worthy for asking. Usually, an arrogant person uses knowledge to make himself or herself feel bigger by making his or her audience feel smaller. In other words, arrogance is often a cover-up for insecurity.

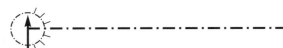

A simple quality that can help you avoid stepping over that line is *self-confidence*. If you are confident that you know what is correct, you don't have to trumpet your correctness from the rooftops. Unfortunately, self-confidence is one of the most elusive qualities to understand: If you don't have it, you usually don't realize it. It took us years to gain the self-awareness that precedes self-confidence, so if you are having trouble with an impression of arrogance, we can certainly understand.

You can help to reduce the root cause of arrogance by simply lowering the stakes on your quest for technical credibility.

As sales consultants, we want to be right as much as possible. But no one can be right all the time. There will inevitably be technical aspects that you are less familiar with. Sometimes, sales consultants will try to cover for their lack of mastery with arrogant bluster. Remember, you don't have to be right about *everything*. Be humble. Arrogance is an *attitude*, not an attribute. The exact same information can be presented in an arrogant or a welcoming manner. You can watch your audience to see if your manner seems to be causing resentment toward you. If they seem to resent you, perhaps you are not giving your knowledge as a gift, but instead are attempting to trade it in exchange for their worship.

You should also use your sales team and colleagues as detection mechanisms. Recap sessions about a sales call should include feedback on how well you did with the audience. Listen carefully to the comments of the other members of your sales team, since their impressions can help you correct potential problems with your manner before they hurt you any more.

Arrogant people are often described as *prima donnas*, which originally referred to the lead female singer in an opera company but has come to mean anyone who insists on taking the spotlight and placing themselves above others. An arrogant attitude is one of the chief attributes of a prima donna.

As you may suspect, the authors of this book have occasionally been accused of being prima donnas. In most situations, however, we have been able to balance this perceived downside with the value that we brought to the table. As one of my favorite managers once said, "You're a prima donna, but you're worth it."

But this is a risky strategy—one that we have both abandoned. The manager I just quoted was perceptive in being able to see my value, despite my prima donna airs. I was lucky in that respect. But at other times, I was not so lucky, with managers who either did not perceive my value or who became convinced that my attitude was inappropriate before they saw the contributions I could make. In other words, I ceded control over the perception of my ultimate value to my manager. And, as we have emphasized in many other contexts in this book, you should avoid ceding control if possible.

You can avoid being perceived as arrogant by treating everyone in your audience with respect. Some sales consultants work very hard to treat their primary contacts well, only to blow it by treating the less central people in the room with arrogance. You shouldn't, for example, act superior to your sales rep, even if your knowledge is far more advanced. People don't like an arrogant jerk, even if you are not being arrogant to them.

Overconfidence

The sin of overconfidence is not the same as the sin of arrogance. When we speak of overconfidence, we don't mean overconfidence in your own abilities; we mean falling into the trap where you are overly confident of the outcome of a particular sales situation.

You may come to a point where you feel a deal is yours. The successful completion of a sales cycle can involve an exacting amount of focus, so feeling that you have won a deal can cause you to let your attention to the deal lapse slightly. These lapses can take the form of not preparing properly for sales events, not strictly following the criteria advanced by the prospect, or not being attentive in returning phone calls.

As a sales consultant, you typically feel that a deal is closed when you win the technical evaluation. But we estimate that more than 25 percent of all deals are lost *after* the winning of a technical evaluation. Do not let overconfidence contribute to ignoring a prospect after the completion of a technical evaluation.

Some sales consultants can feel overconfident far earlier in the sales cycle. You may see that your solution is such a perfect fit for the prospect that he or she falls squarely into your sales sweet spot. *You* may recognize this, but your *prospect* may not, so overconfidence may lull you into taking this prospect for granted, only to see the deal evaporate. There are several common manifestations of overconfidence that you should avoid:

Don't get too casual.

If you are working closely with a prospect during a long evaluation, there is a natural tendency to become friendly with the evaluation team members. This is especially true when you are winning the deal. It is all too easy to let your guard down and become too casual in your mannerisms in these situations. Resist the urge to get overly informal, personal, or casual with your prospect.

Complete all of your open items.

Sometimes, the client will give you the technical nod and start negotiations even though there are still some open technical issues. Make sure that you follow through on these items ASAP and get them closed out. It is embarrassing to have a contract be held up because you failed to follow through on some open issues. Make sure that you document all open items and that you also document your response to these issues as well. Prospects can make mistakes too, but it is up to you to keep track of the issues and responses.

Avoid the "don't try this at home, kids" trap.

As sales consultants master their product, they have a tendency to feel that there is nothing they cannot make the product do. We see this happen all too often during product demonstrations in which the sales consultant attempts to try something on the fly. If you must attempt something that you are unsure will work, at least cover yourself in advance by mentioning that you are going out on a limb, *before* you try it. If you succeed, it will be more impressive, and if you fail, it will seem less crucial. You can always escape by taking the blame yourself, rather than having the failure appear to be a weakness of your product.

This is different than making it appear as if you are trying something new. I have always added new tricks to my demos that look as if I am trying something on the fly for the prospect. For example, one of the application development tools that I supported could produce code that would run on multiple platforms. I would often agree to move a program from one platform to another as part of the demo, while explaining that "I don't usually do this, but..." Of course, I had practiced showing this feature dozens of times, but it looked as if I were doing it for the first time. This is different than actually trying something new on the fly.

As one of my favorite sales reps used to continually say:

No job is complete until the paperwork is finished.

And, in fact, even the completion of a single deal simply begins the process of the next sales cycle. Therefore, you should never let overconfidence reduce your commitment to an account. This is often the hardest part of the job. You will find that the paperwork may sometimes take weeks to be completed, lasting long after the evaluation phase is over. However, during this tenuous phase of the deal, you still need to treat the prospect as a *prospect* and not as a customer. Until the paperwork is signed, the deal can be lost. Make sure that you continue to focus on your prospect during this crucial period.

Lack of Organization

The warnings about overconfidence bring to the fore a lingering doubt that you may have about your job: Isn't there entirely too much to do? If you can't overlook even those accounts that you believe have closed, how will you ever have time for all your tasks?

There is no doubt that your job is excessively task-driven, with your workload dramatically varying from day to day and week to week. Your in-box is sometimes overflowing with competing requests. In order to maximize your productivity and your value to your company, you must be able to prioritize your tasks. Prioritization is a skill that will improve as you work with sales reps and others in your company, but a prerequisite for prioritization is organization. After all, if you cannot organize your tasks, you will not be able to prioritize them appropriately.

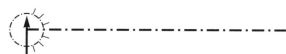

You should make sure that you have a system for capturing and retaining requests for your services, contact names and numbers, and all the other information that you use in your environment. A variety of tools can help you to organize your professional life. In the next chapter, we review some of these tools. Regardless of whether you choose to use one of the tools described, you must be able to keep a handle on your workload and its accompanying data, or else you will find yourself not only failing as a sales consultant but also unhappy in your job. As one forgotten task after another rears its ugly head, you will be continually pummeled for your lack of organization.

As with some of the other sins described in this chapter, there is a flip side to the strength of organization—in this case, it is the flaw of inflexibility. You may be an ace at organizing your requests, with every individual task scheduled down to the minute. This is all well and good, as long as you can accomplish the task without anyone else's help. However, if you require a prospect to provide you with some information, or you are waiting for a headquarters resource to call you back, you may find your schedule suddenly collapsing around your feet.

Another facet of inflexibility is the inability to reprioritize on short notice. Sales emergencies do arise, so you should be able to use your tools to revamp your schedule quickly if necessary.

Organization is a key virtue, but if you ignore the fact that the people with whom you interact have their own sets of priorities, you will find your organizational abilities causing you an excessive amount of frustration.

There are a couple of common organization mistakes that sales consultants make:

- Underestimating the workload.

When you are planning out your schedule or working out a priorities list with your team, be realistic in the estimates that you make for each item. If a task is going to take a half-day of your time, don't be a cowboy and tell the sales manager that you can do it in an hour.

- Cutting things too close.

Assume that Mr. Murphy, the creator of Murphy's Law, is going to have some effect on your tasks. Avoid lining up too many tasks close together. This kind of time management will give you some leeway when things go awry. We discuss the topic of organization in depth in the next chapter.

Taking the Sales Representative's Role

The person you work with most closely is your sales rep (or reps). Much of the time, you will be working toward the same goal—the successful completion of a sales cycle. However, you should not confuse this commonality of purpose with a commonality of roles.

The sales representative and the sales consultant have separate roles in a sales cycle.

We have characterized this difference earlier in this book as having to do with money. Most of the financial aspects of a deal are the exclusive province of the sales rep. He or she is concerned with the actual price of your offering, the discount structure, and even the number of different products that make up the total order.

As a rule of thumb, don't talk about money with the prospect.

Even if you know some of the answers to financial questions, it is not your responsibility to handle this part of the deal. And since the financial aspects are some of the most important and unyielding aspects of the deal, a small misstep can have dire consequences for your company.

Imagine a case where you quote a 10 percent discount, when, in reality, there has been a brand new rule handed down from headquarters that allows a discount of only 8 percent on this particular type of deal. Your sales rep will have the difficult job of actually raising the price of the solution when the contract is finalized.

It is also not your job to close the deal. Just as it would be inappropriate for you to hand a contract to the prospect to sign or to check the prospect's credit status, it is not really appropriate for you to take the final step in the sales process.

This doesn't mean that you can totally ignore all portions of the sales rep's role in a deal. You will notice that the cardinal rule listed above talks about separate roles but not necessarily *clearly defined* roles. There are some parts of a sale that you will both engage in, such as qualification. Different sales reps will, for instance, have different levels

---

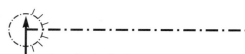

of technical abilities and comprehension. Some reps will always defer to you on technical questions, while others will tackle some or all of the questions. The exact boundaries between your sales rep's job and yours are typically worked out as you develop a relationship with the rep through working together.

> If you are unfamiliar with the style of a particular rep, it is best to defer to him or her more frequently, rather than less frequently. The worst that can come out of this approach is a belief by the customer that you are excessively polite.

However you work with a sales rep, you should try your best to make sure you are not stepping over each other as you deal with customers and prospects. You should act as a well-trained relay team, smoothly handing the baton back and forth in the context of the customer interaction. As with a relay team, a smooth handoff may not, in and of itself, win the race, but a bungled handoff can cause your team to lose, or at least make it harder to win.

You may also find that prospects are often leery about taking steps that move them toward a sale—a step that your sales rep is trying to get them to take. They will try to divert the conversation to technical issues when your sales rep attempts to close or ask tough qualification questions. Take note of this dialogue:

Sales Rep [Sue]: *"Joe, now that you have had a look at SuperServer, do you think it is going to meet your needs?"*

Prospect [Joe]: *"Well, there are some issues... Say, Jack [sales consultant], how does SuperServer handle locking?"*

Sales Consultant [Jack]: *"That's a great question, Joe. I think we have a white paper that talks about locking. Sue, are you familiar with the document that I'm talking about?"*

Sales Rep [Sue]: *"I know just the one you are talking about, Jack. Joe, I will be sure to get that for you. Now, how does SuperServer stack up against your requirements?"*

The prospect is trying to deflect the question by digging back in on technical issues with the sales consultant. In these situations, it is important to answer in a professional manner. But get the control of the call back into the hands of the sales rep. In the preceding example, the sales consultant asks the sales rep if she is familiar with the white paper; the sales consultant is trying to draw the sales rep back into the conversation.

Your job as a sales consultant is to drive control back to the sales rep when the prospect attempts to back away from the tough financial or closing-type issues.

This can be difficult. Sometimes, the rep will have to get tough in order to get the needed information. You don't want to make his or her job more difficult by allowing the prospect to steer the conversation back to technical issues.

Poor Transitions

The previous "sin" introduced the idea of transitions between you and the sales rep. In fact, there are transitions all throughout your job, especially within your interactions with the public. For instance, when you are giving a demo, you are center stage. All eyes will be on you. When you end your demo and move into a question-and-answer section, you have to switch gears to allow your audience to drive the interactions. And since you have focused attention on your demo, you will have to work extra hard to move into the background and allow your audience to step forward.

Interactions have a type of progression. When you are leading a discussion, you will tend to continue to control it, even after your role has changed to a less prominent one. Many sales consultants really have to work at learning how to transition to a different mode of communication.

There are some techniques than can help smooth out the transitions between different forms of communication. One technique that we have used successfully is simply to switch "output" devices.

You can't turn off your brain, but you can turn off your mouth.

We do this by keeping an open notebook, where we write down the comments that we might have said out loud. With this approach, you can still communicate without disrupting the dynamics of the situation. When you have just left the spotlight of attention, even small side remarks can act as a distraction from the main purpose of the meeting.

— · — · —

> When I have reviewed the type of comments I write down in these situations, an overwhelming majority of them are not very important—certainly not worthy of the distraction they would have caused by injecting them at the time. I am also careful not to spend too much of my time scribbling away in my notebook, because this, too, is distracting.

— · — · —

You may also experience some difficulties transitioning between different types of tasks that make up your workload. There is a world of difference between working with prospects in a demo situation, coding a benchmark, answering e-mail, or writing a response to a Request For Proposal. It never hurts to give yourself a few minutes of breathing room to get into the right frame of mind for a job. Taking a brief walk or making a trip to the water cooler can make these types of transitions easier.

Transitions can also get sloppy if you get tired. It never hurts to take a break between items on an agenda (such as the presentation and the demo). Most sales consultants work out a code with their sales rep so that the rep can jump in and call for a break when the consultant gets tired. This gives you a chance to huddle with your sales rep informally and to recharge your batteries quickly for the rest of the meeting.

— · — · —

> I often use an inconspicuous hand signal as my cry for a break. Whether I am getting tired, or I sense that the audience needs a break, I roll my pen between my two palms to signal that I need to "take five." All my reps are keyed in to this little signal.

> Of course, I have to remember *not* to roll my pen that way unless I need the break. The key is to pick an inconspicuous signal, but one that is not something that you normally do.

— · — · —

Letting External Problems Intrude

You may be a sales consultant, a superhuman presence in this world, but you are still a human. As such, you are bound to have your share of problems. In fact, some of your problems will invariably be related to your work environment. Perhaps your sales rep has not treated you with the courtesy and respect you feel you deserve and have given to him or her. Perhaps your manager has just given you what you feel is an insufficient bonus or raise. Perhaps your luggage was lost on the way to the meeting. Or, more seriously, perhaps someone in your family is ill and you are very concerned.

Sales consultants typically bring their passions into their work, which can also lead to bringing their problems into a sales situation. We have seen sales consultants engage in passive-aggressive behavior when it comes to work problems. Rather than dealing with their issues directly, they wait for an opportunity to strike back at someone indirectly. For instance, if they are angry with their sales rep, they may try to show them up in front of a prospect or customer.

Your prospect does not know about any of the external problems affecting you. Frankly, your prospect also doesn't care—at least when it comes to external problems caused by others in your company. Your prospect will notice the repercussions of those external problems, though, and will almost inevitably react badly to them.

Of course, you are not the only one who can let problems intrude on a sales cycle. A sales rep I was working with, who was a particularly emotional guy in a particularly emotional mood, felt that I had slighted him at a customer meeting. He literally took on the demeanor of a pouting child—arms folded tightly in front of him, mouth set in a grimace—for the rest of the meeting.

The prospects at the meeting couldn't help but notice his attitude. In fact, several of them interrupted the meeting to ask if he was OK. Unfortunately, the overwhelming impression we made at that meeting had nothing to do with our products; all they could think about was the behavior of the rep. We had forfeited valuable selling time with a public display of conflict on the sales team.

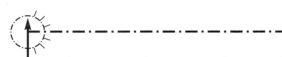

We don't pretend that any sales consultant, or any person, for that matter, is a stone. Things happen and you react emotionally. But try as best you can to leave your problems at the doorstep when you walk into a meeting with your prospects or your customers. Your problems will still be waiting for you when you come out of the meeting, if you wish to pick them up again. If necessary, take a few minutes to explicitly relax your mind before starting a meeting.

You don't have to break Cal Ripken's consecutive-games-played record, either. If personal problems have gotten you down, get your manager involved and take yourself out of the game for a day or two. This is a very common problem when a technical market begins to heat up. I have worked for companies in hot market spaces in which we were making two presentations a day, five days a week. At a certain point, your motor wears down. Recognize the signs of exhaustion and take a break.

Your ability to perform well with customers, despite having issues with your sales rep or company, will also help to resolve some of these issues that come between you and your sales rep in a positive way, for two reasons. The first reason is strategic. By handling a meeting with a customer well, you will help to remind your sales rep and, down the line, your company, of your incredible value in closing business.

Colleagues (especially sales reps) will sometimes forget your value.

Suppose that your sales rep has done you wrong, and you are still steaming when you go into a customer event. If you handle the event well, the rep can't help but start to think, "Gee, he [or she] did a great job—I had better put some extra effort into fixing our relationship." Well, maybe...

Think how much better that potential result is than the opposite effect, which would be caused if you went into the meeting and showed the rep up or performed in some other manner that disrupted the effectiveness of the meeting. Your rep will very likely start to think, "You know, this sales consultant can't be counted on to help in the sales cycle"— and this can be the start of a downward spiral of a lack of respect and effectiveness.

The second reason to try to perform well, despite problems, is primarily tactical. Putting your problems aside during a customer meeting is a lot like counting to ten when you are angry. By giving the problem a rest, you tend to separate it from the raging emotions it immediately inspires. This technique doesn't necessarily make a problem go away, but it does give you some perspective, which, in turn, allows you to address it in a more effective manner than in the heat of the moment.

If you really feel that a problem is going to affect your performance in a customer interaction, you should simply try to postpone the interaction, or at least reduce your importance in the event so as to minimize the disruption. If something is bothering you in your personal life, such as a family problem or tragedy, most people will understand your feelings and respect your wishes. If you are having a problem with your sales rep, it is much more professional to let him or her know that the problem may affect your performance than simply to go into a meeting and possibly sabotage the sale.

Wrapping Up

As a sales consultant, you are gifted with enormous strengths. In our attempts to be the best sales consultants we can be, we can fall into one of the seven deadly traps discussed in this chapter. Since these failings are common to our chosen field, we must make it a habit to continually check ourselves for any symptoms of these sins.

In the next chapter, we are going to discuss some techniques for optimizing your time and improving your productivity, both of which can help you to avoid some of the common mistakes that we've identified in this chapter.

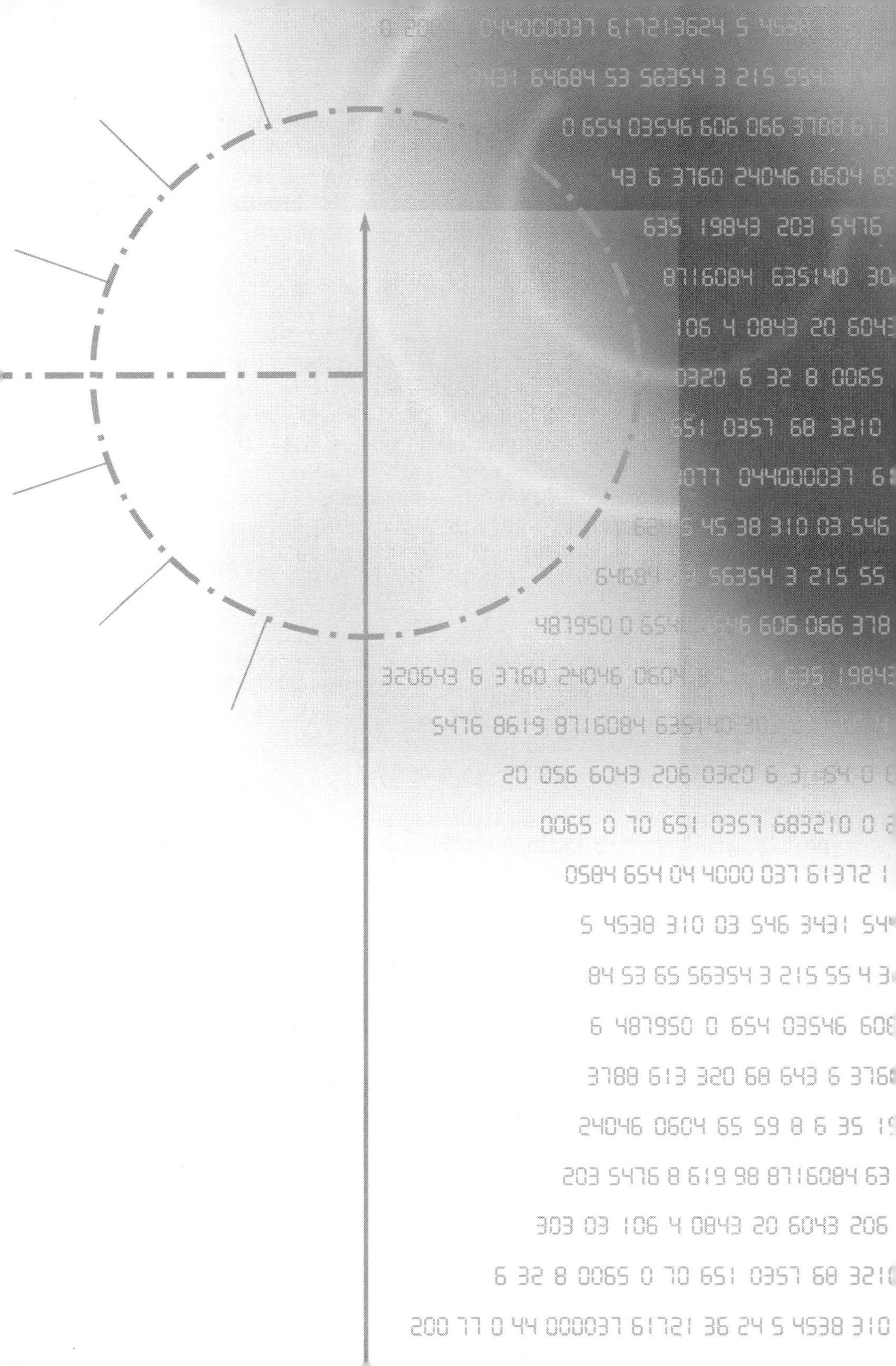

Productivity Enhancers and Time Management

The role of a sales consultant is diverse, and you will no doubt be asked to juggle many tasks at the same time. While you will certainly experience some slow periods, by and large you likely will never be in a situation in which there is a shortage of things to do. Couple a busy schedule with the constant deadline of having to meet sales targets, and you have a recipe for disaster. In this chapter, we'll take a look at tips and techniques for managing your time more effectively.

Basic Principle of Productivity

There are numerous resources for you to turn to in pursuit of excellence in productivity and time management, but it has been our experience that the role of the sales consultant requires some special consideration. One of the most important principles for you to learn is how to maximize your time. To do so, you must have an accurate idea of how long it takes you to perform any given task.

In Chapter 7, "Mastering the Demo," we introduced the concept of activity-based costing. Businesses use activity-based costing as a means of accounting for expenses, which are then compared to the actual costs incurred. The purpose of such an exercise is to determine where the money is going on an activity-by-activity basis. We introduced you to this concept as a means of focusing you on maximizing your time for a very specific activity—prospect demos.

You want to ensure that you are spending valuable demonstration time on prospects that you actually have a measurable chance of closing. You and your sales rep partner have a fixed window of time, to achieve your annual revenue target. Most technology companies work on a quarterly basis, which is why you should look at your quota in three-month blocks. It's possible to miss your revenue targets all year long, and then to make quota with a monster deal, but most sales reps focus on making their quarterly revenue numbers.

> ## *The basic measure of sales consultant productivity will always be based on sales quota.*

If you and your sales rep make or exceed quota, almost all other sins that you might have committed will be forgiven. You essentially are measured on quota, above all other factors. There may be cases in which the company attempts to measure customer satisfaction and tie this factor back to your compensation—but this is much more common for the technical support department than it ever will be for you. The trick for you as a sales consultant is to budget your time so that you can make quota.

Marking Your Time

Before you do anything else, you need to get a handle on exactly how much time you will spend on each activity.

Consider the following list of activities:

- Customer support—on-site
- Customer support—telephone/Web
- Demo preparation
- Demonstrations
- Presentation
- Seminar
- Trade show
- Qualification meeting
- Travel
- Trial management
- Site visit

- E-mail
- Paperwork
- Sales meeting
- Training

This list is a fairly comprehensive total of the types of activities that you will undertake as a sales consultant, but it is by no means complete. The nature of the product that you sell and support will dictate the exact list of activities that you undertake on any given day.

The starting point for managing your time and productivity is to record all of your work over a given period of time. Some tasks will not vary between companies, but other tasks, such as the amount of time that you spend giving demonstrations, will vary widely as you move from product to product or company to company.

Begin by recording the time you spend on each activity and each client.

You want to make a list of activities that is comprehensive enough to cover major tasks, but you do not want to make this list so extensive that it becomes difficult to manage. Using the preceding list as a guideline, you can come up with a ballpark set of tasks.

These tasks form the first component of a two-part matrix for monitoring your workload. The second component consists of the customers and prospects who are in your pipeline. The two elements form the basis on which you will want to gauge the time that you spend.

- What are you working on?
- Who are you doing it for?

Sales consultants who have come from a consulting background will be much more familiar with this angle for measuring their time and productivity. If you have any experience in a job in which you are required to bill clients for hours spent, you will be familiar with this method. However, in the world of consulting, you may have found that the degree of detail for which you need to mark your time is not as fine. As a sales consultant, you will almost always be working on multiple items during the same workday (with the possible exception of days when you provide on-site support for a prospect evaluation). Thus, it becomes much more important to record accurately exactly how much

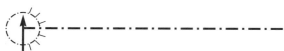

time you spend on various tasks. You will also want to record for *whom* you are doing the work. We're not expecting you to bill the prospect for work performed, but you need to develop some base statistics about the type and amount of resources that will be required to close business.

There are many systems for recording your time, and you may even have developed your own system. For the purposes of example, we are going to use our own personal system so that you can see exactly how we propose to measure time. In today's world, the best way to manage this task is to use a personal digital assistant (PDA). A PDA is the easiest and most comprehensive solution to the problem of recording your time and activities. (Later in this chapter, we'll also talk about it as a tool for maintaining contact information and scheduling data). PDAs have come a long way over the past few years, and are now a reliable way for you to capture and maintain data. They may still be a little cumbersome for the average person, but you are not the average user—you're a sales consultant.

> Our machine of choice (at the moment) happens to be the Palm IIIx from Palm Computing, so we'll use this as our example. There are a number of good Windows CE-based PDAs, as well as the popular Psion, and there is no reason why these won't work for you as well. We just happen to use the Palm Pilot.

Essentially, you need three components in order to make an automated time management system work for you:

- A hand-held PDA
- PDA application
- Host application

The first component is the hand-held PDA. Now, you might be tempted to say that a laptop computer is a far superior solution. The problem with a laptop, however, is the ease-of-use issue. When the laptop is up and running in front of you, it is very easy to use. But there will be many instances in which you will need to record tasks when your laptop is not readily available. In such cases, the odds are pretty good that you will not be able to take the time to crank it on and enter the data. What you are more likely to do is to jot down a quick note in your notebook with the idea of adding this data to your laptop application later on.

**Having two separate mechanisms
for recording data will also lead to problems.**

Any credible time-management expert will tell you that having multiple entry points is a problem. It is inevitable that the two systems will get out of synch and that you will forget to enter data from your notebook into your laptop application. That's why we like the PDA concept. PDAs start up in a flash and are easy to have handy. The good ones have some sort of stylus and a touch-screen keyboard so that you can quickly enter the appropriate information. We have mocked up a version of such an interface in Figure 18.1.

Figure 18.1
Time-tracking
interface.

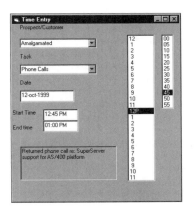

The idea is to be able to easily and quickly mark down everything that you do in a given day. You should be able to make an entry in less than thirty seconds from the time you open up the PDA until you save the entry. Remember, you need to track two key items: the task type and the prospect/customer the task is for. Figure 18.1 shows a mocked-up timetracking interface, but there are a number of commercial applications available for each of the major PDAs on the market.

Try to choose an application that allows you to enter the maximum information with the minimum amount of effort. In our sample application (which mimics the interface that we actually use), you can enter tasks and customers by picking from a list. You can set start and end times by clicking in the box and then using the time fields to set the start and stop time for the activity. It's that simple. Open up a new record when you start a task, and then mark the end time when the task is complete. The PDA

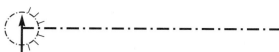

application is the main user interface that you will interact with on a daily basis, but it is not the only software that you need.

Ideally, you will want to have a host application on your laptop/desktop machine that you can use to upload and analyze the data. We like this approach because it maximizes the ease of use for each portion of the task. You want entering and modifying the data on the PDA to be very easy. On the desktop side of the equation, you will want to have an application powerful enough to give you good reports and charts about your activities.

> One of the reasons that we like PDAs as a hand-held solution is that they typically have applications that understand how to synchronize your desktop database with your hand-held database. The less complicated it is for you, the more likely it is that you will "stick with the program."

Normally, you will want to track all of your major activities, including the time you spend answering e-mail, handling support questions, and giving demonstrations and presentations. As a normal output of this process, you will get two kinds of information, as shown in Figure 18.2 and Figure 18.3.

Figure 18.2
Table of tasks/times.

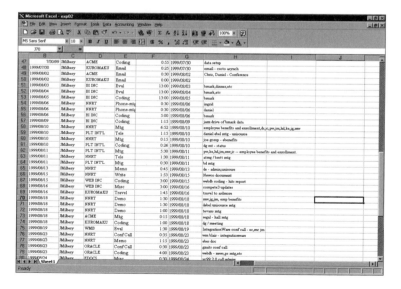

Productivity Enhancers and Time Management — Chapter 18

First, you get a database of tasks and customers that you should be able to sort by task type and customer/prospect code. We generally add a customer entry for our own company to keep track of tasks that are not prospect-specific, such as working on the demo or handling paperwork. While your own company is not truly a customer, most PDA-software packages do not differentiate between your own company and customer entries.

In Figure 18.2, we have used "Kuromaku" as the internal company name. All of the other items are actually tasks, prospects, and times from a week in the life of a real sales consultant.

The mix of tasks will vary according to how far along you are into a sales quarter. At the beginning of the quarter, you are more likely to be working more product demonstrations than evaluations. Obviously, this is not strictly true, since prospects can fall across quarters, but it is true more often than not.

It will help if you can get a more visual cue as to how you are spending your time. Most of the packages that track time have support for graphics, as shown in Figure 18.3:

Figure 18.3
Weekly time chart.

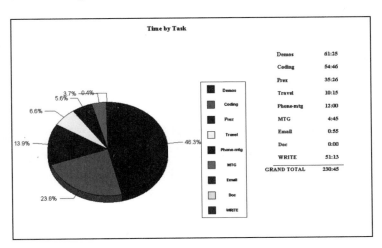

We have used a shortened list of task codes to make the examples easier to read in book format, but the basic process is accurately portrayed. From the graph, you can get a better idea of exactly how much you have spent on any given activity during the period covered by the report. As you delve down into the details, you will be able to develop estimates as to how much time you spend on each activity. In the example case, we have used the task "coding" as the entry for supporting customers in the installed base. You will notice that we spent almost 24 percent of our time handling customer problems with our installed base over the period of a month. This, in turn, translates into almost fifty-five hours over a month of business days, or an average of more than thirteen hours per week.

While such a large amount of customer-support time may not be typical, the figures used in this example are actually taken from a real month of our time. At first blush, you probably would not have guessed that as a sales consultant you would spend so much time supporting customers. Once you begin tracking the time that you spend on individual activities, you can do a much better job of managing your time.

The first step to improving time management is to have an awareness of how you spend your time.

It is the hidden costs that will cause you a lot of grief. You will probably find that you spend lots of time working on things that you never expected, and it's doubtful that you would have guessed that you were spending this time in such abundance. Once you have a handle on where your time is going, you will have a much better chance of adequately prioritizing your activities.

Managing Time and Setting Expectations

Once you begin to track the time you spend on the various tasks, prospects, and customers, you will have a better idea of how to manage and schedule your time along four separate tracks:

- Deal resources
- Customer support
- Lead generation
- Training and internal projects

As a sales consultant, your primary job is to help close new customers. From a time-management perspective, this translates into the amount of resources needed to close a deal. Add up all of the hours that you spend on a prospect for each activity—including qualifying, presentations, demonstrations, evaluations, meetings and phone calls. The resulting figure is the amount of your time required for closing any given deal. This number will rarely be the same for each and every deal, but you will quickly be able to produce a reasonably close average. You can use this average to allocate your time appropriately.

For example, assume that it takes fifty hours of your time on average to take a prospect from the qualification meeting to closure. Assuming an eight-hour work day and sixty working days per quarter, this translates into a total of 480 hours per quarter. Simple math says that you can work a *maximum* of nine deals to closure in any given quarter (480/50).

Now, we know that deals don't necessarily start and end strictly on a quarter-by-quarter basis; you will have deals in every phase of the sales cycle at any given point in time. But this relatively simple calculation should drive home the already important point about the scarcity of your resources. This figure is also useful for gauging your maximum workload—but this is only the starting point. Consider the second element on our list—the amount of time that you have to spend on customer issues. Go back to our earlier example, under which we were spending an average of thirteen hours per week on support issues. This translates into 156 hours over the course of a quarter, which leaves you with only 324 hours of "deal" time, or *six deals per quarter*. Add in the time that you spend making seminar and trade-show presentations, and the amount of selling time drops even further. You also have to add in all of the time that you must spend handling paperwork, training yourself on advancements in your product, and managing your demo machine. In the end, you are not left with as much time as you might think.

There is a natural tendency to underestimate the amount of time that you need for any given activity. The solution to this problem is to track your time religiously so that you can develop accurate estimates. You need to be honest about this process. Take the time and effort to accurately record the work that you do. Your PDA will make it really easy to time these tasks and record them for you on a daily basis.

Nothing takes a minute, not even a minute.

There is no task that you perform as a sales consultant that takes only a minute. If you include the time that you spend dialing and being on hold, you cannot even order a pizza in under a minute. If you keep an accurate log, you will have a better idea of exactly how long any given task is likely to take. You can use this information to better plan out your schedule.

Handling Your Workload

We like the idea of having one piece of equipment for managing your workload. Your PDA serves as your time tracker, your address book, and your calendar. Keeping it all in one place will get you in the habit of using the PDA. It is portable enough to keep with you at all times. In addition to keeping track of your time, there are a number of other things that you can do in order to manage your time more effectively.

Set priorities.

Armed with your time chart and PDA, you can sit down with your sales rep at the end of the week to plot out your strategy for the forthcoming week. If you have too much on your plate, you will have to work with your sales rep to set priorities. Make sure that you are in agreement about which items you are going to drop. One of the biggest items in this category will be customer support. If you find yourself averaging ten to twelve hours per week on customer issues and you are facing a week that is completely filled with presentations and demos, you are headed for trouble. Remember that all customer contact must be timely, so leaving customer calls to sit for a week is a recipe for trouble. Make sure that you communicate this problem to your sales rep. Some items can take a lower priority if necessary, but many items cannot be put on the back burner easily. You have to be honest with yourself and your rep about your commitments if you are going to stay ahead of the game.

Delegation is often a myth for sales consultants.

There is some amount of delegation that you can make within a larger organization. In particular, you can *sometimes* get another sales consultant to cover some of your prospects using the telephone or e-mail. Customers can be routed to the technical support organization. However, you may find that these alternatives are filled up as well, in which case there is no place to turn. At the end of the day, you are responsible for your prospects, and they have to take priority. It may not be possible to delegate work to other team members. Even when you can delegate, you will still have to leave time in your schedule to circle back and check on the status of open issues. Your customers are your responsibility, even if you have to delegate individual tasks to other resources.

Set expectations.

We have said it before and we will say it again: Set proper expectations. If you are in the middle of an intensive road trip, you might not have the bandwidth to follow through on all issues. You can eliminate problems by letting people know where you are and what your schedule is. Start by changing your voice-mail message on a daily basis. You don't have to tell callers where you are, but do let them know that you are out of the office. If you are not going to be able to check voice-mail and/or e-mail regularly during the day, make sure that your message includes this information. Do not include your pager number if you do not plan to respond to it. At the end of each day, check your voice-mail and respond to all of your messages. You do not need to promise to help if you know you cannot, but you *are* expected to respond in some fashion.

— · — · —

> If you will not be available during working hours while on the road, you might suggest on your voice-mail that you will be able to respond to e-mails faster. Include your e-mail address on your voice message.

— · — · —

Handle the tough stuff first.

When you are tackling a list of items, you should concentrate on handling your least favorite tasks first. It is too easy to keep pushing the tougher tasks onto the back burner and then to fall behind. If you start with the tough stuff first, you will find it is easier to get through your entire list of tasks much more quickly. Everyone has customers that he cannot stand talking to. I found it would take me longer to get through my regular list of items if I knew that I had to call on one of my problem customers. I found endless reasons to drag out my other tasks so that I would run out of time. Once I started disciplining myself to deal with my least favorite customers *first*, however, I found I actually *gained* time by not having to avoid these calls! I also found it easier to handle these problem customers by setting proper expectations.

Just say "No."

Despite the fact that Nancy Reagan turned this phrase into a cliché for all time, it's still good advice. It's OK to say "No" to sales reps, prospects and customers. You will find that it is easier to say "No" if you are organized and keep track of where you spend your time. It is not necessary to give a detailed excuse. A firm "No" is better than a wishy-washy "Yes" that you have every intention of forgetting or ignoring.

Managing Your Time in the Life Cycle of Your Product

Throughout this book, we have stressed how the Technology Life Cycle affects both you and your prospects. As your product develops and matures, you will find that you will have a tendency to spend time on different activities in accordance with your product's position in the marketplace. Individual technologies will have their own peculiarities, but there are still some basic trends that you can expect to see.

During the early phases of your product's life cycle, you can expect to spend much more time dealing with prospects in evaluations and trials. Almost every activity that you undertake will require more time than it will when both your product and the market are more mature, since you will encounter many more new situations.

New technology requires more resources to demonstrate and explain, since many of the concepts will be new both to the market and to your prospects. During this phase of the Technology Life Cycle, you can expect to spend much more time working closely with your prospects during trials and evaluations. Your company will probably be short on technical support and consulting resources. Therefore, lots of problems are going to fall to you for resolution.

Plan on handling fewer accounts with higher involvement in the early stages of the Technology Life Cycle.

You have to be very careful not to stack up too many tasks closely together at this phase of your product's life cycle. Resources across your company as a whole are likely to be very tight and problems are going to be more difficult to solve. You will probably spend more of your time

---

fixing problems than anything else. Even your customers will have to be treated as prospects, since you will need to use them as stepping stones to closing new accounts. Sales consultants routinely overcommit in these situations because they consistently underestimate the amount of time they spend working on tasks for these accounts.

The problem starts out innocently enough, since you have only a few prospects to work with. You spend extra time helping these prospects and customers with your technical expertise. Initially, there will be fewer prospects and customers, and you will tend to have more time on your hands. As the market begins to heat up, though, you will find that you do not have enough time for covering all of your tasks. Existing customers get mad because you are not spending as much time with them as they are used to. In effect, your earlier responsiveness has set their expectations higher than is proper.

> It is vitally important that you track
> the time you spend with each prospect
> and customer during this period,
> so that you can work with your sales rep
> to set priorities and meet expectations.

What makes your life even more complicated is the fact that your prospects may have all sorts of unusual needs from a demo perspective. Remember, a wealth of different features and benefits are fighting for awareness during these early stages, and your prospects will probably need some extra time to appreciate your special advantages. Odds are pretty good that you will also be spending precious cycles trying to make the product address some issues that are unique to each client. In either case, you end up spending more time customizing your presentation for each prospect. This is a time-consuming effort.

Once the market hits its stride, the focus moves from prospect support to presentations and demonstrations. As the general market begins to see the advantage in using your technology, the number of concurrent prospects will begin to pick up. The market will be better educated as a whole, and this will reduce the amount of hand holding that you need to undertake. Technical support and consulting services have been staffed more completely by now, and you can leverage their resources to help manage trials and product evaluations. Your company is on a run to grow the installed base significantly, and this translates into lots of demos.

Your prospects will have a better idea of what they are looking for, so your demonstrations should become shorter and more focused on product differentiation.

As the market matures, demos become the standard task of the day.

As the market matures, you will find yourself in a much more balanced position. If the early market was support-intensive and the middle market was demo-intensive, the mature market is the perfect balance of both. Your technical support organization is much more mature and well staffed, but your buyers are likely to be late majority adopter, who will need more personal attention. Although you will still need to make lots of presentations and demonstrations, they will be much more consistent than before. Prospects in this marketplace tend to want the same types of solutions. A standard demo will generally address their requirements.

It is important for the sales team to gauge where they are in the market and adjust accordingly. In the early phases of the market, the sales team should be careful not to take on too many prospects at the same time. Although it is very hard to walk away from prospects, you have to face the reality that it is going to be impossible to cover as many accounts as you will be able to in the latter stages of the market.

Wrapping Up

Time management is a very personal issue, but the role of a sales consultant requires some very specific optimizations. Sales consulting is a job in which you will be asked to manage an overly large and changing set of tasks. If you are religious about keeping track of your time, you will have a much better chance of meeting expectations on a quarterly basis.

CHAPTER 19

Sales Consulting in the E-World

In this book, we have given you a framework of understanding which you can apply to a wide variety of technical sales. But the world of technology is constantly changing, and in the recent past there has been a sea change in the way that technical products are marketed and sold—the e-world.

We use the term *e-world* to represent a galaxy of terms relating to selling products over the World Wide Web, which is most frequently referred to as e-commerce. E-commerce virtually always takes place through a Web site maintained by a company. Although there are different varieties of e-commerce, such as business-to-consumer (B2C), business-to-business (B2B), and the use of online exchanges, the broad characteristics of sales in the e-world are shared across these varieties.

Although any type of product or service can be sold over the Internet, technical products particularly lend themselves to this approach for two reasons:

1. Technical products are, by and large, easily demonstrated and delivered over the Web. With the bandwidth that is available to most corporate customers today, even large applications can be downloaded in a matter of hours.

2. Technical buyers are very likely to be competent users of the Web to preview and purchase products.

In other words,

E-commerce is ideally suited to the sale of technical products.

In some ways, there is nothing new about the e-world. People are still looking to make a purchase to address their needs, and most of the events in the sales cycle still occur. But the introduction of the Internet has reshaped the entire sales process in some fairly significant ways.

Major Change in Sales Process

It's not your father's sales cycle any more. It's not even your older brother's sales cycle, for that matter. Although you will find that all of the events in a standard sales cycle are still present in the e-world, the way each of the stages in the cycle is implemented has been significantly modified.

The overall effect of electronic commerce on the sales process has been to compress the process. This has had two basic results. The time allocated for some parts of the process has been reduced, while the overall scope of the sales cycle now encompasses a wider variety of interactions.

Time Allocation

Prior to the advent of electronic commerce, the time allocation for a sales cycle was fairly standard, as shown in Figure 19.1.

Figure 19.1
Traditional
sales cycle.

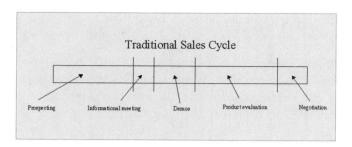

The prospecting portion of the sales cycle typically took a relatively long time. Prospects would become familiar with products and technologies as they slowly worked their way down the sales funnel. Once a prospect became an "A" prospect, the "hands-on" part of the sales process began, with an introductory meeting or phone call, a demo, and frequently a product evaluation. Once your company "won" an evaluation, the sales representative would begin the negotiation and closing portion of the deal, which could again stretch out over several weeks, depending on the size of the deal and, often, the closeness of the end of a fiscal quarter for your company.

The typical sales cycle for e-commerce sales is shown in Figure 19.2.

Figure 19.2
E-commerce
sales cycle.

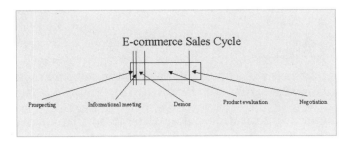

To start with, this new chart is a lot shorter. A well-implemented Web site, coupled with public awareness of the site through advertising, links or search engines, should attract its own customers, so the prospecting portion of the sales cycle is greatly reduced.

Since prospects can find information about your products online, there is virtually no need for an informational meeting. Similarly, many products are well-suited to online demonstrations, so this portion of the sales cycle is eliminated.

The reduction in these earlier segments of the traditional sales cycle also has the effect of increasing the occurrence and importance of the product evaluation. Since the product evaluation will serve as the primary vehicle for product proofs and one-to-one interaction with the vendor, there are probably relatively more situations that call for product evaluations in the world of e-commerce than were required in the previous sales cycle.

Finally, you can see that the negotiation process has been greatly reduced. Part of this is due to the availability of online payment processes. A well-implemented e-commerce site can automate the purchase process, which reduces the time and effort required to close a deal. The growing popularity of e-commerce has also led to an increased popularity of standardized and public price lists as well as terms and conditions, which tend to reduce the amount of negotiation required in the closing process.

Customer Interaction

The most dramatic impact of e-commerce on the sales cycle is physical. Since a prospect can find your products, learn about your products, see your products in action, and compare your products with your competitors' offerings online, it means that you will have much less face time with a prospect in the sales cycle.

Less face time means less time to gather information from a prospect. This reduction makes the time that you do spend talking with a prospect—in person, over the phone, or through e-mail or online chats—much more critical. All of the skills you developed as a sales consultant in the traditional world of technical sales must be leveraged to make the best evaluation of a sales situation, despite the reduced opportunities for customer interaction.

The availability of information online also means that there are fewer barriers for potential customers to find your products. In the best case, easier access means a much larger set of prospects. In every case, the lack of customer interaction means that you will have much less of a chance to separate prospects based on your assessment of the likelihood of their sales. Anyone can fill in an online response form and state that he is the key decision-maker for a purchase. You have no way of knowing if that response came from the chief information officer of a major company, sitting at his or her desk in a suit, or a teenager, sitting at home in his or her pajamas.

In fact, this response could have even come from a chief information officer sitting at home in his or her pajamas. Your Web site is always open for business. The professionalism that used to be concentrated in an eight-hour work day is now required from your site twenty-four hours a day, seven days a week, and in every aspect of the site.

Effect of the E-World on Sales Consultants

The sales process for the e-world is different, but what is the effect of those differences on the role of a sales consultant?

First of all, if the sole purpose of a sales consultant is to give product demonstrations, that role can be easily eliminated through an online version of the demo.

> For that matter, if the sole purpose of a sales rep is to find prospects and do paperwork, their role also virtually evaporates.

But sales consultants provide a great deal more value than simply being "Demo Demons." You are the primary translator between the technical capabilities of your products and services and the needs of your prospects. In the reduced sales cycle of the world of e-commerce, your evaluative skills are in even greater demand.

A company may choose to use your talents in different ways in this new world. You may find that you maintain a high level of customer contact, but that this contact will be in the form of managing product trials and less involved with introductory meetings and demos.

You may also find that your skills are needed behind the firewall, helping to design and implement your company's all-important Web site. Or you could find yourself performing the same type of function as before, but online instead of face to face. For some more enlightened companies, this changed role can result in more flexibility for you in your job. You, perhaps, could work from your own home, in your pajamas.

As the sales cycle is compressed, the space between potential customers and your company is significantly shortened and broadened. In the more traditional sales cycle, you and your sales rep were the primary representatives of your company. The key qualities required in a sales consultant—credibility, responsiveness, and the ability to relate to people—are now required of a much broader range of employees. If the design of your company's Web site is not easy to navigate, it will have the same impact as a sales consultant who is unable to communicate the strongest features of your product. If a Webmaster is slow in returning e-mails, it will have the same impact as a sales consultant who is tardy in replying to phone messages.

Everyone in your company is a sales consultant in the e-world.

And, most importantly, these effects will be spread over a much larger, and undifferentiated, group of prospects. There was very little chance that the technical buyer for a large account would just drop by your office outside working hours for a demo or some detailed information on your products. But those same important people will be among the masses visiting your Web site, and they will be just as affected by the quality of that site as the teenager in his or her pajamas.

The net result of this is that the qualities required in a good sales consultant are now required in a much broader group of roles within your company. Couple the increased range of roles with the gold rush for sales over the Internet and you end up with a much larger demand for your services than before.

George Gilder, a well-known technological visionary, has said that any company that can maintain its marketshare will increase its volume one-thousand fold in the next five years.

First Principles Revisited

We can see the effect of the changes wrought by the e-world by re-examining the first principles presented in Chapter 1, "Your World".

The first overriding principle of the sales cycle is the need to maintain control of the sales process. In the highly compressed world of e-commerce, the need to maintain control becomes one of the primary differentiators between a successful e-world vendor and a failure. The overall design of your company's Web site will have a lot to do with maintaing this control. A Web site that is easy to navigate and provides logical access to information and processes, such as requesting products or information, will gently guide a visitor through the steps of a sales interaction.

The other first principle refers to the limited resources in any sales cycle. In the traditional world of technical sales, both the resources of the selling company and the purchaser are finite. In the new e-world, the primary limitation on a Web-based interaction is the visitor's time. In the e-world, it is often said, your competition "is only a click away." It's like doing a demo, but with your competitors doing demos in the next room, and your prospects having the ability to roam from room to room as they see fit.

This scenario could rapidly lead to chaos in the sales cycle. But your capabilities can greatly aid in creating and maintaining an Internet presence that is as effective as your best efforts in the field.

The limitations in the sales cycle are also imposed very harshly on the amount of face time you have with a prospect, especially early in the sales cycle. For e-commerce sites, however, there is a countering resource available. Most Web sites can capture the interactions that any browser has with your Web site. These interactions make up a "clickstream" of data. A Web site can analyze the clickstream to create a more personalized and engaging interaction with your prospects.

—·—·—

One reason to try to keep a visitor at your Web site longer is to be able to collect more clickstream information for identification and analysis.

—·—·—

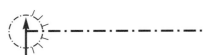

There are additional opportunities to merge data collected from a clickstream over time to create visitor profiles. Profiles can be used not only to customize a visitor's experience, but also to do proactive marketing, such as recommending other purchases or sending out merchandising offers.

An Opportunity for Growth

The impact of the e-world and the new economy means some fantastic opportunities for sales consultants. The traditional lines between the role of the sales representative, the sales consultant, and the business development manager have begun to overlap. This affords you the chance to take on some additional responsibilities for your company. Many of the hottest start-up companies have created a hybrid role that is part sales rep and part sales consultant. You can leverage your sales consulting skills in these positions while you hone your sales techniques. You will find yourself working with counterparts at other companies who are coming from the same background. Industry analysts have recognized the importance of this trend to the overall success of the business-to-business market.

The days of long, protracted application development and implementations are gone. Large projects have been broken down into manageable mini-projects that often are less than ninety days in length. In order to meet these tight deadlines, vendors are working in close partnership. Business development managers are being chartered with the task of creating these partnerships—and the role of the business development manager is being filled from the ranks of sales consultants.

Many of the skills that you have mastered as a sales consultant are critical in fulfilling the role of the business development manager. Highly technical decisions must be made in short time frames, and these decisions can have an enormous impact on the success of your company.

Wrapping Up

Everything changes, but everything remains the same. In many ways, there is even more opportunity for the skills of a sales consultant in the e-world, although those skills may be funneled into slightly different roles and positions. There are even more opportunities for a position that is already a center for a wide range of options.

In fact, you may find that you can contribute more in a slightly different position within your company—that of a Web designer, a person who analyzes data collected through a Web site, or an online customer advisor. The more dramatic stakes in the world of e-commerce give you the opportunity to leverage your abilities in a whole new set of ways. You may find that one of these other positions suits your particular mix of strengths and preferences even more than that of the traditional sales consultant.

This chapter also wraps up this entire book. We trust you have found it useful. We have tried to give you a fairly comprehensive set of "best principles" that you can use to hone the natural talents you bring to the role of a sales consultant.

As we mentioned in the first chapter of this book, one of the great things about sales consulting is the virtually endless variety in the job. You will be interacting with an ever-changing group of prospects and customers. Since you sit in the sweet spot of technological change, you will continually be faced with the need to update and deepen your technical knowledge. And your interpersonal skills can be continually refined as you polish them on the wheel of experience.

It has always been our experience that the better a person does a job, the more rewarding that job is. Your job is a major part of your life, and increased job satisfaction usually has a direct impact on your overall quality of life. We hope that this book has, in some small ways, enriched your life through the guidelines within its pages.

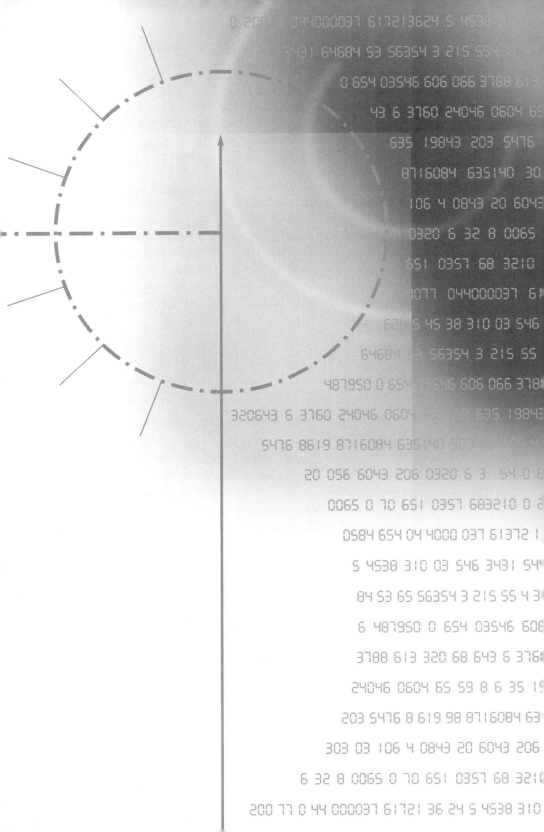

Index

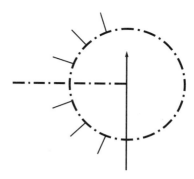

NOTE: Italicized page numbers refer to illustrations or figures.

A

activity-based costing, 155–157
administrative support team, 12
advising, establishing credibility by, 71
apologizing, 80–81
Application Service Providers (ASPs), 291
appointments, promptness for, 14
architecture discussion, product, 168–169
arrogance, 339–341
ASPs (Application Service Providers), 291
assessment, Bulldozer/BMW, 141–142
associated disciplines, fluency in, 136
audiences
    See also demonstrations, product;
        presentations
    dealing with difficult, 86–89
    earning attention of, 83
    keeping attention of, 84–85
    of presentations, 164–166
    of slide presentations, 172
    using humor with, 86–87

B

benchmarks, 226–230
benefits
    objections about, 243, 252–253, 254
    personalizing
        acceptance by prospects, 109–111
        need to, 99–100
        preparation for, 99–105
        presentation process for, 105–109
    turning features into, 97–100
body language, reading, 73, 323

breaks, 345
budget considerations. *See* cost issues
Bulldozer/BMW assessment, 141–142
business cards, use in presentations, 165
business problem. *See* problem statement
buyers
    economic, 54–55, 57
    end user, 55–57
    and political considerations, 65
    and product types, 63
    and schedule problems, 65
    standard assignments, 65
    technical, 52–53, 57
    working with, 59–60

C

calls, unanswered, 330–331
cardinal rules, 3
categories of sales consultants.
    See personality types, of sales consultants
chalk talk presentations, 173–179
"clickstream" information, 373
closing process, reacting to, 32
coaches, 146
"colleague" personal style type, 78, 79
colleagues, responsibilities of, 10–11
committees
    design of Request For Information by, 263
    standards committees, 319
communications, enhancing, 81–84
competition
    discovering, 299–302
    information about
        finding, 311–113
        using, 303–308
    making weaknesses known, 297–299,
        309–311

---

problems with, 205–206
process overview, 29–30
purpose of, 182–183
questions during, 203
seminars and trade shows, 208–210
"show-and-tell", 133–134
"test-drive" kits, 184
time management for, 353–354, 365–366
tips for, 202–207
trying new processes during, 342–343
warming up, 206
diagrams, drawing during presentations, 173–179
differentiation, product, 169
dishonesty. *See* lying
dress and grooming, 13–14
dry-erase markers, 178
"dynamo" personal style type, 79

E

early market prospects, 37
and "Demo Demon"
type sales consultants, 43–44
economic buyer as, 61
end users as, 61
and "Implementer" type sales
consultants, 46
and "Maverick" type sales consultants, 41–42
technical buyer as, 60
ease-of-use. *See* learning curves
e-commerce, 367–368
and basic sales principles, 373–374
effect on sales consultants, 371–372
and new opportunities, 374
and time allocation, 368–369
economic buyers, 54–55
concerns of, 57
as early market prospects, 61
influence in comparison
with other buyers, 59–60
as mature market prospects, 63–64
as popular market prospects, 62–63
educating prospects, after objections, 245–246
emotions, letting influence sales deals, 349–351

employment, changing, 48–49
end users, 55–57
as early market prospects, 61
influence in comparison
with other buyers, 59–60
as mature market prospects, 63–64
as popular market prospects, 62–63
engineering staff, customer access to, 278
equipment, for presentations, 163–164
evaluations, product, 30–31, 211–214, 217
and competition, 236–239
corporate site visits, 230–233
and customer references, 217–218
customer site visits, 219–221
meeting immediately before, 212–213
overconfidence after won, 341
parallel evaluations, 236
prototypes, 225–226
team members for, 224, 233–236
technical proof points, 214–217
evaluation teams, transitional, 65–67
expectations, setting, 360–362, 363

F

facilities, presentation, 163–164
faults of sales consultants
See also personality types, of sales
consultants
arrogance, 339–341
lack of organization, 343–344
lying, 336–339
overconfidence, 341–343
personal life problems, 349–351
poor transitions, 347–348
taking role of sales representatives, 345–347
features
of competition, 300
demonstrating, 133–134
explaining
need to, 94–97
during product demonstrations, 125–129
when no need to, 93–94
objections about, 243, 251–252, 254
personalizing
acceptance by prospects, 109–111
importance of, 99–100

preparation for, 99–105
    presentation process for, 105–109
    technical requirements, 145–149, 152
    turning into benefits, 97–100
feedback, in product demonstrations, 205
financial issues. *See* cost issues
"first principles", 16–20
flags, red (in this book), 4
flip-charts, 174, 249, 256
fluency, in associated disciplines, 136
forecast, sales, 27–28
formality, 13–14
functional explanation of products,
    120, 129–132
funnel, sales, 23–26

G

gatekeepers, appealing to, 330–331
genuineness, 78, 80
gestures. *See* body language
gimmicks, 288
grid, objection, 244–245, 246–247
grooming and dress, 13–14
groups, working with, 90

H

headquarters, visitation by prospects,
    230–233
highlighted text (in this book), 3–4
honesty
    See also lying
    in answering Requests for Information, 272
    and competitive information, 305
    during prospect qualification, 150–151
    reasons to be, 336–337
    in relationships, 77–78
humility, 340
humor, using in presentations, 86–87

I

identity of buyers. See under buyers
    (specific buyer types)
"Implementer" type sales consultants,
    39, 45–46
insecurity, and arrogance, 339–340

installing software,
    handling objections regarding, 253–254
interest in customers
    importance of, 9
    ways of showing, 73–75
Internet. *See* e-commerce
introductions, before presentations, 166

J

jobs, changing, 48–49
jokes, using in presentations, 86–87

L

laptops, versus PDAs, 356–357
lateness, 14
leads
    See also customers; prospects;
        relationship, professional
    becoming prospects, 27
    ranking interest level of, 23–26
    and sales funnel, 23–26
learning curves
    being honest about, 338–39
    handling objections regarding,
        248–249, 250–253
lectures. *See* presentations
life cycle, technology.
    See Technology Life Cycle
listening
    establishing credibility by, 71
    importance of, 15
loosing the sale, reacting to, 32
lying, 77–78, 150–151
    See also honesty
    inadvisability of, 336–337
    lies of exaggeration, 338–339
    lies of omission, 337–338

M

markers, dry-erase, 178
market data, 168
match-up, technical, 152–154
mature market prospects, 38
    buyer roles among, 63–64, 66
    and "Demo Demon"
        type sales consultants, 45

and "Maverick"
type sales consultants, 41–42
mature market segment, 63–64
popular market segment, 62–63
and sales consultant types
"Demo Demon" type, 39, 43–45
"Implementer" type, 39, 45–46
"Maverick" type, 38–39, 40–43
and time management, 364–366
telephone calls, unanswered, 330–331
"test-drive" kits, for
product demonstrations, 184
testing. *See* evaluations, product
text, highlighted (in this book), 3–4
timeliness, 14
time management, 343–344, 360–362
See also productivity
and e-commerce, 368–369
handling workload, 362–364
and product life cycle, 364–366
and sales forecast, 27–28
time limitations, 19–20
tracking time, 354–360
timing of sales process, 16, 33
trade shows and seminars, 208–210
training
product, 115–120
during product trials, 223
Transaction Processing Council
(TPC) suite, 226–227
transitional evaluation teams, 65–67
transitions, poor, 347–348
trials, product, 221–225
See also evaluations, product

trust, in relationships, 75–77
See also relationship, professional
building by answering questions, 82
truth, in relationships, 77–78
See also honesty; lying
types of sales consultants. *See* personality
types, of sales consultants

U

unique selling proposition, 297–299
user groups, 286–289

V

value-added resellers (VARs), 289–290
"visionary" personal style type, 79
visitation by prospects
corporate site visits, 230–233
customer site visits, 219–221
voice-mail messages, 363

W

whiteboard presentations, 173–179
handling objections with, 249
versus slide presentations, 178–179,
202–203
winning the sale, reacting to, 32
"wired" deals
determining, 323–324
handling prospects with, 325–326
Request For Information (RFI), 265
World Wide Web. *See* e-commerce

MUSKA&LIPMAN

Order Form

Postal Orders:
Muska & Lipman Publishing
P.O. Box 8225
Cincinnati, Ohio 45208

On-Line Orders or more information:
http://www.muskalipman.com
Fax Orders:
(513) 924-9333

Qty.	Title	ISBN	Price	Total Cost
_____	*MP3 FYI*	1-929685-05-X	$14.95	_____
_____	*Digital Camera Solutions*	0-9662889-6-3	$29.95	_____
_____	*Scanner Solutions*	0-9662889-7-1	$29.95	_____
_____	*Learn to Program Visual Basic—Objects*	1-929685-16-5	$39.95	_____
_____	*Learn to Program Visual Basic—Databases*	1-929685-17-3	$39.95	_____
_____	*Learn to Program Visual Basic—Examples*	1-929685-15-7	$29.95	_____

Subtotal _____

Sales Tax _____
(please add 6% for books shipped to Ohio addresses)

Shipping _____
($5.00 for US and Canada, $10.00 other countries)

TOTAL PAYMENT ENCLOSED _____

Ship to:

Company _____

Name _____

Address _____

City _____

State _____ Zip _____ Country _____

E-mail _____

Educational facilities, companies, and organizations interested in multiple copies of these books should contact the publisher for quantity discount information. Training manuals, CD-ROMs, electronic versions, and portions of these books are also available individually or can be tailored for specific needs.

Thank you for your order.